7.50

Industrial Management:
East and West

edited by
Aubrey Silberston
Francis Seton

The Praeger Special Studies program—
utilizing the most modern and efficient book
production techniques and a selective
worldwide distribution network—makes
available to the academic, government, and
business communities significant, timely
research in U.S. and international economic, social, and political development.

Industrial Management: East and West

Papers from the
International Economic
Association Conference
on Labor Productivity 1971

PRAEGER SPECIAL STUDIES IN INTERNATIONAL ECONOMICS AND DEVELOPMENT

Praeger Publishers New York Washington London

Library of Congress Cataloging in Publication Data

Conference on Labor Productivity, Ravello, Italy, 1971.
    Industrial management: East and West.

    (Praeger special studies in international
economics and development)
    Includes bibliographical references.
    1. Industrial management—Congresses.
2. Economic policy—Congresses.   I. Silberston,
Aubrey, ed.   II. Seton, Francis, ed.   III. International Economic Association.   IV. Title.
HD29.C655   1971   658.4   73-2922

PRAEGER PUBLISHERS
111 Fourth Avenue, New York, N.Y. 10003, U.S.A.
5, Cromwell Place, London S.W.7, England

Published in the United States of America in 1973
by Praeger Publishers, Inc.

A conference on Industrial Management: East and West was held at Ravello, Italy, from August 23 to September 2, 1971. Some 30 economists, divided equally between Western and Eastern countries, participated. The conference was held under the auspices of the International Economic Association, and the arrangements for it were made by a Program Committee, originally appointed by the Association. The Ravello meeting was the eighth organized by the Labor Productivity Committee (first established in 1960) of the International Economic Association.

This volume contains the main papers presented at the conference. The authors were given an opportunity to introduce corrections, and the English of the papers by the non-English-speaking participants has been tidied up. Apart from this, the papers are as they were given at Ravello.

The papers given at the conference covered topics suggested by the Program Committee. The aim was to compare and contrast the managerial problems arising in the different types of economy represented by the participants. Given the different backgrounds of those who presented the papers, it was to be expected that the contributions should range from those concerned with managing the entire economy to those concerned with managing individual firms. The arrangement of the book reflects this, starting with economywide problems and then concentrating on the level of the industry and the individual firm. There is a separate section devoted to techniques of management.

The International Economic Association acknowledges the financial assistance of the Ford Foundation in meeting the expenses of the conference and of publication.

The members of the Program Committee at the Ravello Conference were:

Professor John T. Dunlop, United States (Chairman)
Professor Abram Bergson, United States
Professor Walter Galenson, United States
Academician Nicolay P. Fedorenko, USSR
Academician István Friss, Hungary
Dr. Rikard Lang, Yugoslavia
Professor Pieter de Wolff, Netherlands
Mr. Aubrey Silberston, United Kingdom

The participants were:

Almon, Clopper, U.S.A., Professor, University of Maryland

Andrews, Kenneth R., U.S.A., Professor, Graduate School of Business Administration, Harvard University

Bendeković, Jadranko, Yugoslavia, Economic Institute, Zagreb

Bergson, Abram, U.S.A., Professor, Harvard University

Cipolla, Carlo, Italy, Professor, University of Pavia

Dunlop, John T., U.S.A., Dean of Arts and Sciences, Harvard University

Ellman, Michael, U.K., Department of Applied Economics, Cambridge University

Faxén, Karl-Olof, Sweden, Swedish Employers' Confederation, Stockholm

Fedorenko, Nicolay P., USSR, Director, Central Economic Mathematical Institute, Academy of Sciences, Moscow

Friss, István, Hungary, Director, Institute of Economics, Hungarian Academy of Sciences, Budapest

Gabrovski, Konstantin, Bulgaria, Institute of Economics, Academy of Sciences, Sofia

Galenson, Walter, U.S.A., Professor, Cornell University

George, Kenneth D., U.K., Faculty of Economics, Cambridge University

Grieve Smith, John, U.K., British Steel Corporation, London*

Hansson, Reine, Sweden, Swedish Employers' Confederation, Stockholm

Isaev, B. L., USSR, Central Economic Mathematical Institute, Academy of Sciences, Moscow

Jacquemin, Alex, Belgium, Professor, University of Louvain

Kolev, Konstantin, Bulgaria, Institute of Economics, Academy of Sciences, Sofia

Lang, Rikard, Yugoslavia, Director, Economic Institute, Zagreb

Machrov, N. V., USSR, Central Economic Mathematical Institute, Academy of Sciences, Moscow

Marosi, Miklos, Hungary, Karl Marx University of Economics, Budapest

Matthews, Robin, U.K., Professor, Oxford University

Naslund, Bertil, Sweden, Professor, Business-Economic Institute, University of Stockholm and European Institute for Advanced Studies in Management, Brussels

Nikic, Gorazd, Yugoslavia, Economic Institute, Zagreb

_____

*Mr. Grieve Smith, Dr. Rabi, Mr. Hansson, and Dr. Marosi were unable to be present, but their papers were read and discussed.

Rabi, Béla, Hungary, Chief, Department of Capital Investment and Construction, State Planning Administration, Budapest

Sarmir, Eduard, Czechoslovakia, Institute of Economics, Slovak Academy of Sciences, Bratislava

Seton, Francis, U.K., Nuffield College, Oxford University

Silberston, Aubrey, U.K., Nuffield College, Oxford University

Williamson, Oliver E., U.S.A., Professor, University of Pennsylvania

de Wolff, Pieter, Netherlands, Professor, University of Amsterdam

van der Zijpp, I., Netherlands, Professor, University of Amsterdam

CONTENTS

PART III:
TECHNIQUES OF MANAGEMENT AND CONTROL

LIST OF TABLES

LIST OF FIGURES

Figure		Page

MANAGEMENT AT
THE NATIONAL LEVEL

1

PRACTICAL EXPERIENCES
OF ECONOMIC
REFORM IN HUNGARY
István Friss

For a few years economic reforms have been an everyday
practice in Comecon countries. They have been reforms independent
of each other, introduced at different dates, and with different contents.
Yet they have many common, or at least similar, features. This is
not surprising since every country is building up socialism. What
are the common features? In each country there is an increased
emphasis on commodity and money relations, and in several countries
there is the growing role of the market, the regarding of profits as
the main indicator of enterprise efficiency, the introduction of a
charge on tied-up assets, and an increase in enterprise autonomy.
All these features are also part of the Hungarian economic reform.
There are countries where the economic reform can be characterized
precisely or mainly by the manner in which one or two of the features
quoted, or all of them, have been implemented: with what tools, in
what ways, to what extent. In the case of Hungary, the situation is
different.

Each of the features listed also can be found in our country,
but we do not believe that the measures and their method of implementation are inalienable parts of the reform. Recently, for example,
one of our deputy ministers proposed to abolish completely the 5 percent charge on tied-up assets and the 8 percent wage tax, and to
introduce instead a tax on value added (the difference between the
net value of sales by the enterprise and the material costs connected
with them).[1] Our minister of finance, however, in one of his recent
articles, went even beyond that. He argued that "a significant
correction of money and price relations, a revision of the role and
principles of the price system, of the rate of exchange (or, rather,
the special price criteria used for foreign trade decisions) and of
interest, will enable the formulation of a radically new and better

system of allocation of resources, based on new foundations and correctly reflecting socioeconomic and political objectives."[2] These two examples suffice to prove that money and price relations, credit conditions, the regulation of enterprise incomes, price coefficients, etc., can be considered only as tools. They are economic regulators—levers—serving the implementation of our plans, but they are not the substance of our reform.

There exists, however, an essential feature of our reform, not to be found in the reforms of other Comecon countries, that cannot be eliminated. Beginning with January 1, 1968, the national economic plan is no longer broken down to the enterprise level—enterprises do not receive obligatory targets and instructions. This is so novel a feature in the planning practice of the member countries of Comecon that there were even some Marxist economists, particularly abroad, to whom we had to confirm repeatedly that we had no intention of renouncing national economic planning as the main tool of implementing our economic policy. We were not even surprised when our reform was interpreted in capitalist countries—particularly initially—as implying that, by abolishing detailed plan instructions, we had parted with Marxism and shifted to some new kind of capitalist economy. As a matter of fact, history unequivocally proves that the demand for a uniform plan of the state governing the activity of millions appeared with Lenin at a time when it was still out of the question to break down the plan to enterprises. The main content of this demand was the principle that each economic activity should be subordinated to a plan expressing the most important interests of society. Decades of practice have acquainted us with the advantageous aspects of breaking down plans to enterprises, but also with its disadvantages. From among the latter I will mention only one, since I believe this single one justifies our choice of another solution. Our experience has awakened us to the realization, later proved theoretically, that though plans broken down by enterprises are really deduced from the national plan, there cannot be full agreement, full harmony, between the national economic plan and enterprise plans. The situation is universal—and any different situation can hardly be conceived—that enterprise plans are drawn up by the authorities responsible for branches (or industries), which operate more or less independently of each other. The more detailed the plan for the enterprise, the less it can be harmonized with the plans and instructions relating to connected activities, but drawn up in other industries. The plan obtained has to be fulfilled by the enterprise not because it follows from the national economic plan, but because it (the enterprise) has been ordered to fulfill it. And there can be no question of it being fulfilled because the enterprise deems it purposeful, useful, and serving national economic interests. This cannot be judged by the enterprise; at least no conclusion to this effect can be drawn from the plan handed down. Whereas what we would like to achieve is that enterprise managers should themselves shape the whole activity of their enterprise with the participation of all the work force. They should work out what and how to produce and sell if they want to act rationally; whether they should invest, and how much and for what purpose; what wages they should pay; where and at what prices they should sell; where they should purchase; what organizational forms they should employ; how they should develop the enterprise. They should experiment and look for the best solutions. They should—after thorough consideration and democratic debate—do what they find useful, expedient, and for the good of the enterprise and society. There are many means available to society to subordinate the economic activities of enterprises, institutions, and individuals to the most important economic objectives. These tools can even take the form of detailed instructions issued to individual enterprises. In general, however, it is more expedient, instead of issuing direct instructions to individual enterprises, to secure the attainment of the objectives deemed most important by prescribing prices, enterprise income regulations, investment rules, foreign trade rules, credit rules, etc., that conform to these objectives. Within the framework of these general regulations, the managers and all the personnel of the enterprise must be given every possibility to unfold their talents.

When speaking about the practical experiences of our reform, I make a distinction between how the reform as a whole—its basic idea—has stood the test, and how we have succeeded in implementing the economic regulators—the levers. I would observe, by way of introduction, that the basic idea of the reform has proved to be correct, and later on I will discuss it in detail. In economic debates nobody in our country suggests any more that we should revert to the old system. As against that, some of the regulators, have proved to be right and some of them wrong. Even after repeated corrections, they are still far from meeting the necessary requirements.

To give the right background, I think something else must be mentioned. Our economic policy must reflect the needs and requirements of social progress, in their order of importance. These must be expressed by the plan and served by the economic regulators. Thus, the establishment and ranking of the most important social needs and requirements, that is, the setting of the fundamental objectives of the national economic plan, is the task of the social bodies exclusively competent in these matters. Their decisions must rely on the widest and deepest scientific and political investigation and judgment. Among other things, they have to consider all economic resources, the whole complex system of society, domestic and international political and market relations, the results and direction

5

of technical progress. The objectives of the plan cannot be derived from this, not even with the aid of the most sophisticated mathematical methods and the most perfect regulators. But once the objectives have been defined by relying on the required scientific and political analysis and judgment, then the most refined mathematical methods and the most perfect regulators must be used to attain the given objectives most rationally, with the fewest mistakes or losses. After having decided on the most important aims, dozens of different governmental and social organizations still have to take decisions in important and wide fields. Among other things, scientifically based and responsible decisions must be made about the regulators themselves. If a decision—taken either by higher bodies or at medium levels of control—is incorrect, if it is not adequately founded scientifically, it if leaves important economic or other interrelations out of account, then, for all the effort and good work of economic leaders and workers, unavoidable smaller or greater evils are bound to follow.

As I have mentioned, our reform has stood the test of practice. The most important indicators of economic development corresponded to the plan and were satisfactory in the first years of the reform. We expected no wonders and emphasized that the introduction of the reform might entail difficulties and that its favorable effects could unfold only in the course of some years. The experience of the first years confirmed our ideas. National income increased in 1968 by 6 percent, in 1969 by 8 percent and in 1970 by 5 percent. In 1968 the 6 percent increase of national income was achieved with a 1 percent decline in national income originating from agriculture, and in the next year the global 8 percent was achieved with a 12 percent increase in agricultural output, while in 1970 the 5 percent overall growth concealed a 12 percent decline in agriculture (mainly owing to floods and other natural calamities). Production per man-year in the socialized sectors increased in 1968 by 2 percent, in 1969 by 1 percent and in 1970 by 8 percent. In evaluating these conspicuously low and unsatisfactory figures, it must be taken into account that in the meantime industry had moved to a shorter working week. The increase in output per man-hour was more satisfactory: 5, 6, and 7 percent in the three consecutive years. The increase in per capita real income of the whole population was uniformly 6 percent in each of the three years. The growth of real wages per employee was 2 percent in 1968, 5 percent in 1969, and 4 percent in 1970. In the years 1966-70, an average of 65,000 apartments were built annually, with 67,000 built in 1968, 62,000 in 1969, and 80,000 in 1970. Foreign trade in 1968 came to 42 billion forints (Ft),* with a deficit of Ft 200 million,

---

*11.4 forints equalled 1 dollar in 1971. Tourist rate, 28.5 forints equalled 1 dollar in 1971.

while in 1969 the volume of trade was Ft 47 billion with a surplus of Ft 1.8 billion. In 1970 trade amounted to Ft 57 billion, closing with a deficit in the balance of trade amounting to Ft 2.2 billion.

Our statistics can trace the structural shifts in production only to a limited extent. As far as can be ascertained, such changes did not occur on an extensive scale. Where they did occur, this happened mainly as a result of central decisions—for example, in the vehicle building program or in computer techniques. Where many new products were introduced, for example in some branches of engineering, the older articles generally continued to be turned out as well, and thus the range of production—too wide even before—further expanded. We may also conclude that there was an improvement in the efficiency of industrial production from the fact that, in each of the three years, national income generated in industry (i.e. value added) increased faster than the gross value of industrial output. In 1968, industrial output increased by 5 percent over the preceding years, and its contribution to national income by 6 percent; in the next year the corresponding figures were 3 and 4 percent, and in 1970, 7 and 9 percent. Thus in three years industrial output grew by 16 percent whereas its contribution to national income grew by 20 percent. Partly because of an improvement in the pattern of foreign trade, and partly because of more successful foreign trading activity, a ruble or a dollar could be procured in succeeding years for slightly decreasing numbers of forints. In this, of course, world market trends also played a role.

I believe that all this suffices to prove my previous statement: the reform has, on the whole, stood the test of practice.

I will now pass to some of the problems experienced with the armory of the reform, the economic regulators. Anyone who has some idea of the almost boundless number of economic regulators will find it natural that from this mass I concentrate on only a few problems, because only some of them can be dealt with in the framework of one chapter. I have chosen three formidable problems, each of which touches upon vast fields: (1) the price system, (2) income distribution in enterprises, and (3) investment and the structure of the national economy. I think it is necessary to restrict my subject in this way, though the objection will be obvious that the total neglect of very important fields—for example, foreign trade, credit, and the whole of agriculture—makes a survey of the complete system of regulators impossible. However, I cannot aim at completeness even in the three fields chosen. Yet I believe I will serve my purpose better with this restriction, i.e., of bringing our present economic problems nearer to those interested, than I could have done with any detailed review of the regulators.

It has been with this aim that when writing about the problems chosen, I have deviated from the method frequently used by authors writing on this range of subjects. I will say relatively little about what should be achieved or what we would like to achieve, or what the desired results should be. I refrain from considering whether some of our recent measures have solved the problems on account of which the measures were undertaken. Rather, I would like to make the readers feel and understand the difficulties and problems we encounter with every step we take. As we continue, certain trends emerge that point to possible solutions and perhaps even a definite indication of what is to be done, or at least what must not be done.

THE REGULATION OF PRICES

The price reform was a fundamental part of our economic reform. Together with most of the other important measures of the reform, it was implemented as from January 1, 1968. But we attributed to it greater importance than to the other reforms. Why? Because one of the most important requirements of our reform has been that the main measure of enterprise efficiency should be profits. We also set ourselves the aim of increasing the role and importance of commodity and money relations, of the market and competition. But if relative prices are incorrect, then enterprise profits, commodity and money relations, and the market and competition may also lead us astray.

Are the relative prices incorrect? Can they lead us astray? What should be meant by that, or, more exactly, what had been meant by that prior to the implementation of the reform?

In 1966 it was written in the "Principles of the Reform of the Economic Mechanism," published together with the party decision relating to the economic reform:

> It is a fundamental principle of prices that they should correctly direct and stimulate producers and consumers in their economic decisions. They should thereby promote a rational use of economic resources, the adaptation of production to effective demand, the spread of modern products, the development of an efficient pattern of consumption, and equilibrium between demand and supply. Prices fulfill their basic function if they develop under the combined effect of the following main factors:
> -costs of production
> -value judgments of the market
> -government preferences, reflecting the requirements of economic policy.

These factors combine to determine prices and also influence each other. Owing to changes over time in production costs and market demand, this is possible only in a price system where prices are fixed by authorities over a small range of commodities and, further, where government price control works in a flexible manner.

So many requirements, so many false hopes. It is no new phenomenon, either in our own economic experience or in that of others, that we cannot exactly assess in advance our possibilities or their limits, and that contradictions among the various requirements—correct in themselves—escape our attention. But perhaps in no other field do we include in our objectives as many understandable but not well-founded hopes as we do in the case of prices. Some of our hopes are realized, others melt into thin air and their unfounded character becomes exposed. Some of our requirements are met; others prove to be not feasible.

I do not list among the contradictions the statement that prices fulfill their basic function if they develop under the joint effect of production costs, the value judgments of the market, and government preferences. I would argue that no matter how they fulfill their function, these major factors make their combined effect felt on the trend of prices. They make it felt even if there are fixed administrative prices everywhere, that is, using the above terminology, if government preferences prevail at the expense of production costs and market value judgments. The latter have an influence in that they are taken into account—as far as possible—when prices are fixed. But they also work even if they are left out of account in price formation. In the latter case this leads to disturbances—some commodities disappear from the market, others become unsalable— so that they either become sources of lasting loss at the national economic level or they enforce the changing of fixed prices.

It must also be perceived that the three main factors mentioned are not of equal importance. In a certain sense—we shall presently see in what sense—production costs have priority over the value judgments of the market and over government preferences. If the commodity is useful because it statisfies effective social demand, its production costs must be covered. Its market price can fall below production costs only transitorily—if there is no government interference. If there is competition among producers and there is no government interference, the market price cannot deviate much from production costs, even in an upward direction. If the officially fixed price is lower than production costs, the difference must be returned to the producer from some source. If the fixed price is higher than production costs, this will act restrictively on market demand, and hence on the volume of output.

Consideration of national economic welfare provides a strong case for relative prices to correspond to production costs—to relative social inputs, using a more general term. On the one hand, this requirement corresponds to the principle of the distribution of income according to the work done. It is not sufficient that workers should receive equal wages for equal work, it is also necessary that they should be able to buy for the equal wages commodities that comprise equal social inputs. Moreover, only such relative prices satisfy the requirement that the interests of the consumer should go hand in hand with the social interest, as they would not if what was cheaper for the consumer were more costly to society, or vice versa.

It seems, therefore, as though what emerges on the market would also be correct and desirable in principle. It would be fine if we could rest satisfied with that. Unfortunately, we cannot. I have said above that, in the absence of external interference and if there is competition among producers, market prices cannot lastingly deviate from production costs. But what if there is no competition and external interference does exist? In this case, the deviation may be lasting. As a matter of fact, in our country, as is known, external interference does exist, and competition among producers seldom prevails in the market. Nor does past experience hold out hopes that we shall succeed in the foreseeable future in attaining greater competition among producers. In this case, the relative prices deemed desirable will not emerge.

The situation is further complicated by foreign trade. This is of great importance for a country like Hungary, with an area of not quite 100,000 square kilometers, rather densely populated, at a moderate level of industrial development, and lacking the majority of important industrial raw materials. We can maintain industrial production only with the aid of imported raw materials, intermediate products, machinery, and components. In order to import them, an adequate quantity of domestically produced commodities must be exported. But neither the purchase prices of commodities bought abroad nor the sales prices of our commodities sold abroad depend on domestic production costs, the value judgments of our domestic markets, or government preferences. The competence, practice, and skillfulness of our foreign trading organs can influence the prices of these commodities bought and sold in foreign trade only to a certain extent. Yet these foreign purchase and sale prices are some-how all built into our domestic price system.

What is more: From the national economic viewpoint an important argument is that relative prices should correspond to relative world market prices. When talking above about production costs and social inputs, we tacitly understood domestic costs and inputs. But social inputs may relate also to the world market—to

internationally relevant production costs and inputs. Various circumstances restrict competition even on the world market, but competition
generally exists and in this competition the latest technical achievements, the most advanced production processes, and the products
satisfying the greatest demand gradually prevail, though not smoothly
and not with the same degree of efficiency. World market prices
reflect the results of this competition. If we let them exert their
influence, relative world market prices transmit to us the reflection
of more advanced technology and hence stimulate technical progress.

Thus, we have already found two principles for determining
relative prices that, according to our experience, frequently contradict
each other. Unfortunately, this is not the end of our difficulties. We
must not forget that we did not create our economy anew on January
1, 1968. Big changes were started, but under historically established
and determined conditions. This equally holds true for the structure
of our society, for the quantity, distribution, and level of development
of our productive forces and means of production, as well as for the
prevailing prices influencing production and consumption. We could
not radically throw prices into confusion, and especially not consumer
prices. This followed naturally from the important principle of our
reform that the real income of not a single major section of the
population must be allowed to diminish. As will be seen, this principle
has set very narrow limits to any kind of price change.

The relatively great diversity of our price system conceals
this strong constraint, and this may easily mislead a superficial
observer. We have various types of prices: fixed prices, maximum
prices, prices moving between officially prescribed limits, as well
as loosely controlled prices and free prices. It is somewhat misleading, however, if we examine the pattern of consumption by the
population according to degrees of price freedom as a percentage
of turnover. We then perceive that one-third or more of articles
sold—including cultural and technical goods as well as building
materials—are sold at free prices. This ratio is even higher with
clothing, where it reaches 80-90 percent of turnover. On the whole,
about one-quarter of total retail trade falls into the category of free
prices.

However, the fundamental problem is not that many fixed prices
remain, but that these prices can be maintained only with an extensive
system of state contributions and price subsidies. Almost all staple
foodstuffs receive such price subsidies. The price subsidy is 56
percent for beef, 46 percent for pork, 59 percent for bottled milk,
53 percent for fuels, almost 50 percent in public utilities, more than
40 percent in cinemas, more than 50 percent in laundries, 80 percent
for railway passenger transport, 84 percent for urban transport in
Budapest. Obviously, raising these prices would directly affect the

11

living standards of workers. It is also obvious that raising the prices of certain goods affects consumers in different ways. There are people who eat a lot of meat, and others who eat little; there are people who travel a great deal by streetcar and others who never do. Thus, if we adhere to the principle that we must not diminish the real income of any single major section of the population, we can hardly change these important prices.

Not only are the prices of important consumer goods fixed but also those of the most important raw materials. This also gives rise to problems. I will deal with the most important of these when I discuss the movement of world market prices.

According to our experience, if Hungarian working people were asked, the great majority would vote for unchanged consumer prices. Unchanged consumer prices indicate the stability of the purchasing power of the forint; it is easier to allocate household expenditure and assess the extent of rises in income. Against these advantages stand the disadvantages already mentioned. From among two people with identical work performance and with the same money income, the one who avails himself of government price subsidies to a greater extent gets more in reality. With our present prices, the interests of society and the individual consumer may sharply deviate from each other since the individual consumer is interested in economizing socially necessary costs only to the extent that he himself pays for them, and at times he may lavishly waste socially necessary labor.

All this refers, of course, to relative prices and not to the price level. The latter is a problem apart and it cropped up during the preparation of the reform. "After the price reform we have to reckon in the future with a smaller rise in the general price level," according to the previously quoted "Principles." Why had this to be reckoned with from the beginning? Because in the system of independent economic accounting, every economic unit is interested in raising the prices of its own products. A certain, usually concealed, rise in prices frequently occurs even with fixed prices. Thus, when fixed prices were abolished in many fields, an intensification of these efforts by the economic unit to raise its prices had to be expected. This does not mean that we are at the mercy of rising prices: Both the method and the possibility exist for stabilizing the price level. But, in principle, a rising price level may also have the favorable effect of diminishing disproportions in both prices and wages. Therefore, it seemed expedient to reckon with a certain small rise in the price level, together with a correspondingly greater rise in incomes.

Has the moderate rise in the consumer price level coincided with an improvement in relative prices and wages? The consumer price level has risen moderately, according to the statistics, by an annual 1-2 percent. But an improvement of relative prices has not come about nor, most probably, of relative wages. There are no comprehensive surveys available on relative wages, but regarding relative prices it can hardly be doubted that if certain prices, particularly those requiring government price subsidies, remain fixed at a very low level while others are rising, the disproportion can only grow, even though in the meantime we have undoubtedly succeeded in improving the relationships in some less important fields.

Constant contradictions also are caused by the movement of world market prices. In general, these movements do not point in the same direction: There are both price rises and price reductions. In some periods, however, either price rises or price reductions are dominant. Difficulties are caused mainly by rises in world market prices, especially of important raw materials that in many cases have fixed domestic prices. In the final analysis, they entail a rise in the consumer price level. If the state wishes to prevent this rise, the state budget must be debited with the amount of the rise. In this case, however, the burden on the budget will grow and, presumably, so will the budget deficit, with uncomfortable consequences for the economy. If the state, on the other hand, does not shoulder the burden, it becomes uncertain whether the rise in the price level can be kept within the limits of the prescribed 1 to 2 percent.

I will mention only one more of the many problems and difficulties related to prices. When introducing the reform, we aimed at a much closer relation between international market prices and domestic prices. In principle, Hungarian buyers pay for foreign goods, and receive for their goods sold abroad, as many forints as derive from foreign prices multiplied by the appropriate foreign exchange rates. But there are two kinds of foreign markets. On one of them the generally acknowledged currency is the dollar and on the other the ruble. Thus we have established exchange rates for dollar prices and for ruble prices. But relative dollar prices are entirely different from relative ruble prices. This gives rise, naturally, to further contradictions, since there are many commodities that we buy or sell both for dollars and for rubles. Also, we use in production materials and components bought on both the dollar and ruble markets, while the finished product is either consumed at home or sold for dollars or rubles, perhaps at very different prices.

My purpose has been merely to indicate the multitude of problems related to prices. These problems have not been solved either by the price reform or the measures taken since then, nor could they be solved by them. In order to find a satisfactory or acceptable solution, many problems have yet to be clarified, discussed, and decided. Work has started in this direction. We cannot predict what the results will be, and at most it can be stated that our experience and discussions have pointed in two important directions. On the one hand, all our

13

experience has proved that we cannot put up for much longer with the extreme disproportions derived from consumer price subsidies. Since we cannot liquidate them soon, a long-term plan must be drawn up for their abolition. On the other hand, it seems necessary to bring our relative prices nearer to world market relative prices, which means that many changes will be needed. However, this raises the problem of transforming the whole pattern of our economy, especially that of production, and thus also requires the preparation of a long-term plan.

I will not digress in detail on this problem, but, for the sake of making clear the wider implications, I will mention that the revision of our price system must fit into our system of international economic relations. Thus our price system is closely related to the problems of our currency and monetary system, including that of convertibility. These problems, however, cannot be discussed without analyzing the main problems of equilibrium in the national economy—the relation between purchasing power and commodity supplies, the balance of trade and international payments, the equilibrium of the investment market, and the balance of the state budget.

THE REGULATION OF ENTERPRISE INCOME

The regulation of enterprise income decisively affects the behavior of enterprises, and, because of this, every aspect of the national economy. It has been asserted that one of the important characteristics of our system of control and management is the use of the profit motive in enterprises, or rather, that the main indicator of the success of an enterprise's work is its profit. In general and in principle this holds true. It is also true that the executives of enterprises and the workers themselves are interested in raising profits, since this enables them to raise their own incomes and also makes possible more investment in the enterprise. But earnings do not rise to the extent that the profits of the enterprise rise. They rise only to the extent allowed by the rules governing enterprise income. Yet employees are mainly interested in increasing their own incomes.

One of the main ways of regulating income distribution is the division of enterprise profits into parts serving investment, profit sharing, and reserves. This division is rigid and general, although in some branches of production—for example, in mining, electrical energy, transport, state farms, building materials, construction, and food—the proportions are different from what they are in industry generally. Changes were made in the rules in 1970 and again at the start of the fourth five-year plan. The changes have not affected the division of profits into investment, profit sharing, and reserves, but they have changed the proportions of each of these parts and to some extent also the method and extent of taxation.

The utilization of the investment share has a decisive role in shaping enterprise structure and in technological progress. I will deal with these problems separately in the following section. The part destined for reserves does not raise particular problems in practice, and I will, therefore, deal here only with profit sharing.

It is the development of this last part that has most actively interested those working in the enterprise. This is only natural, since it is from this part that—after deducting payments for taxes and other obligations—the profit-sharing fund of the enterprise is built up, and this adds to the earnings of the workers over and above their wages. No wonder that the executives and the workers anxiously watch the development of the profit-sharing fund and take this into account when formulating the investment, market, wage, and price policies of the enterprise. If there are no profits, there is of course no profit-sharing fund and no cover for benefits in addition to wages. But the profit-sharing fund is reduced not only if the profits of the enterprise diminish, but also if the average level of wages paid by the enterprise rises.

In discussions about the reform, prior to its introduction, a dominating role was played by the question of differences in earnings. On the whole, there was agreement about making all members of the enterprise interested in the results it achieved. It followed that all members must share in its profits. But this leads, of course, to differences in earnings: Those working in more efficient enterprises making higher profits will earn more than those working in smaller enterprises earning lower profits. However, there was also agreement that this difference should not be too great: A turner working in an enterprise with high profits should not earn twice as much as a turner working equally well in an enterprise with smaller profits. In the case of enterprise executives, relatively great income differences seemed justified, depending on the size of profits, since in the final analysis they may have a decisive role on the results achieved by the enterprise. It seemed correct that they should receive a relatively big share of profits; that is, in a favorable case their profit share should form a considerable part of their income. On the other hand, it did not seem right to give such weight to profit sharing in the earnings of workers and lesser employees. If, however, a large part of their incomes consisted of wages, efforts had to be made to ensure that wages could not be raised excessively by enterprises. Following these ideas, the development of the profit sharing fund and its allocation was regulated in such a way as to make, on the one hand, a sharp distinction between executives, middle managers, and

15

ordinary workers. On the other hand, whenever average hourly wages rose in comparison to the initial level of wages, an amount equal to the total of the excess wages had to be paid from the profit-sharing fund into the state budget.

The hopes and ideas attached in 1966 to the planned new system of regulation were well illustrated by the following reasoning in the Directives:

> These rules for raising the wage level . . . affect staff management in a different way from the present direct, administrative regulation of average wages. If enterprises are increasingly interested in profits, they will not increase staff unnecessarily, since this would reduce profits and the part to be retained by the enterprise. The profit-sharing fund to be built up from profits would be reduced, and this would be distributed to a greater number of workers, i.e., a smaller wage rise and a smaller share would be allocated to any individual worker. Thus a strong profit motive works against efforts at increasing staff.

The practical results have not at all come up to expectations. We have succeeded in attaining the objective that wages should not become too different, but at a price that was not worth paying. The side effects left out of account were graver than the main effects we had reckoned with. The sharp distinction between top executives, middle managers, and ordinary employees soon had to be abolished since it led to strong objections from workers. Even more disagreeable results followed from the rule that prescribed that the profit-sharing fund should be reduced by the total amount of excess wages due to a rise in average wages. The earlier administrative method of controlling average wages ceased, but what took its place served to maintain the average level of wages more stringently, as a result of the iron law of economic necessity. The hope proved to be vain that a greater interest in profits among executives and workers would raise obstacles to wage increases that were not technically justified. The need to keep the average level of wages from rising (in order to prevent a reduction in the profit-sharing fund) was irresistible. Related to this was the other unavoidable requirement for the wages of certain categories of workers to be raised in order to secure the necessary wage relativities. Consequently, there was widespread recourse to the device of keeping average wages constant by employing unnecessary workers at low wages. Whereas earlier there was a shortage of labor only in a few trades, it now became general, and so the need to raise wages manifested itself more strongly. Additional efforts were made to counterbalance this by the future employment of unnecessary workers with low wages. Finally, the general shortage of labor has had a wide-ranging and unfavorable effect on work discipline.

This situation forced a change in the method of wage regulation as early as 1970. The financial sanctions against raising average wages were somewhat reduced and others were attached directly to increases in the work force. Further changes were made in wage regulation with the start of the fourth five-year plan. Depending on the combined growth of per capita wages and profits, the wage level could be raised, to a certain extent, if conditions were favorable. Above a certain level the penalties grew steeply, i.e., progressively higher payments had to be made from the profit-sharing fund. The problem has not been solved satisfactorily even after these changes. The rules have become so complicated that they are difficult to follow. The situation has improved, but economical use of the work force has not yet been attained. In general, it will pay an enterprise even today to employ cheap labor with average earnings of Ft 1,600-1,800 a month— a level higher than a wide section of workers outside production proper can earn—for example, kindergarten teachers, employees in transport and trade, junior health staff, etc. It is fundamentally the shortage of labor that puts limits on raising the number of employees, and there are hardly any enterprises where the aim is to reduce the number.

Frequently efforts at increasing profits have the effect of boosting staff numbers. The simplest method of increasing profits in an enterprise is to increase production without changing the pattern of production, technical equipment, or production methods. Thus production is increased with old machines by employing more labor. To experiment with something new, in order to increase the productivity of labor, is much more difficult and involves greater risk: Trials are needed, often for a considerable time and using labor and money, without any guarantee of success. If, moreover, enterprises belonging to different branches of production wish to increase their profits by raising the productivity of labor, they have to face—apart from other difficulties—another deficiency of our wage regulation system. This is that it requires equal treatment between workers, in conditions where there should be unequal treatment, since in different branches of production there are very different possibilities for raising the productivity of labor.

Thus the problem of income and wage regulation in enterprises is invariably on the agenda. The tendency emerging—although not quite unequivocally and not accepted by many—is to loosen or abolish the existing close relationship between profit sharing and the wage level, i.e., to have separate rules for profit sharing and for determining the wage level. But, most likely, we shall have to go farther than that. Four or five years ago, for fear of uncontrolled effects, we bound the hands of the enterprises too much in regard to wage regulation, although this was opposed to the spirit and the main direction of the reform. I believe the following question is justified: Is it not correct to allow enterprises, in harmony with the spirit of the reform, and subject to certain general rules, to decide for themselves the wages that seem right for each enterprise?

INVESTMENT AND THE PATTERN OF PRODUCTION

The economic reform reserved the right of decision on major investment projects to the state, but it also set as an objective that, with their growing autonomy, enterprises should play a greater role in investment. By 1970 half of the investment decisions in industry, and indeed in the whole socialized sector, came within the scope of enterprises. The argument was that, if the viewpoints of the market and of profitability were taken more into account in investment decisions, the production of articles in demand would expand and the production pattern of enterprises would gradually be improved.

I have already mentioned that it is difficult to follow statistically the changes in the pattern of production. According to a report of the Central Statistical Office, "an unequivocal and considerable change in the pattern of output by products can be observed in those industries where output is prescribed by central decision, by programmes approved and promulgated at a high level."[3] In addition, however, certain surveys made in enterprises and some efficiency indicators have shown that many enterprises are using their new opportunities correctly. They have liquidated bottlenecks, modernized and innovated, and have thereby achieved favorable results.

Of course, even in this field development is not free from problems or contradictions. Our system of regulation has brought about unforeseen side effects in this area also. The realization of our ideas has been rendered difficult, hindered, and sometimes even brought to nothing by developments in both prices and profits, as well as in the market, different from those planned or expected.

For the most part, the initial level of prices brought about higher profits than planned, independently of the economic efficiency of enterprises. As a result, greater profits and investment funds than expected became available to the enterprises. When introducing the reform, in order to facilitate the transition, efforts were made to secure equal conditions for enterprises, as far as possible, irrespective of their up-to-dateness, equipment, labor productivity, product quality, or the demand for their products. Later, the financial devices used to solve production or foreign trade difficulties also helped to bring about similar conditions between enterprises. In this manner, more or less equal development possibilities were provided for the majority of enterprises. All this has led to greater investment demands than were expected or could be accommodated, and also to a wide dispersion of investment claims. The distribution conformed broadly to the old pattern, and, therefore, instead of these measures helping to bring about a change in structure toward greater efficiency, they have hindered it.

The many financial devices, price subsidies, and refunds built into the price system greatly hinder a correct evaluation of the real efficiency of enterprises. Nor has growing market freedom come up to expectations, because hardly any real competition has been experienced among our productive enterprises. The case of electric light bulbs is a rare exception, since imports have provided competition for domestic production. Recently the question of competition in heavy industries was discussed at a ministerial meeting, and, according to the newspapers, it has been established that "real competition can be felt only among the enterprises producing detergents. This is shown by the fact that at present the capacity for producing synthetic detergents is greater than the demand. Competition has induced enterprises to improve quality, introduce new types, and, simultaneously, to reduce prices." These are favorable consequences of a state of affairs that may perhaps give rise to less complacency: namely, that perhaps—although this has not yet been investigated— unjustifiable overcapacity has been created in detergent production.

Of course, it is not only price regulation that has side effects in the fields of investment, development, and the shaping of the production pattern, but also wage regulation. Owing to our system of wage regulation, investments that implement technological progress—typically using highly paid skilled workers—are unprofitable for enterprises. This is not a secondary problem. Higher labor productivity derives from more developed technology and improved machinery, materials, and production processes. Our present economic regulators do not sufficiently stimulate this kind of progress, and this applies not only to wages, but also to foreign trade controls in the form of customs duties.

Nothing would be more erroneous, however, than to blame the system of economic regulators for the deficiencies of the investment market. If, as a result of central and local decisions, more investment has been started than can be accommodated by the capacity of the construction, building material, and related industries, or by our manpower situation, and if, as a consequence, extreme tension prevails in the investment market, with well-known harmful effects, it is not the economic reform or the regulation system that is responsible, but those who have taken incorrect decisions.

This has to be said, not to defend the economic reform, but in the interests of truth. The economic reform is not in need of defense. It has stood the test of almost four years of practice. It has proved its viability. It can no longer be denied that a planned economy can be run in this way, that planned development, the implementation of important and correct decisions, and consistent progress toward the main objectives of the economy can be secured without specifying plans for individual enterprises, and without issuing them with obligatory targets. We should not and could not expect the reform to supply important and correct decisions by itself, automatically. No competent person has ever stated or believed that the reform is called upon to supplant the control and management of the economy, based on a scientifically founded economic policy. The advantages and usefulness of the reform must be looked for elsewhere. Previously, the fetters of plan indicators made it impossible for the talents of our executives to unfold, or at least it kept them within narrow bounds. The reform opened a wide field for their creative activities. The new method of management is becoming second nature for a growing number of them, and they are using the possibilities offered by the reform to give more and to achieve more. The competent organs of our society must now ensure that the least possible amount of the huge energies so released is wasted, and that, to the greatest possible extent, they should be harnessed to really important and correct decisions.

NOTES

1. Imre Vince, "Prices, Taxes, and Subsidies Following the Reforms in Economic Control and Management; Doctoral Dissertation, Budapest 1970.

2. Lajos Faluegi, "The System of Regulation and Preferences," Gazdaság, March, 1971, pp. 15-16.

3. Industrial Development by Industry and Product Pattern between 1966 and 1970 (Budapest: Central Statistical Office, 1971), pp. 9-10.

PROBLEMS OF ECONOMIC REFORM IN THE USSR
Nicolay P. Fedorenko

The comprehensive and thoroughgoing reform now under way in the Soviet Union covers all sectors of the national economy: industry, farming, construction, transport, trade, science, etc. It affects every link in the organizational structure of production: shop floor, individual enterprises, enterprise-associations, chief administrations ("glavks"), and ministries. It involves drastic changes in the traditional style and methods of central state agencies in every sphere: planning, economic administration, credit, and finance.

Individual enterprises of the socialist economy are now endowed with wider powers to decide on the allocation of economic resources and to determine the nature of the economic links binding them to suppliers on the one hand and to customers on the other. This often induces foreign press correspondents to voice the suspicion that the current reform implies a departure from the basic tenets of socialist production management and the weakening of the planning principle in the Soviet economy.

The essential aim of a system of economic management serving society is the creation of conditions in which the individual enterprise, while independently pursuing its own specific interests and maximizing profits, is at the same time acting in the interests of the national economy as a whole. The first task of a centralized planning apparatus is to give enterprises clearly defined economic parameters, such as prices, capital charges, interest rates, and penalties for breach of contract. Guided by these parameters, enterprises can then take economic decisions on their own. Far from infringing the planning principle, such a system is instrumental in raising the effectiveness of planned socialist production, as it brings greater scope for enterprise initiative and participation by all working people in the search for hidden potential for industrial growth.

Thus it can be seen that Soviet methods of production management are in essence faithful to the planning principle. Let us clarify this proposition by an example. Under socialist conditions it is of prime concern to society that the technical equipment of every enterprise should be adequate. This can be achieved in a variety of ways. One could, for example, regulate the introduction of new technology into an enterprise in the strictest detail, giving it concrete instructions on how machines and various types of equipment must be used in the productive process. But it is also possible to proceed on different lines: One may set the enterprise the task of paying into the state budget, say, 6 percent of the value of the fixed capital at its disposal. The enterprise will then be able to apply the new technology unaided, as it can confine consideration to those production methods that will yield a profit of over 6 copecks per ruble invested. In this way the 6 percent capital charge becomes one of the planners' guidelines for the enterprise in shaping its investment policy. In essence the capital charge is a "directive" by the planners for guiding enterprises toward the efficient use of the resources allotted to them; but it is given to the "addressee" in the form of an economic criterion rather than an administrative order. Similar functions are fulfilled by economic criteria of a different sort.

The essence of the new reform is precisely this synthesis of centralized planning and enterprise initiative. The reform covers the whole gamut of economic activity in our country and deals with the basic theoretical and practical problems of drafting and implementing plans. It is directed toward improving centralized planning and economic management and involves a very real increase in the powers of individual enterprises and of enterprise-associations acting on a commercial and self-financing basis. Particularly important changes have taken place in the nature of the enterprise's links with the state on the one hand and with its suppliers and customers on the other. A distinctive feature of the new situation is the sharp increase in the responsibility that both managers and workers now carry for the present and future economic health of the enterprise. This greatly strengthens the incentive to obtain adequate returns for resources expended. Enterprises are now in the position of having to finance expenditure out of their own income. This refers to current expenditure in the first place, but increasingly also to capital investment aimed at increasing output and improving quality and product mix. Accordingly, a part of the enterprise's profits are channelled into the "production development fund" into which some 30 to 50 percent of annual depreciation charges (for capital renewal) are also paid. The allowances for capital repair are almost totally retained by the enterprise.

If the enterprise lacks sufficient means of its own, it may apply for credit, either long- or short-term. This is granted for outlays to improve or modernize products, settling creditors' accounts, introducing new techniques, capital investment, etc. The availability of the enterprises' own resources supplemented by outside credits provides the basis for stable and permanent operations on commercial and self-financing principles.

Greater independence in the financial relations between enterprises is also reflected in new special powers enabling them to enter into direct agreements with their suppliers and customers, thus enhancing the role of contractual economic relations in the process of balanced growth. Fines for breaches of contract, for failure to honor delivery dates, etc., have also been upgraded in importance. If an enterprise revises an order previously given, it must inform the supplier affected in good time or compensate him for the losses incurred in producing for the canceled order.

The operative principle of the new mechanism is the direct link between economic performance and the worker's individual reward. One part of the profit is allocated to a "material incentive fund" and another to a "fund for social and cultural amenities and housing construction." Essentially these allocations represent a variable part of the wage whose size does not exclusively depend on the effort of the individual, but varies with the efficiency of the whole work force of which he is a member. In order to increase their receipts, enabling them to channel more money into the incentive fund, enterprises must sell their products and make a profit. This in turn requires continuous study of the conditions of social demand, well-timed research aimed at improving output and attracting customers, and technical progress of a cost-reducing kind. Given the size of the work force, any increase in the rewards to labor depends on the quality of work, the choice of product mix, and the technical progress achieved. These factors are no longer regarded as external to and independent of the enterprise, but are increasingly felt to be the outcome of the enterprise's concern for its customers and its degree of specialization and rationalization of production.

The degree to which the powers of enterprises have been widened can be gauged from Table 2.1, which lists the indicators planned from the "center" before and after the reform.

The necessary conditions to support the new system of management planning and incentives are the following:

First, the improvement of the system of wholesale prices. This occupies a special place in the planning reforms. Planned losses, previously allowed in certain branches of industry, have now been abolished, and the excessive and irrational multiplicity of profit rates for different brands of products has been eliminated. The

TABLE 2.1

Centrally Approved Indicators

Previous System	New System

I. 1. Gross output
   2. Commodity output
   3. Main product mix
	I. 1. Sales volume
	   2. Product mix in aggregative terms

II. 1. Total wage bill
   2. Average wage
   3. Number of workers and employees, broken down by category
   4. Labor productivity
	II. 1. Total wage bill

III. 1. Unit cost of commodity production (index for comparable products)
   2. Cost per unit of each article
   3. Cost of commodity output (per ruble of output)
   4. Gross profit
	III. 1. Accounting profit
	
	   2. Rate of profit (ratio of profit to value of the fixed capital)

IV. 1. Payments to the budget	IV. 1. Payments to the budget
V. 1. Allocations from the budget	V. 1. Allocations from the budget

VI. 1. Volume of capital investment
   2. Itemized lists of the most important construction projects
   3. Commissioning of plant, equipment, and buildings arising from total investment activity
 	
Etc.
	VI. 1. Volume of centralized capital investment
	   2. Commissioning of plant, equipment, and buildings arising from total investment activity

Source: Compiled by the author.

price reform of 1967-68 made allowances for capital charges and rental payments and for an improved balance between supply and demand. The new prices give incentives for improvements in the quality and up-to-dateness of products. In the case of a number of articles, enterprises and local agencies have been given wider price-setting powers. Further work on methods of improving price formation is now under way.

Second, if the fullest benefit from the reform is to be derived, its principles must be applied throughout the economy. By the end of 1969 almost 40,000 industrial enterprises were using the new method. The reformed enterprises accounted for nearly 90 percent of industrial output and for more than 95 percent of the profits of all industry. State farms, railways, and the whole of motor transport have now been transferred to the new system.

Supply agencies (responsible for the supply of raw materials and components) and construction organizations started the conversion process in 1970. When this is completed they will be able to fulfill their customers' requirements much better and improve their spatial distribution and the network of permanent supplier-customer links. The Central Institute of Mathematical Economics of the USSR Academy of Sciences is working on a methodology for optimizing commodity flows between enterprises and determining the size and composition of stock holdings. This has to some extent already been put into practice and has proved effective.

Third, it is urgently necessary to give greater importance to supplementary payments to workers for results achieved collectively, and to make these payments as high as possible. Investigations are under way on the possibility of varying bonuses by category of worker and it is becoming clear that the performance indicators on which the bonuses are based will also have to be differentiated.

Fourth, the economic reform would be unthinkable without a parallel reform in the system of training and retraining skilled manpower. New programs have been worked out for the teaching of various branches of economics in colleges of higher education and technical schools, more economists are being trained, and new special subjects are being introduced (programming, mathematical economics, etc.). Courses for the retraining of managers have also been organized and special departments for production management established. Lecturers are at work full time in every enterprise, giving seminars and organizing study groups on new aspects of economic life. It would be difficult to overestimate the importance of this work.

Fifth, the effectiveness of the reform depends directly on the application of commercial principles of accounting and self-financing as one moves "vertically" up the administrative ladder, i.e., on the extension of this principle to the relations between enterprise and enterprise-association, between association and glavk (chief administration), and between glavk and ministry. In other words, all the links in the chain of economic management must be transferred to this principle of operation.

Enterprise-associations are a means of centralizing production in the hands of state organs run on commercial principles. At the same time the functions of individual enterprises must be revised in order to ensure the optimum pattern of concentration and specialization. In this way centralization can help toward greater economies of scale. The effectiveness of this link depends on the technical possibilities and economic bases for the integration of similar types of enterprises into associations, regardless of whether they were enterprises previously under a single administrative department or under different ministries (this refers to multiindustry associations, including "kombinats"). At the present stage of economic development the forming of associations is the most important, if not the decisive, way of maximizing the concentration of productive forces in our planned economy, with all the benefits in terms of efficiency which that implies. One of the most important aspects in the growth of efficiency to be expected from large-scale associations run on commercial principles is the greater range of opportunities opened up for the development and widespread use of automated management systems based on the extensive use of mathematical methods and computers. This can be fitted easily into the automatic management-information system that is being set up for the economy as a whole. When computerization is confined to the level of the small individual enterprise, it is often constrained by limited access to information on new processes and developments taking place outside the enterprise, and then it requires the intervention of higher levels of management to be fully effective. Soviet and foreign experience shows that only a change-over to a system of enterprise-associations will produce the sort of fully integrated automated management system that can speedily recoup the research and development costs and the operating expenses incurred.

The existence of associations opens the way to a further major advance in economic reform. Very small enterprises often cannot be transferred to fully commercial (self-financing) operations with the autonomous control over "technical progress funds" that this implies. This is so because modern advances in technology are very frequently unprofitable before the scale of production has reached a sufficient level and delivery in large batch-sizes has become possible. Associations create more favorable conditions for the introduction of new technology and give greater stability in respect to finance and the setting of technical norms, as well as increased scope for the standardization of these norms.

Associations, once formed, must be put under a perfected regime of commercial accounting and self-financing that allows for a degree of autonomy exceeding that of individual enterprises. They must be given almost unconditional decision-making powers in the sphere of investment (whether in fixed or working capital), research and development, etc. One of the most important advantages of self-financing associations of this sort is the emergence of systematic accounting relations between themselves and their constituent enterprises, and the parallelism of the interests pursued at both levels.

Associations also produce a beneficial effect by centralizing a number of operations previously performed by individual enterprises at an inadequate level of profitability, e.g., research and development project-making (i.e. the formulation of investment projects), licensing, accounting, and subcontracting of specialized or auxiliary operations.

The creation of associations must not be reduced to a mere renaming of the glavks and to an excuse for channeling funds from enterprise profits into bonuses for the staff of the glavk. It must be based on the optimal methods of increasing productivity through centralization, and this is the sole criterion that should be followed, whether it leads to the inclusion of enterprises previously outside the glavk or to the exclusion of enterprises previously within it.

The association is a new form of management and administration that can be highly specialized or extremely diversified in nature; it may have members throughout the USSR or be limited to a given area. Before it is set up, plans must be approved for reorganization, increased specialization, the closing of inefficient workshops or services—in fact the construction of a whole new improved structure and methodology of management for the interrelated whole, ensuring organic links between all the constituent enterprises.

The extension of the rights of associations leads to the transfer to a higher administrative level of planning and management functions that are wider than have been exercised at that level before. Associations will arrange economic links between enterprises, study the demand for their output in greater depth, and will be able to avail themselves of larger loans than enterprises can at present. The change-over to associations will enable Gosplan and the ministries of the USSR to concentrate on those aspects of medium-term planning that are the most important at the level of the nation as a whole.

Soviet industry has several hundred associations. The number of self-financing associations in Leningrad, for instance, has stood at 47 for a number of years, including 224 single enterprises, project-making, and research and development agencies. These account for nearly a third of total production in this major center of industry. Since 1970 the Moscow chief transport administration has operated

27

as a self-financing association. It employs about 30,000 people in its enterprises and operates on a completely self-financing basis, with full responsibility for recouping its own outlays. In 1970 a whole branch of industry—instrument-making—was transferred to full self-financing by way of an experiment. It was stated at the 24th Party Congress that during the next few years the process of forming self-financing associations would extend to the whole of industry.

Let us now look at the course of the reform and its initial results. It started in January, 1966 with the transfer to the new system of 43 enterprises belonging to 17 different branches of industry. Later on, further groups of enterprises were transferred. In the current five-year period (1971-75) the transfer of the whole national economy to the reformed system will be completed. The economic results achieved under the reformed system are shown in Table 2.2.

In the past five years affected by the reform, economic performance has been far superior to that of the preceding five years. Scientific and technological progress has accelerated and so has the growth of production and of labor productivity. We now enjoy increased managerial efficiency and a better pattern of specialization

TABLE 2.2

USSR: Selected Economic Indexes
(1965 = 100)

	1965	1966	1967	1968	1969	1970
Gross social product	100	108	117	125	131	142
National income	100	108	117	127	133	143
Industrial output	100	109	120	130	139	150
Gross agricultural output	100	109	110	115	111	121
Capital investment	100	107	116	125	130	142
Ton/kilometers carried by all forms of transport	100	106	115	124	129	138
Volume of retail sales	100	109	119	129	138	148

Source: Compiled by the author.

28

in the economy. This has led to an improvement in welfare and in the cultural standards of the nation.

The accounting profits of industrial enterprises in 1968 amounted to 31 billion rubles (the planned figure being 30.6 billion rubles). In 1969 it reached 43.4 billion (as planned) and in 1970 it reached 49.7 billion (as against 49.9 billion in the plan). In the same years, industry achieved the following rates of profit:

1968	21.2%	(as against 20.8% in the plan)
1969	22.5%	(" " 22.5% " " ")
1970	23.2%	(" " 23.2% " " ")

The growth in profits and rates of return was due to reduced production costs, increased labor productivity, and, to a lesser extent, increased employment and output. There was also a rise in the rate of return on capital, more specifically on the working capital of industry.

The growth of incentives was also of great importance. Incentive funds of various kinds more than doubled in 1970 and reached the following levels in that year:

Material incentive fund	7.1 billion rubles
Social and cultural development fund	1.3 billion rubles
Production development fund	3.4 billion rubles

When account is taken of free state services (education, health, reduced prices on children's clothing, etc.) the real income of the working population can be seen to be even higher.

The growth in production efficiency had beneficial effects on the budget revenue of the state. In 1969 these were as follows: capital charges from enterprises, 8.5 billion rubles; rental payments, 2.3 billion rubles; profits channeled into the budget, 15.9 billion rubles. In 1970 the figures were 9.4 billion, 2.4 billion, and 19.1 billion rubles respectively, implying an overall growth rate of 15.7 percent.

The growth of managerial efficiency in the past few years was in the main induced by technological progress and the improved organization of production. These are due to the introduction of continuous operational planning, network analysis, and mathematical data processing with the aid of the most modern electronic computers. There has also been some increase in output per unit of capital in enterprises subject to the reform.

We are well aware that the full potential for improvement in economic management has scarcely been tapped as yet. It must be understood in the first place, however, that we shall only reap the full advantages of the reform when all enterprises and all levels of management have been integrated into the new system, i.e., when the entire national economy acts as an organic whole. It is obvious that an enterprise transferred to the new system while its suppliers or customers are still on the old will not be able to function to the fullest advantage. In the second place, it will certainly take time to carry out the capital investment that enterprises and whole industries require in order to eliminate the bottlenecks in the way of growth; it will take time to increase the flexibility of the material and technical supply system without which the smooth and effective use of plant and equipment is severely hampered. In the third place, it will take time to develop fully the new pattern of specialization and concentration, and to train personnel in the skills required for successful operation of the new system.

In the initial phase of the reform we can tap production potential that is obvious and near the surface—surplus inventories, redundant plant and equipment, deficient production methods. These measures are certainly effective in improving economic efficiency, but they are not the most crucial or the main improvements. The main effects to be expected from the reform are a permanent and stable return from technical innovation, the revitalization of economic activity, reduction in production costs, improvement in quality, responsiveness of product mix to consumer demand, and the benefits accruing to the nation from a reduction in prices.

The economic essence of the current reform (its pith and marrow) is the upgrading of incentives toward greater efficiency in all production units and at all managerial levels. The reform aims above all at a high level of material and moral commitment in the work force of each enterprise, directed toward the most efficient use of all resources (material, human, and financial). It aims at a proper and clear-cut linking of workers' incomes with the performance indicators chosen for the production and management of each enterprise.

AN INTEGRATED ACCOUNTING
SYSTEM FOR DESCRIBING
THE FINANCIAL RESULTS
OF ECONOMIC ACTIVITY
B. L. Isaev

All Soviet measures taken in recent years for the improvement of economic management have been inspired by the same basic idea— that of exploiting the superior potential of the socialist economy in order to maximize the effectiveness of the country's productive apparatus and ensure the optimal utilization of its human material and financial resources.

One of the hallmarks of the economic system of the Soviet Union, deriving from the very nature of its socialist economy, is the centralized character of economic administration. In the modern world any centralized form of management must of necessity be integrated and systematic in its nature: It must be able at any moment of time to bring about the desired state of the economy by means of central action at strategic points without disturbing the autonomous functioning of individual economic units.

The principle of democratic centralism, which is the cornerstone of current economic reforms, demands for its consistent application a shift of emphasis in the centralized decision-making process toward those performance indicators that reflect the circular flow of economic transactions in value terms. The target for central decisions is no longer a multiplicity of specific output assignments for individual commodities and enterprises. It is gradually shifting toward the planning of overall structural proportions, such as may be required for the optimal harnessing of the economy to chosen objectives, and to the creation of an economic environment in which individual enterprises can freely operate under the guidance of such instruments as prices, wages, taxation, interest rates, and regulated constraints on the use of specific resources or revenues. All this gives pride of place to those economic indicators and criteria that reflect the financial aspects of the productive process.

The introduction of electronic computers and the development of mathematical economics have created a need for special systems of automatic data processing. These are known as AMSs (automated management systems) and are currently being built up within individual ministries and departments for use at the level of enterprises for industrial branches. Each of these systems defines primarily the performance indicators appropriate to the respective level of the economic hierarchy, but the AMS simultaneously incorporates (explicitly or implicitly) certain elements reflecting performance at the macro level, also including financial criteria of economic performance.

Both theoretical considerations and practical experience suggest that the problems that will gradually have to be faced are those of finding a proper synthesis between the principles underlying AMS (mainly methods of recording and summarizing primary data in a purposeful manner) and the principles of macroeconomic analysis in general. Without such a synthesis the central administration would lack the necessary informational base for decisions affecting the economy as a systematic whole. It would also lack a methodological basis for the mutual tying-in of different AMSs.

To ensure this tie-in in all its rigor with respect to the macroeconomic indicators of financial performance, the following prerequisites are essential:

1. A general framework for information flows adequately reflecting the state of economic theory and of actual relationships in the economy, which must form part of all information systems.

2. The insertion into this framework of certain standard elements ensuring an automatic "dovetailing" of all systems within an overall system of macroeconomic information flows.

As far as the overall scheme of macroeconomic information flows is concerned, the solution of the problem may be approached with the aid of the "method of balances" and the "theory of circular production flow." As far as the integration of different AMSs is concerned, it may be approached with the aid of standard methods used for the rigorous definition of the most important accounting and managerial objectives.

Elements of economic information are generated with every social transaction that takes place, involving a transfer of value of definite magnitude a from subject i to subject j. The embodiment or carrier of the value so transferred will be a concrete object or some real economic service, to be denoted by α. This object or service must be referred to a definite period of time t. Such an event may be recorded in a special notation with all its characteristics, say $_t a_{ij}^{\alpha}$. If the analysis is confined to a given period of time (i.e., t is chosen), then the whole network of value transfers within the economy may be characterized by the totality of all sets i, j, and α. A general framework for macroeconomic information can be built up by grouping the subjects (i, j) and the objects (α) of economic transactions in the desired manner. This methodology serves to create an integrated system of accounting.

Complete accounting records of economic transactions of the type a_{ij}^{α} may be displayed in the shape of square matrixes of format i x j x α. In practice it is useful to establish accounts of the following types:

1. Pairwise transactions between subjects regardless of the objects transacted ($\sum\limits_{\alpha} a_{ij}^{\alpha}$) or in respect of special types of transactions $\underset{m}{m}(\sum\limits_{m} a_{ij}$

2. Receipts and expenditure of subject k for each type of operation α

$$\sum_{j} a_{kj}^{\alpha} = \sum_{i} a_{ik}^{\alpha}$$

3. A link between all spenders and all recipients involved in transaction ℓ

$$\sum_{i} a_{ij}^{\ell} = \sum_{j} a_{ij}^{\ell}$$

All these types of linkages are recorded in the so-called global material financial balances (or, in more general terms, in integrated systems of balances that cover several aspects of the analysis).

The theoretical and experimental research work now being done in a special laboratory for financial planning models within the Central Institute of Mathematical Economics of the USSR Academy of Sciences is concerned with the construction of an integrated system of accounting, reflecting the results of economic activity at all levels of the economy— from the global national level down to that of individual enterprises. One of these models, based mainly on relationships of type 1 and 2, has found practical application in an experimental way. At the same time, work has been completed on an accounting scheme for macroeconomic information flows that combines all three types of economic analysis mentioned above. The model incorporates the relationship between two aspects of economic performance, as shown in Figure 3.1.

In the material-financial-balances worked out in the Central Institute of Mathematical Economics the symbols i, j, and α carry the following information:

33

FIGURE 3.1

Schematic Diagram of Interconnections between Physical and
Financial Aspects of the Integrated Accounting System

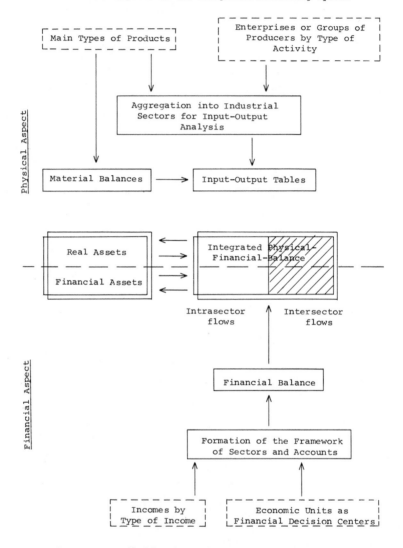

Source: Compiled by the author.

i, j—The subjects of economic transactions, i.e., recipients and spenders of money, categorized by type of activity, position in the administrative structure, function within the productive process, or territorial location.

α —The character of the transaction. In the case of material or physical flows, this concerns various types of production, use categories, or types of investment. In the case of income flows, it refers to types of income; in the case of financial flows, different types of credits and financial assets or liabilities. At the highest level of aggregation α corresponds to the basic processes of the economy.

This system of material-financial-balances is designed for both interindustry and interregional planning.

The accounting tables that are now being constructed on the basis of this methodology are considered as supplements to the "balance of the national economy." This is a set of records reflecting in the main the results of the production process for a given year in accordance with the Marxian scheme of production and reproduction. The integrated accounting system, which covers several aspects simultaneously, provides a supplement to this information in the shape of detailed data on the circular flow within the economy in fully articulated form. The integration of the same methods into AMSs will enable such types of accounting schemes to be used at all levels of the economic hierarchy. The general scheme of accounting tables is shown in Figure 3.2.

The global material-financial-balance (GMFB) at the highest level of aggregation is compiled in two variants: one according to industrial branches, and the other according to republics. The republic GMFBs give details of the industrial breakdown of performance indicators appearing in the global interrepublic GMFB, while the sum of all industrial indicators at the republic level will equal the global figures in the highest level interindustry GMFB. The basis of the national system and the network of GMFBs are the matrixes of production and financial flows culled from the reports (and plans) of individual enterprises. These form the lowest levels of information. The system contains within itself possibilities for modifications in the accounts of each administrative level (without disturbing the links in the system), which may be made in pursuance of the specific interests of individual rungs in the administrative system of the Soviet economy (the accounting matrix of the state budget, the accounting matrix of global payments of the state bank, the national balance of payments matrix).

The compilation of integrated physical-financial-balances requires the standardization of the primary financial information flows in the AMSs of industrial sectors.

FIGURE 3.2

Integrated System of Accounts for Analysis and Planning of the Economy

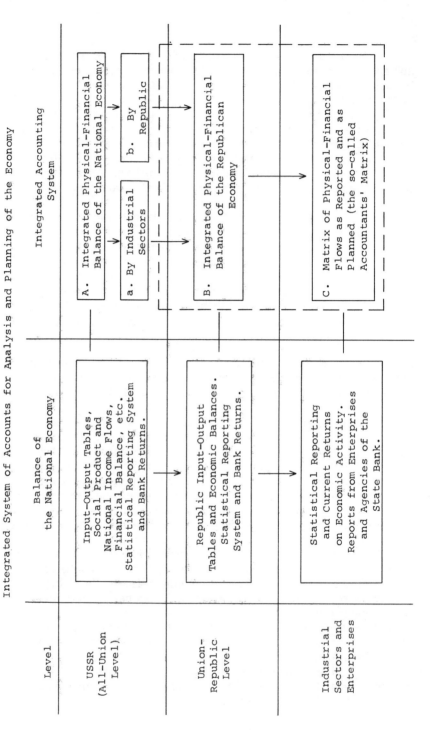

Source: Compiled by the author.

36

The primary data on the financial operations of enterprises must be recorded in such a way as to ensure comparability with the financial information used in all AMSs at present existing or to be set up in the future. This can be achieved by a standardized system of coding, identifying economic units and their operations, and labeling all data with the corresponding code numbers. This standardized system may be built up on the basis of enterprise accounts and takes the following form.

Standard accounting frameworks must be worked out for each industrial sector of the national economy.

Within the enterprise, economic information is recorded in the form of a matrix. This matrix is a classificatory scheme of the standard accounting framework and is constructed in such a way that the most detailed subdivisions of accounts occurring within it correspond entirely to the needs of the enterprise. At the same time, however, it must allow aggregation in a manner that is significant from the point of view of the national economy as a whole, and provide the means of isolating those information flows regarding the operating of the enterprise that can serve as the direct "feed-in" into a similar matrix at the next higher level of the economic hierarchy. For all practical purposes the accounting matrix at the enterprise level is the integrated physical-financial-balance of the enterprise and its constituent entries correspond to the entries in the normal commercial accounts.

The code number of each operation reported by the enterprise is a label that locates the corresponding entry in the matrix. The original reporting system records against the value of each transaction the code numbers of the transactors and that of the type of operation involved, each number referring to a specific location in the matrix framework. Since all transactions between Soviet enterprises are recorded by a single clearing center—the state bank—such a system of data flows will permit the latter to gather all the relevant information in a form that can be directly incorporated into the integrated physical-financial-balance.

In those cases where the economic transaction involves a money payment, the bank will dispose of information on the identity of the transactors as well as the type of transaction performed. At the same time, the code number of the enterprise that carries information on its administrative and sectoral position, its location and other characteristics, will enable the bank to undertake any desired analysis of interindustry flows, i.e., according to administrative sectors, regions, or functional aspects of the economy. The code number of the operation that defines all the characteristics of its position in the enterprise's accounts enables the bank to process this information additionally according to the financial aspects of the transaction.

In sum, therefore, the bank obtains all the information necessary for an integrated tableau of the process of production, distribution, redistribution, and final utilization of the national income, and of all the links between industrial branches and enterprises that are being formed in this process.

Even in those cases where the economic operation is internal to the enterprise and does not involve payments or other effects outside the enterprise, it will be recorded in the accounting matrix. If the reports sent by enterprises to statistical organs are made in matrix form and based on the accounting matrix, a "tie-in" between the information flows of the Central Statistical Administration and those of the state bank will be ensured.

The use of standardized code numbers for enterprises in all automated data processing systems will enable administrative organs operating under different systems to exchange information and will thereby substantially widen the scope for economic analysis within each AMS. The use of code numbers for each type of operation based on standard accounting matrixes would create standardized frameworks for the consistent description and analysis of financial relationships within the economy as a whole. Both types of code number thus would be great steps toward the integration of economic reporting systems, whether statistical, accounting, or production-operational, and thus would solve a pressing problem at a time when automated information and processing systems are being created throughout the national economy.

CONCENTRATION AND
SPECIALIZATION
IN INDUSTRY

Kenneth D. George

INTRODUCTION

The study of concentration and specialization in industry has long been of interest to the economist. Up to a point it is recognized that increasing the concentration of economic activity can result in benefits to society—by allowing economies of scale to be attained, especially those achieved through increasing the division of labor both between and within firms, and also by the attainment of those wider economies that cut across industry boundaries and that apply to the concentration of economic activity in particular regions. But there are problems as well—problems of market power, the monotony of work in industries where the division of labor has been carried furthest, and external diseconomies in regions where economic activity has come to be most highly concentrated. We are concerned, therefore, not only with the aggregate or overall level of industrial concentration and the extent to which a small number of firms dominate individual markets, but also with the geographical concentration of economic activity.

In this chapter it will be possible only to outline some of the main issues, looking first at the level of aggregate concentration, secondly at the concentration of activity in individual markets, and thirdly at some aspects of the regional problem.

AGGREGATE CONCENTRATION

One of the most striking features of the manufacturing sector of developed economies is the extent to which activity is concentrated in the hands of a relatively small number of firms. In Britain, in 1965, the 100 largest companies held approximately 60 percent of net assets in the quoted public sector of manufacturing and distribution.[1] In the United States the share of manufacturing assets held by the 100 largest manufacturing companies in 1968 was 49 percent, and by the 200 largest 60 percent.

Apart from the level of aggregate concentration there are two other important questions. First, what is the rate of turnover among the leading firms? Second, has there been any clear tendency for the aggregate level of concentration to increase over time?

Some evidence on turnover is to be found in a study by N. R. Collins and L. E. Preston for the U.S. economy over the period 1909-58.[2] They found that of the 100 largest firms (in terms of assets) in manufacturing, mining, and distribution in 1909, 36 remained among the top 100 in 1958. The changes that have occurred are, of course, closely related to structural change in the economy. In particular, firms that were heavily engaged in food and clothing gave way to those in the newer industries such as automobiles and petroleum refining. It is difficult, however, to draw any clear-cut conclusions from such absolute measures of turnover. Indeed, whereas some are likely to be impressed by the fact that as many as 36 firms managed to keep in the top 100 over as long a period as 50 years, others might want to emphasize the fact that 64 firms failed to maintain their leading positions. There is no doubt at all, however, about one thing, and that is that over time the rate of turnover has declined. In the period 1909-19 the average number of exits from the top 100 firms in manufacturing, mining, and distribution was 4.0 per annum; in the period 1919-29 it was 3.1; and in the periods 1935-48 and 1948-58 it was 1.5 and 1.6 per annum respectively. This trend toward the more entrenched position of the giant corporations is likely to have been due in large measure to the growing professionalization of management. The increasing importance of the divorce between ownership and control in the large corporation has been associated with the emergence of a management class whose main interest is to preserve the firm as an organization. In general, it has been in the interests of this class to avoid very risky projects, including too heavy a reliance on the production of a narrow range of commodities, and instead to seek greater security and status by emphasizing the growth of the organization, including growth by diversification.

As far as trends in aggregate concentration are concerned, the evidence of the postwar years for the United States and Britain suggests that there has been some tendency for the degree of dominance of the largest manufacturing firms to increase. In the United States the 100 largest manufacturing firms in 1947 accounted for 23 percent of value added, in 1958 the figure was 30 percent and in 1966, 33 percent.[3] In Britain, the 100 largest companies in manufacturing and distribution increased their share of quoted public sector net assets from 44 percent in 1954-65 percent in 1965. These trends have been due partly to the rapid expansion of industries in which large firms predominate, partly to increased merger activity within industries, and partly to the increasing importance of diversification in the growth of large companies.[4] The third of these factors—the growing importance of diversification—deserves further comment. In particular, it is worth looking at the significance of this development for resource allocation and for monopoly policy.

The factor that perhaps stands out more than any other is the way in which diversification has become more a "strategy of development" than simply a response to adverse market conditions. Perhaps this is largely due to the greater professionalization of management that we have already noted, and in particular to the fact that management has become more long-sighted. Whatever the strength of this argument, there is little doubt that diversification has been facilitated by developments in management techniques and especially as a result of the greater use of computers and the adoption of the decentralized or multidivisional form of organization.

But what of the consequences of all this for the process of competition and for the performance of the competitive system? On the one hand, there are those who as yet see little need to be concerned about the large diversified company and indeed point to some actual or potential advantages. Thus, for instance, it is pointed out that even if the aggregate level of concentration were much higher than it is today this would be quite compatible with each large firm lacking significant monopoly power in individual markets. In this case large firms owe their size not to positions of dominance in one market but to the extensive diversification of their operations. Individual market shares, therefore, may be relatively low and competition between firms in each market intensive.

Looking at the diversified firm in a more dynamic context it may be argued that it improves the performance of the economic system in two important although related ways. First, because it increases the degree of competitiveness by facilitating entry into industries where the barriers to entry are too high for the smaller more specialized firm. Secondly, because there is some tendency for the direction of diversification to be toward industries characterized by above-average profitability and growth rates.[5] Given the fact that large companies finance a high proportion of their capital expenditure from retained profits, the diversified company may, therefore, facilitate more rapid resource reallocation and thus contribute toward a more adaptable economic system.

This advantage of flexibility in the allocation of investment funds may also be promoted by the internal organization of the large diversified firm, and especially by the division of function between different levels of management. Here the multidivisional form of organization is of particular importance. To such an organization the formulation of investment plans will be made by branch or divisional managers who compete for the finance available to the firm. Top management, however, is responsible for allocating funds, and the fact that it has not been deeply involved in the formulation of plans means that it is not committed to them and, therefore, is free to accept, reject, or modify them. By contrast, in more specialized firms where the division of labor in management is less and where top management is more closely involved in the formulation of plans, the degree of commitment to investment projects might be such as to lead to greater inflexibility.

All this is not to say, however, that there are no problems of coordination in the large firm. Clearly there are, and they frequently lead to substantial internal inefficiency. Problems of communication between different levels of management become more severe as the organization gets larger; vested interests within the firm may be powerful enough to succeed in delaying needed changes; the capacity of the top executive to coordinate effectively is limited, especially for firms operating in constantly changing environments. The decentralization of management, the development of more sophisticated accounting and budgetary techniques, and the use of computers have helped to reduce the problems but they have not eliminated them. Clearly, it is dangerous to generalize. There are examples of large diversified firms that seem to be very efficiently managed, but also several cases that could hardly be put forward as models of efficiency. My own view is that even in an age when it is fashionable to speak about management as a team effort, a great deal of the efficiency or inefficiency of very large companies depends on the presence or absence of the organizing genius of one or two people.

It remains to mention some other problems relating to the large diversified firm.

The first, and most familiar, is the danger of cross subsidization. Thus, the large diversified firm can use its financial power to discipline specialist rivals who engage in price cutting. The smaller producers, recognizing the much greater financial strength of the new entrant, may well be forced to modify their competitive policies for fear of retaliation from the large firm, and the latter may in effect become a price leader.[6] Price cutting subsidized by profits from other markets where the firm has monopoly power may also be carried further in an attempt to eliminate rivals from the market or to forestall the entry of new firms. There clearly are limitations to the profits that can be sacrificed in this way and whether such a strategy is worthwhile will depend on whether entry barriers can be raised sufficiently to ensure higher long-term profits. However, it must not be forgotten that the mere entry of a large diversified firm into an industry previously consisting of specialist producers only will change entry conditions for other specialized firms, making them more difficult than would otherwise be the case.

More important, however, is the use of excess profits in one market to engage in heavy advertising in another so as to extend a firm's sphere of monopoly influence. The danger is particularly great where marketing rather than production skill is the main basis of diversification. It is in the field of marketing that large firms have perhaps the main advantage over smaller ones—especially where such factors as brand names, national advertising, and style changes are important. In this case a small number of diversified firms may well build up a position of dominance in several industries, using their monopoly position in one industry to finance heavy sales promotion expenditures in another. Furthermore, once established in a dominant position the heavy marketing expenditures are themselves an entry barrier to new competition. It has to be recognized, of course, that such developments, although leading to positions of greater dominance for large firms, could still be consistent with substantial competition between large firms themselves. Thus exploitation of a monopoly situation by one large firm carries with it the danger of attracting competition from another. It is highly unlikely, however, that the dominant firms will achieve the same pattern of diversification. Rather, it is likely that in a number of cases the main activity of one firm will be a secondary activity of another and that, recognizing the dangers of spoiling one another's markets, firms will tend to develop "spheres of influence."[7] If mutual interpenetration of markets does occur and profits are eroded then this may be followed either by restrictive trading agreements or by mergers or other (perhaps government-sponsored) schemes designed to "rationalize production."

As large firms increase their dominance, their interdependence as buyers and sellers also increases. There will be a tendency, therefore, for an increasing proportion of interfirm transactions to be based not on a comparison of price, quality, etc., from different sources of supply but on bargaining power. That is, preference in purchasing of inputs will be given to a firm that is a good customer for one's own products. Such arrangements may be undertaken even at some sacrifice in terms of higher cost. But even where price, quality, and reliability of supply are equal, reciprocal buying arrangements still have anticompetitive effects. They inevitably favor the larger firm, and increase the entry barriers to new firms, since the latter have no large purchases they can use to secure orders.

Finally, it must be recognized that even if, given the high proportion of finance that is generated internally by the large firm, the diversified form of organization facilitates more rapid resource allocation, there is the more fundamental question of whether high levels of self-finance should be accepted as inviolate, or whether firms should be forced to compete more for funds in the market. In this situation the allocation of resources would be subject to more stringent market tests and would be less influenced by forms of organization and types of management control.[8]

Where the balance of advantage and disadvantage lies in relation to the present positions of the large diversified company is difficult to determine. There is certainly need for much more research into many of the issues. In the meantime, policy has to be formulated. My own view is that it would be better to err on the side of adopting a hard line rather than a soft line toward big business, and the area where this can most appropriately be done is in policy toward mergers. It would be silly to adopt any measures against diversification as such. The major cause for concern is the way in which expansion by diversification is achieved, and here there should be a very definite presumption in favor of internal growth and against mergers. This does not impose any undue burden on large as compared to small firms. Indeed the former have greater financial, managerial, and marketing resources on which to base expansion. But when growth takes place in this way it is more likely to be grounded on efficiency factors and less likely to be based on financial and market power than is the case with expansion by merger.

MARKET CONCENTRATION

We have seen that most of the problems relating to the large diversified firm are likely to be found when such a firm has market power in individual markets. What, then, is the general picture as far as individual market concentration is concerned?

In the United States, the present position in the manufacturing sector, as reflected by census data, is approximately that shown in Table 4.1. This shows that high concentration accounts for only a minority of industries. Thus in 1963, 74 out of 416 industries had a 4-firm concentration ratio of 60 percent or over, and accounted for 21 percent of total value added in manufacturing. The weighted average concentration ratio is approximately 40 percent. Although the evidence is far from perfect it seems that the picture is broadly similar in Britain where again high concentration accounts for a significant minority of markets, and where the average level of concentration also seems to be similar to that in the United States.[9]

TABLE 4.1

Distribution of Manufacturing Industries by 4-Firm
Concentration Ratios, United States, 1963
(416 4-digit industries)

4-Firm Concentration Ratio	Number of Industries	Percent of Total Value Added
0-19	89	20.8
20-39	161	38.0
40-59	92	20.5
60-79	47	9.9
80-100	27	10.8
Total	416	100.0

Source: U. S. Senate, Subcommittee on Antitrust and Monopoly, "Concentration Ratios in Manufacturing Industry, 1963" (Washington, 1966).

In the postwar years the trend in concentration has been upward. In the United States this trend has been slight but certainly noticeable.[10] In the United Kingdom the upward movement probably has been more marked, although here again the evidence is incomplete. Certainly, however, the majority of industries for which comparisons can be made showed upward movements in concentration between the three census dates 1951, 1958, and 1963.

Census information must, however, be used with great caution. The industry boundaries "drawn" by the census often diverge, sometimes substantially, from those that actually identify groups of closely competing firms. The existence of regional markets within the national economy, and of strong product differentiation within a census industry will mean that the boundaries of the latter are drawn too widely, so that concentration is underestimated. On the other hand, where imports account for a substantial proportion of domestic consumption the census industry will tend to overestimate the degree of concentration since it takes into account only domestic production. As far as the United States is concerned there seems little doubt that the net effect of these influences is for the 4-digit industry data to underestimate the true level of concentration in the manufacturing sector.[11] In Britain, on the other hand, imports are far more important, and in several industries the volume of imports is such as to rob domestic concentration ratios of much of their usefulness. After making an allowance for the effects of regional markets, strong product differentiation, and imports it may well be that the true level of market concentration is higher in the United States than it is in Britain.

There is another respect in which published concentration ratios also conceal an important aspect of industry structure. In referring to the share of the four or five largest firms they conceal the dominant position often held by the largest (or two largest) firm in an industry. Such positions of dominance occur most frequently in smaller industrial countries such as Australia and Sweden, but they are also an important phenomenon in the United States and Britain. And these situations of dominance by one or two firms seem to be the worst offenders in terms of exploitation of monopoly power. Also, 4-firm concentration ratios do not show the extent to which the remainder of the industry is concentrated. There is some evidence that suggests that, given the level of 4-firm concentration, economic performance tends to be better the higher the concentration of the rest of the industry in the hands of the fifth to eighth largest firms. Certainly, one would expect that unless there is collusion, as in the case of the British cement industry, economic performance will be better where there is effective competition between half-a-dozen or so firms than where there is dominance by one or two firms.

To what extent, however, can high concentration be explained by the existence of economies of scale in production and distribution? There is a fair amount of evidence that suggests that the long-run cost curve of the individual firm at first sharply declines then flattens to produce conditions of constant or slightly increasing returns to scale. The important questions, therefore, are the size of firms at which all substantial economies are exhausted and how large this size is in relation to the size of the market. The present state of knowledge on these questions can, I think, be summarized as follows:

First, most of the important economies of scale seem to be realized at the plant level. These economies are based on such factors as the division of labor, the use of specialized machines, and the benefits of long production runs.

Second, attempts to measure the importance of plant economies by the use of such methods as statistical cost analysis, survival tests, and engineering estimates, have tended to show that concentration is in most industries much higher than would be the case if each of the four leading firms had one plant of minimum optimal size.

Third, an important explanation of actual concentration levels is the extent to which leading firms engage in multiplant operations. There is little evidence, however, to suggest that multiplant economies—e.g., in management, marketing, research, and development—are important. What evidence there is has tended to show that multiplant economies are rather modest.

This suggests, then, that as far as economies of scale are concerned, the existing levels of concentration in most industries are "unnecessarily" high, by which we mean that productive and distributive efficiency would be just as good at substantially lower levels of concentration in many industries. It might equally be said, of course, that high concentration could be adequately explained by efficiency factors. After all, there is not much evidence of diseconomies of scale in the production of a given product, and when this fact is combined with the desire of management for the growth of the organization it can quite easily be seen why high concentration might emerge on the basis of efficiency considerations alone.

It must also be emphasized that the bulk of the evidence that I have attempted to summarize is based on U.S. data, so that the conclusions need not be applicable universally. In particular, differences in the size of markets does have an important impact on concentration levels, an impact that is seen most clearly by comparing the United States with small industrial markets such as Australia, Canada, and Sweden. Whether the difference in size between the United States and British markets for comparable products is large enough to justify higher concentration in Britain is more difficult to determine.

Differences in the size of markets also contribute to the explanation of differences between countries in the degree of specialization within plants. The diversity of processes carried on within the same plant is generally smaller in America than in European countries and this difference has been given great prominence in productivity comparisons between America and Europe. The larger the market and the more consumers can be persuaded to accept standardization, the more will specialized techniques be employed. Conversely, the smaller the market and the greater the demand for variety, the greater the risk involved in the use of specialized production techniques and the more likely it is that firms will adopt the more flexible techniques of production.[12] Of course other factors, and particularly transport costs, are also important in determining the size of markets. But whether it is on account of the demand for variety, or the smallness of the domestic market, or the size of the market, it is economical to supply from one plant (because of transport costs) for any of these reasons all the potential economies of scale may not be realized.

Although efficiency factors may go a long way in explaining patterns of concentration and specialization I do not think they tell anything like the whole story. There are other important factors to be taken into account as well.

Foremost among these is the desire to gain market power. This may be achieved as the result of internal expansion, but more often it is the outcome of expansion by acquisition and merger. The way in which mergers can change the structure of markets is impressive. The classic example of course is the first merger boom in the United States at the turn of the century. More recently, however, mergers have transformed British industrial structure in such sectors as vehicles, electrical engineering, and clothing and footwear. Furthermore, one cannot but fail to be impressed by the economies-of-scale benefits of mergers. After all, most of the important economies of scale occur within the plant and the only immediate effect of a merger is to bring two previously separately owned plants under common ownership. If there are important technical links between the plants there may be scope for significant cost savings, but this does not seem to be very common. For instance, an investigation carried out by the Economic Council of Canada into acquisitions made by manufacturing companies during the period 1948-61 came to the following tentative conclusions. In as many as 47 percent of the cases on which information was obtained, negligible or no economies of scale were realized. Even in horizontal acquisitions alone the figure was as high as 35 percent. In only 10 percent of all cases (15 percent for horizontal acquisitions) were any economies claimed as a result of integration of plants and use of raw materials.[13] Again, a study by Newbould suggests that efficiency considerations are much less important than those of market power in explaining merger activity.[14]

Of course, from the point of view of the firm, expansion by merger has several advantages especially in terms of the speed of expansion and the ease of entry into new fields. But this does not mean that there are corresponding benefits for the economy as a whole. Thus, although a firm can increase its growth rate by means of merger, there is no corresponding acceleration of real growth in the economy unless the merger means that the combined resources of the larger unit can be used more productively because of economies of scale or complementarities in production and distribution; but this, as we have seen, is not usually the case. Indeed, one of the worrying features of unusually high merger activity is that it may well result in a reduction in the rate of capital accumulation and of real economic growth as compared to what it should have been with greater emphasis on internal expansion.

In the short run, adverse effects on growth may result because of the greater proportion of managerial resources required for coordination of activities within the firms that have been enlarged by merger. More serious longer-term effects may arise as mergers result in growing monopolization of industry. The danger is greatest where a competitive situation is transformed by a series of mergers into a dominant-firm situation. In the initial situation, firms have competitive investment projects and the losses resulting to one firm from another's investment plans do not deter the latter from expanding capacity. If the situation is transformed into a monopoly then these losses are internalized with the result that investment will be reduced. Similar effects may occur where the number of competitors is small enough for investment plans to be based on cooperation rather than competition. Of course, the situation is not so simple as to allow one to conclude that any tendency toward less competitive investment plans should be resisted. Competitive investment plans may lead to large fluctuations in investment and a failure to achieve a reasonably smooth adjustment of capacity to demand. But whereas such tendencies may be reduced by greater cooperation between firms, the monopoly dangers must also be realized.

Two other factors related to market power may have a strong influence on industrial concentration. The first is that for certain commodities, especially in the field of consumer goods, there may be advantages of large-scale sales promotion. Since the "pulling power" of a large sales effort is more effective than that of a small one, sales promotion activities benefit the larger firms. Therefore, it will generally pay for a firm to grow large enough to make effective use of the national advertising media. Similar considerations may lead it to establish links on a national basis with distributive outlets. Once existing firms have established such links, a very effective barrier is created to the entry of new competitors. Such advantages are probably largely responsible for the findings in the United States that the tendency toward higher levels of concentration has been more marked in consumer goods industries than in the field of producer goods.[15]

The second factor is that of "countervailing power." In this case the existence of large firms with market power on one side of the market is an incentive to the growth of large firms on the other side, so that the latter can both protect themselves from the market power of their suppliers or buyers, and also share in any monopoly gains.[16] Evidence does not support the view that the emergence of countervailing power is a general tendency applicable to all situations. Nor is it clear that where countervailing power has emerged this is due to market power on the other side of the market. But whatever the reasons for the emergence of countervailing power its existence is important, and nowhere more so than in the development of large multiple retailers.

This introduces a point that is of substantial importance not only to capitalist economies but also to any socialist economy where, for instance, the consumer goods sector is organized on the basis of free-market transactions. Many of the problems associated with big business seem to be particularly prevalent in manufacturer-dominated industries. The question is whether the interests of consumers can be met more effectively in an economy where industries are dominated by integrated retailer-wholesaler firms, or at least where manufacturers' power, where it exists, is faced with retail buying power. "In our Utopian economy production is directed by the interests of consumers, and the consumer interest cannot prevail where individual buyers confront producers. . . . The consumer interest, therefore, must be organized, and the most convenient way of doing this is through the agency of wholesale buyers whose business it is to negotiate with productive enterprises and fix the prices at which goods are offered to consumers."17 At best, retailers can take the initiative in deciding, via their orders to manufacturers, what should be produced, these decisions being more in accord with consumer preferences than is the case where they are made by manufacturers. Furthermore, large retailers' orders may be associated with long production runs and thus with the realization of economies in production. At worst, monopoly gains may be shared between retailer and manufacturer with little benefit being passed on to the consumer. However, as long as there is sufficient competition between retailers or there is some other constraint on the abuse of retailers' monopoly power, performance should be substantially better than in manufacturer-dominated industries.

Another factor tending toward higher concentration, especially in industries where investment projects require the expenditure of large absolute sums of money, is imperfections in the capital market. When very large sums are required for investment, large firms will have access to the funds at more favorable rates of interest, and indeed, small firms may not be able to raise the funds at all. At the very least, therefore, such conditions make it difficult for small firms to expand and drastically reduce the number of potential entrants. The problem is greatest where large amounts of finance are combined with important economies of scale—that is, where the minimum efficient size of plant is large in relation to the size of the market and where there are substantial cost disadvantages in entering at a size very much below the optimum. In this case unless the market is expanding very rapidly, even large firms in other industries, which have no relative disadvantage in raising capital, will not be very likely candidates for entry. Even assuming them to have the requisite marketing and technical knowledge, the risks involved in terms of excess capacity are likely to be the decisive factor. In discussing the problem of finance, Sargant Florence has suggested that whereas, historically, the ability to raise large sums has been the main advantage of the joint-stock company, more recently the inability of private enterprise to raise capital for certain projects has been one of the main weaknesses of the system and a factor, therefore, tending toward greater state participation in industry.[18]

This brings me to the role of government in influencing the concentration of industry. The most direct way in which the government can increase the degree of concentration in the economy is of course by nationalization. But apart from this, there are two other factors of considerable importance.

The first is the degree of permissiveness shown by the government toward mergers and acquisitions. It has been suggested by Walter Adams that government permissiveness toward mergers may be the most important single factor explaining merger activity. It was certainly one important factor in the British merger boom in the second half of the 1960s. Apart from this, the government may give an indirect encouragement to mergers as a result of its fiscal policy. Tax discrimination in favor of retained earnings, for instance, may have this effect.

The second factor is the law with regard to patents. The ownership of patent rights can be an important factor in increasing concentration or in entrenching the position of dominant firms, especially in the technologically progressive fields such as chemicals, electrical engineering, and electronics. How important a major patented invention is in causing increases in concentration depends on how quickly, and the extent to which, competitors can respond with rival products or processes. But, this competitive check may be reduced in effectiveness by the accumulation of patents by the currently leading firm in a field. And competitive responses from much smaller firms are, of course, very difficult because of the financial power of large companies and thus their ability to buy patent rights from small firms or individuals, to contest patent rights (the legal cost of the latter putting the small firm or individual at an overwhelming disadvantage), or, of course, to acquire the smaller innovating firm. Patent rights may also entrench existing monopoly situations by means of the handling of licensing agreements. Thus, for instance, a firm may grant licenses to produce only to other large firms that pose a technological threat to it, and withhold such privileges from smaller competitors and new entrants. Licensing arrangements may also be used to control prices and output, thus again entrenching monopoly positions and restrictive business behavior. Whether these disadvantages of the patent system outweigh its benefits, in terms of a greater flow of inventions and innovations, is not easily answered. But there is certainly need for further investigation into the effects of the patent system to see to what extent, if at all, it can be modified so as to improve the balance between social cost and benefit.

Finally, on concentration, I wish to make two more general points of great importance. First, even if economies of scale do seem to indicate a very high level of concentration, there is a problem of the loss of the competitive stimulus. I regard this as being most important in the field of innovation, and in view of the need for several independent centers of initiative. As far as efficiency is concerned, I would not be worried about high levels of concentration or the efficiency of management in large firms if we lived in a world where demand and technological conditions remained unvaried. It is in a changing world that problems of managerial efficiency and the dangers of relying on the decisions of the few arise in their most acute form. For instance, there is need to minimize the danger, always present in tightly knit oligopolistic industries, of development on a narrow front. On this score, the U.S. automobile industry is a major culprit. The leading companies have been far more concerned with the introduction of trivial style changes than, for instance, with improvement of safety and the development of an engine that produces less air pollution. And it took competition from imports to force the U.S. manufacturers to produce a small car. Similarly, large firms in the U.S. steel industry have not been prominent in innovation activity, and much of the technological advance in this industry has also been forced by competition from imports. Competition, therefore, is important in influencing the direction of innovation, and in particular in ensuring that cost-reducing and major product innovations are not delayed in favor of minor improvements to existing products.

Secondly, there is the relationship between concentration and specialization and the place of the individual in industry and in society. Within the factory, labor is treated as another factor to be most efficiently "combined" with machines. The employee has to fit into a very specialized role within an organizational structure that is considered to be the one most suited to achieving the goals of the firm. As specialization increases, the individual is asked to use fewer of his abilities. As Adam Smith pointed out, "the man whose whole life is spent in performing a few simple operations . . . has no occasion to exert his understanding or to exercise his invention in finding out expedients for remaining difficulties which never occur. He naturally loses, therefore, the habit of such exertion and generally becomes as stupid and ignorant as it is possible for a human creature to become."19 The worst consequences of the division of labor as seen by Adam Smith have been avoided by the spread of education and the increase in leisure hours. However, his statement is still of some relevance today. Working hours still account for the greater part of man's active life and job satisfaction is in itself an important aspect of human welfare.

A further consequence of increasing concentration is that the major decisions on plant location and closures will be made at a smaller number of centers and will become increasingly divorced from the local communities that are most closely affected. Thus, for instance, one of the problems of inducing firms to establish branch plants in the less developed areas of an economy is that these often tend to be the ones that are most affected by adverse changes in demand for the firm's products. This kind of problem also exists on the international plane. The growth of multinational firms has resulted, in the case of Canada for instance, in the loss of a considerable degree of national independence in the formulation of industrial policy. But all this brings us to issues of geographical concentration to which we now turn.

GEOGRAPHICAL CONCENTRATION

Just as there are internal economies of scale to be gained as a firm expands to its minimum optimal size, so there are external economies associated with the expansion of the industry (or group of industries) as a whole. Thus, as an industry expands, it will be able to purchase its machinery more cheaply, firms will share the advantages of an increasing supply of skilled labor, transport and banking facilities will become available that would not have been available to an industry of much smaller size, and so on. Some of these factors result in the concentration of industry in one locality or region. Most important in this regard perhaps are the development of a supply of skilled labor and the advantages of proximity between firms with close technical links.

But these economies are not inexhaustible. Indeed, whereas in the case of the expansion of output within the firm there is no clear evidence of diseconomies of size, in the case of the expansion of industry in a given locality there are clear examples of over-expansion and the emergence of external diseconomies of size. The latter are seen particularly in the form of air and water pollution and traffic congestion.

I see no market mechanism that is sufficiently powerful and quick-working to correct this tendency toward excessive geographical concentration. The strongest forces seem in fact to be working the other way and to cause the decline or expansion of individual regions to be a cumulative process, with the expanding areas attracting the more adaptable resources from other regions of the economy, thus making them less attractive for new developments. For instance, the workers who move away from the less prosperous areas are likely to contain a disproportionately high number of the younger, more skilled, and enterprising members of the population. The decline in income associated with this emigration will also lead to a fall in induced investment, both in the private and public sectors, which will reduce income levels still further and make the region less attractive to new firms. The expanding areas on the other hand enjoy the advantages of increasing returns to scale and an up-to-date stock of social capital.

The expansion of prosperous areas, however, takes place as a result of the locational decisions made by employers and employees. These are based on a consideration of private costs that may diverge from those that are borne by society. More specifically, expansion in the prosperous areas will eventually result in congestion costs that are not reflected in the costs borne by individuals and firms. The fact that location decisions are based on actual charges that fall short of marginal social cost means that expansion in the prosperous areas will proceed beyond the social optimum point.

Government policy aimed at counteracting these tendencies has in most Western economies been relatively unsuccessful. This is due largely to the strength of the cumulative factors making for expansion and decline, and also in part to the short-term nature of many of the policy approaches adopted. In Britain, for instance, distribution-of-industry policy was pursued with considerable purposefulness during the immediate postwar years. For most of the 1950s, however, interest in the problem subsided until the recession of 1958 and the growing difficulties faced by industries such as coal mining, textiles, and shipbuilding caused attention to be focused again on the fundamental weakness of the industrial structure of the development areas. During the 1960s, therefore, industrial development certificates were again used more forcefully to restrict expansion in the most prosperous areas, and financial inducements became very much more important especially during the second half of the decade. The 1970s, however, have begun with a drastic weakening of the financial incentives offered to the less developed areas of Britain, whereas the regional problem itself is likely when Britain joins the European Economic Community, to get more difficult to handle.

It is in the field of regional development more than in any other area of policy-making that planning is needed. It is also here more than anywhere else that there is need to take social and cultural factors into account as well as economic ones. The case for regional policy and for a more even geographical spread of industrial activity is only partly an economic one. Efficiency is not an adequate test of economic performance. Economic success must be related to a pattern of living that people find tolerable.

CONCLUDING COMMENTS

Are there any lessons to be learned by East European countries from what has happened in the West? It is dangerous, to say the least, to be dogmatic about any of the main issues. In both East and West, there is no single type of economy but a number of different models with varying degrees of emphasis on free enterprise and planning. Furthermore, our knowledge of structure-behavior-performance relationships is imperfect, often seriously so. Nevertheless, I think that something useful can be said, first in relation to growth, and second in relation to competition and the interests of consumers.

Some of the problems touched upon in the previous section are closely related to economic growth, and a number of economists have argued that the costs of growth in advanced economies are so great as to justify removing it from among the worthwhile objectives of economic policy. However, even though we may regard a fairer distribution of income and wealth, the clearance of slums, the conservation of habitable cities, etc., as more important objectives than growth, it has to be recognized that, given the political and other constraints operating in the economy, most of these more worthwhile objectives are more easily achieved in a growing economy than in a stagnating one. But whether they are achieved or not depends on the government. The managers of firms will not take divergences between private and social costs into account unless they are compelled to do so, and it is one of the important functions of planning to see that such divergences are reflected in decision-making. Hopefully, in the less industrially developed economies, the worst problems of overconcentration and traffic congestion in towns can be avoided by sensible control of industrial location and the maintenance of an efficient urban public transport system so as to restrict the use of private vehicles in town centers.

Another major aspect of planning is, of course, the problem of determining the allocation of resources. In a socialist economy, the broad aggregates of the economy, such as the division of resources between consumption and investment, are determined by planning from the center. But within these basic overall dimensions there is the question of whether resource allocation should be determined by administrative means or be based on free enterprise and a system of market prices. In the case of the former, the maintenance of competitive market structures is not crucial. Indeed, very high levels of market concentration facilitate administrative means of control. However, to the extent that East European countries move toward a system of market prices and free enterprise, it is, I believe, of fundamental importance that attention is directed toward maintaining competition. Of course, this does not imply uniform industry structures. A given concentration ratio and the size-distribution of firms have different significance depending on such factors as the strength of competition from substitutes and imports. But although there is no unique optimum structure for all industries, it is, nevertheless, useful to be able to identify factors that tend to undermine competitive structures. In this respect, our earlier discussion suggests a number of points of some importance for the development of a market system in socialist economies.

First, greater freedom to managers should be set within a framework that puts emphasis on internal growth. There should be a strong presumption against mergers or amalgamations.

Second, in research and development work, any bias in policy should be toward maintaining several independent centers of initiative rather than toward the concentration of resources in one enterprise.

Third, the business of manufacturing should be kept distinct from that of distribution of goods. It is important to ensure the development of powerful and independent retail outlets, again in a competitive environment, so as to safeguard the interests of consumers.

NOTES

1. M. A. Utton, Industrial Concentration (Harmondsworth: Penguin Modern Economics, 1970), p. 88.

2. N. R. Collins and L. E. Preston, "The Size Structure of the Largest Industrial Firms," American Economic Review, December, 1961.

3. U.S. Senate, Subcommittee on Antitrust and Monopoly, "Concentration Ratios in Manufacturing Industry, 1963"; and U.S. Bureau of the Census, "Annual Survey of Manufactures, 1966." Washington.

4. See R. L. Nelson, Concentration in the Manufacturing Industries of the United States (New Haven: Yale University Press, 1963); Michael Gort, Diversification and Integration in American Industry (Princeton, N.J.: Princeton University Press, 1962).

5. Gort, op. cit.

6. See John M. Blair, "The Conglomerate Merger in Economics and Law," Georgetown Law Journal, Summer, 1958.

7. On the spheres of influence hypothesis, see Corwin Edwards, "Conglomerate Bigness as a Source of Power," in National Bureau of Economic Research, Business Concentration and Price Policy (Princeton, N.J.: Princeton University Press, 1955).

8. For a policy recommendation along these lines, see J. E. Meade, "Is the New Industrial State Inevitable?," Economic Journal, June, 1968.

9. See Alan Armstrong and Aubrey Silberston, "Size of Plant, Size of Enterprise and Concentration in British Manufacturing Industry, 1935-58," Journal of the Royal Statistical Society, Series A,

Vol. 128, Part 3 (1965); Joe S. Bain, International Differences in Industrial Structure (New Haven: Yale University Press, 1966).

10. See Joe S. Bain, "Changes in Concentration in Manufacturing Industries in the United States, 1954-66: Trends and Relationships to the Levels of 1954 Concentration," The Review of Economics and Statistics, November, 1970.

11. One attempt to adjust the 1966 census data resulted in an upward revision of the weighted average concentration ratio for manufacturing industries from 39 percent to 60 percent. See William G. Shepherd, Market Power and Economic Welfare: An Introduction (New York: Random House, 1970).

12. A widening of markets by, for instance, tariff reductions will tend to result in greater intraindustry specialization. See Bela Balassa, "Tariff Reductions and Trade in Manufactures among the Industrial Countries," American Economic Review June 1966; and H. G. Grubel, "Intra-Industry Specialization and the Pattern of Trade," Canadian Journal of Economics and Political Science, August, 1967.

13. Economic Council of Canada, Interim Report on Competition Policy (Ottawa: The Queen's Printer, July, 1969), p. 217.

14. G. D. Newbould, Management and Merger Activity (Liverpool: Guthstead Ltd., 1970).

15. See Willard Mueller's testimony in U.S. Senate, Select Committee on Small Business, Hearings, "Status and Future of Small Business," (Washington, 1967).

16. J. K. Galbraith, American Capitalism: The Concept of Countervailing Power (Boston: Houghton Mifflin, 1952).

17. Joan Robinson, Exercises in Economic Analysis (London: Macmillan, 1961).

18. P. Sargant Florence, Ownership, Control and Success of Large Companies, an Analysis of English Industrial Structure & Policy 1936-51 (London: Sweet and Maxwell, 1961), p. 26.

19. Adam Smith, The Wealth of Nations, Book V, Ch. 1, Part III (London, 1776).

5

**LONG-TERM
PLANNING IN
INDUSTRY**
I. van der Zijp

Corporate planning requires a forecast of the trends in society as a whole for the next ten or more years. On the basis of this general forecast, a prognosis must be made of the future development of the markets in which the industry is presently operating or which it could enter in the future. The next step is the selection of the goods to be produced and the markets to be supplied in the future. Corporate strategy must then be elaborated. Detailed plans must be drafted for the various functions of the company: sales, purchases, production, transport, organization, personnel, capital investment, research, etc. The various plans are summarized in a financial prognosis. Management finally considers this prognosis and decides whether other alternatives require consideration. If this is the case, the planning procedure is repeated. If not, the draft plan is accepted as a basis for further decisions about corporate development. The structure of this planning procedure is shown in the diagram on page 63.

In this chapter, we try to survey long-term planning in industry as a whole. It goes without saying that we can only pay attention to the main variables and considerations in the planning process.

THE FINANCIAL PROGNOSIS

A financial prognosis generally consists of an estimate of the balance sheet, the profit and loss account, and the cash survey of an enterprise in a series of future years (usually five or ten years). The accounts could contain the following entries:

Balance Sheet

Assets	Year 1	Year 2	Year n
Fixed assets	B 1(1)	B 1(2)	B 1(n)
Inventories	B 2(1)	B 2(2)	B 2(n)
Receivables	B 3(1)	B 3(2)	B 3(n)
Loans outstanding	B 4(1)	B 4(2)	B 4(n)
Other claims	B 5(1)	B 5(2)	B 5(n)
Cash	B 6(1)	B 6(2)	B 6(n)
Total	B 7(1)	B 7(2)	B 7(n)

Liabilities			
Share capital	B 8(1)	B 8(2)	B 8(n)
Reserves	B 9(1)	B 9(2)	B 9(n)
Accounts payable	B10(1)	B10(2)	B10(n)
Corporate loans	B11(1)	B11(2)	B11(n)
Other liabilities	B12(1)	B12(2)	B12(n)
Profit after tax	B13(1)	B13(2)	B13(n)
Total	B14(1)	B14(2)	B14(n)

Profit and Loss Account

	Year 1	Year 2	Year n
Sales turnover	W 1(1)	W 1(2)	W 1(n)
Interest	W 2(1)	W 2(2)	W 2(n)
Other income	W 3(1)	W 3(2)	W 3(n)
Expenses	W 4(1)	W 4(2)	W 4(n)
	W 5(1)	W 5(2)	W 5(n)
Profit tax	W 6(1)	W 6(2)	W 6(n)
Profit after tax	W 7(1)	W 7(2)	W 7(n)

Cash Survey

Source	Year 1	Year 2	Year n
Pre-tax profit	G 1(1)	G 1(2)	G 1(n)
Depreciation	G 2(1)	G 2(2)	G 2(n)
Receipt of loans outstanding	G 3(1)	G 3(2)	G 3(n)
	G 4(1)	G 4(2)	G 4(n)

Expenditure	Year 1	Year 2	Year n
Investment in fixed assets	G 5(1)	G 5(2)	G 5(n)
Increase of operating capital	G 6(1)	G 6(2)	G 6(n)
Increase of other fixed liabilities	G 7(1)	G 7(2)	G 7(n)
Repayment of corporate loans	G 8(1)	G 8(2)	G 8(n)
Profit tax	G 9(1)	G 9(2)	G 9(n)
Interest on loans	G10(1)	G10(2)	G10(n)
	G11(1)	G11(2)	G11(n)
Change in cash	G12(1)	G12(2)	G12(n)
Initial cash	G13(1)	G13(2)	G13(n)
Final cash	G14(1)	G14(2)	G14(n)

The entries in these balance sheets, profit and loss accounts, and cash surveys are the main variables in long-term corporate planning. These variables can be divided into several categories, which are discussed below.

Strategic Variables

These variables are (1) sales turnover, (2) other income, (3) capital investment, (4) wage costs and social security payments, and (5) purchase costs of raw materials and auxiliary resources.

1. The sales forecast, which will be discussed later, constitutes the basis for long-term corporate planning. Estimation procedures vary according to types of industry. An industry producing a limited assortment of goods can estimate future sales and prices of each finished product separately and can determine future turnover by multiplying the estimated volume by the estimated price of each product and adding up the various amounts.

Industries producing a large assortment of goods must estimate their future turnover in total; they multiply the sales turnover in the current year by two figures: (a) expected changes in the sales volume and (b) expected price changes.

2. Other proceeds, i.e., return on corporate sidelines, are estimated in the same way as the sales turnover.

3. First, the type and volume of the production facilities required for achieving the estimated sales turnover must be determined. Then, the prices and start-up expenses of the equipment

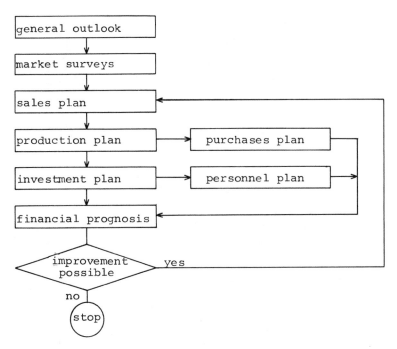

must be estimated. If it is impossible to build the necessary facilities in time because of technical or organizational factors, the estimated sales turnover (1) must be adjusted to the investment possibilities.

4. Wage costs and social security payments can be assessed by a prognosis of: (a) the work force required and (b) future wage costs and social security payments per employee. The estimated work force should be based on future sales turnover (1) and future capital investment (3). If the feasible sales development and facilities expansion is impeded by organizational difficulties or lack of personnel, the estimates under 1 and 3 must be revised.

An enterprise cannot influence the development of wage costs and social security payments per employee on its own. Therefore, wage costs are an exogenous factor in corporate planning and must be estimated on the basis of expected trends in society in general.

5. The estimated sales turnover (1) indicates the volume of raw materials and auxiliary resources to be purchased in future years. An industry producing a small assortment of goods can usually make an estimate of raw material costs by multiplying the estimated production of finished and semifinished products by the volume of required raw materials and auxiliary resources per unit. An industry producing a large assortment of goods must suffice with an estimate of future percentage deviations from the purchases made in the current year.

Besides ascertaining the amount of materials to be purchased, the enterprise must also establish the future prices of materials. If a limited variety of raw materials is used, the price trends of the various materials can be estimated separately. If a large variety of raw materials is used, the average price changes of a combined set of raw materials must be estimated. In that case price variations are usually expressed in percentages of the average price of a combination of raw materials purchased during the current year.

Fixed Assets and Operating Capital

Once estimates have been made of the strategic variables, the following must be assessed: (1) fixed assets, (2) stocks and inventories, (3) receivables, and (4) accounts payable.

1. The present value of the existing fixed assets of a company can be derived from the balance sheet of the current year. Future depreciation costs must be subtracted from this sum. The above-mentioned capital investment in new equipment must also be included in the future balance sheets. Again depreciation costs must be subtracted from the value of the equipment.

2. Future stocks of raw materials and auxiliary resources can be derived from expected purchase costs. If volumes and prices have been estimated separately, the stocks can be determined quantitatively. For example, if past experience has shown that average stocks are equal to one-sixth of the yearly consumption (i.e., a two-month's stock), this fraction can be multiplied by the estimated purchase prices to give the value of future stocks. If volume and prices have not been estimated separately, the value of the stocks of raw materials and auxiliary resources must be estimated in percentages of the total purchase costs in the past.

Future stocks of finished and semifinished products can be estimated quantitatively if annual production has been determined per product. This is only possible for companies producing a small assortment of goods; the volume of stocks can then be estimated as percentages of the annual production and the value of these stocks can be found by multiplying the quantities by the expected future costs per unit. Usually, however, a financial prognosis does not specify costs per unit. In that case—and similarly when the sales turnover has been estimated as a total sum—the value of future stocks of finished and semifinished products must be estimated as percentages of the turnover. (This procedure furnishes correct results only if the profit margin per unit is relatively stable, for the stocks are evaluated at costs per unit, while the sales turnover is multiplied by the prices. However, this procedure must also suffice when profit margins are fluctuating while there is no better alternative.)

Finally, inventories include spare parts and maintenance equipment. The value of the existing inventories can be derived from the balance sheet for the current year. If production facilities are expanded, the increased value of the inventory of reserve parts and maintenance equipment can be estimated as percentages of the capital investment in fixed assets (if the estimates of the price of equipment do not already include a certain sum for spare parts).

3. The volume of receivables can be determined by the average terms of credit granted to customers. If this is one month, for example, then the average value of receivables is equal to one-twelfth times the turnover.

4. The volume of accounts payable depends on the volume of corporate purchases and the average terms of credit allowed by the suppliers of raw materials and auxiliary resources. If the average term is two months, for example, the average value of accounts payable is equal to one-sixth times the purchase costs.

Costs

Costs can generally be grouped into the following categories: (1) costs of raw materials and auxiliary resources, (2) wage costs and social security payments, (3) costs of outside services and taxes, (4) depreciation, and (5) costs of interest, provisions, etc.

1. The costs of raw materials and auxiliary resources in a certain year are equal to the value of the stocks at the beginning of the year plus the purchase price minus the value of the stocks at the end of the year. All three amounts have been mentioned above.

2. Wage costs and social security payments are equal to the amounts specified before.

3. The costs of outside services and taxes must be estimated on the basis of an analysis of these costs in past years. The costs of outside services are usually divided into variable costs and fixed costs. Variable costs are (a) energy, (b) transport, (c) taxes (excluding profit tax), and (d) miscellaneous. Fixed costs are (a) rent, (b) maintenance (excluding wages of corporate personnel and depreciation of corporate facilities), (c) sales (excluding wages of corporate personnel and depreciation of corporate facilities), and (d) general (excluding wages of corporate personnel and depreciation of corporate facilities).

Variable costs can be estimated by determining how these costs are correlated with production, purchases, and turnover respectively. These costs as well as the purchases and the sales turnover may require adjustment to price changes. With the help of the correlations, future costs at current prices can be derived from the estimated future production, purchases, and sales turnover respectively. These figures may then require adjustment for price changes in outside services.

Fixed costs can be assessed in various ways. The costs of future rent are usually determined separately and are based on future corporate policy regarding rent of land, buildings, and machinery. Maintenance costs can usually be estimated in percentages of the capital investment in fixed assets. Sales costs depend on the commercial policy to be followed in the future and must be derived from the sales plan. General costs frequently depend on the number of employees and occasionally on the capital investment in fixed assets. For example, if a correlation is found between general costs and the number of employees, the future trend of general costs can be derived from the expected personnel costs mentioned above.

4. Depreciation costs have been described before.

5. The interest indicated in the profit and loss account as W 2 (1), W 2(2) . . . W 2(n) consists of, first, the balance of the interest paid and the interest received on former loans—this sum can be derived from current terms of interest—and, second, the interest to be received on recent loans to third parties and the interest to be paid on recent corporate loans. An estimate of these earnings and payments can be based on certain assumptions, which will be described below. The estimate of future provisions can be based on the rules customarily applied in corporate administration. The provision for uncovered risks, for example, can be estimated as a percentage of the value of the fixed assets. The provision for bad debts should be equal to a percentage of the expected sales turnover.

Profit Tax

The profit tax to be paid in the future depends on national tax regulations. In the Netherlands, the required corporate tax in any year is equal to a percentage of the difference between income and fiscal expenses. Fiscal expenses sometimes deviate in certain aspects from the costs specified in the corporate profit and loss account. In particular, the amount under "fiscal" depreciation may vary from the amount under "commercial" depreciation. A sound financial prognosis requires not only familiarity with national tax regulations but also knowledge of the dates on which corporate tax is to be paid. There is usually a certain time lapse between the point when the enterprise is liable for tax and the point when it is actually paid. Tax liabilities will be mentioned further below.

Share Capital, Loans, and Dividends

A financial prognosis can be based on various assumptions about future finance. The preliminary assumption may be that a deficit will be offset by increased corporate loans, while a surplus will be invested in loans to third parties. Also an assumption must be made about the dividend policy to be followed in the future. Some enterprises plan to distribute a constant dividend, equal to the average dividend over the past five years, for example. Other enterprises plan to distribute a fixed percentage of the company's profits in dividends. Many other policies are possible. Once the financial prognosis based on these assumptions has been completed, the assumptions should be reexamined. The enterprise may then decide to revise the assumptions and consequently the whole financial prognosis.

Other Claims and Liabilities

An estimate of the value of the other claims and liabilities on the balance sheet and the variations in these entries according to the liquidity survey must be based on various estimates previously described, namely the claims and liabilities ensuing from: proceeds other than sales turnover, investment, wage costs and social security payments, outside services and taxes other than profit tax, profit tax, and dividends.

The most important entries must be estimated one by one with the aid of the essential data derived from past experience (proceeds other than turnover, liabilities toward the suppliers of capital goods, and tax liabilities, for example). The remainder of the claims and liabilities can be estimated as a percentage of past figures, such as sales turnover or balance sheet totals.

Operating Profit and Cash Development

Operating profit and future cash can be calculated on the basis of the above-mentioned amounts and the balance sheet of the current year.

CALCULATION TECHNIQUES

A financial prognosis usually requires several calculations. If long-term corporate plans are to be revised regularly—several times a year, for instance—for adjustment to changed circumstances or viewpoints, a computer will be required. There are many theoretical and practical computer programs for a financial prognosis, but these cannot be discussed within the scope of this chapter.

MARKET PROCESSES

The sales forecast, which is the most important part of long-term corporate planning, is based on a forecast of demand and a forecast of supply in future years. Forecasting the total demand for an existing product is relatively simple. Various statistical techniques for estimating total demand have been developed and are being used by most larger companies. We do not have to discuss these techniques here. Forecasting the behavior of the suppliers of a product poses more problems, which require further consideration.

A significant aspect of supply is that selling is, in practice, a dynamic process. Companies can apply various selling methods; they can choose between different advertising campaigns, operate through various commercial channels, raise or lower their prices, etc. As the reactions of both competitors and purchasers are usually unknown factors, most commercial decisions are based on past experience. Past market trends are constantly analyzed in an effort to determine the steps to be taken in the future. Therefore, future policies are constantly compared with those of the past. The aim of sales activities in general is not to achieve an ideal equilibrium, but to adjust the corporate selling policy as well as is possible to constantly changing market conditions.

In order to be able to study the development of a certain market systematically, it is desirable to draw up a limited number of hypothetical supply processes with which the actual behavior of the suppliers can be compared. For this purpose three hypothetical supply processes are especially useful: "cutthroat competition," the making of agreements between suppliers and "full-cost pricing." We shall consider these cases below.

We suppose that total sales of a certain product rise in the course of time. Further we assume that the members of the branch of industry concerned all have a surplus capacity in a given starting period. (Their sales are smaller than the production capacity available.) In Figure 5.1 the capacities of three suppliers have been drawn. We assume throughout this chapter that the number of suppliers is greater than one. Of course the picture would not change fundamentally if there were to be two, or more than three, suppliers.

FIGURE 5.1

Initial Excess Capacity in Relation to
Industry Demand

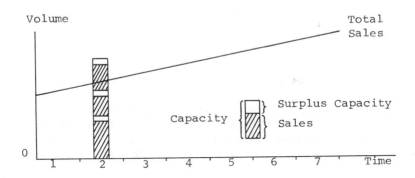

Cutthroat Competition

In the case of cutthroat competition, the manufacturers of a
product constantly lower their prices as long as they have surplus
capacity. The minimum price is, roughly speaking, equal to the
variable costs of each manufacturer. As depreciation nowadays
forms a large component of costs, it will take quite some time before
the price falls to this minimum. It more frequently occurs that the
price falls below the total costs of a number of manufacturers, who
then suffer losses according to normal administrative standards.
Periods of loss for many companies are characteristic of the development of a market with cutthroat competition.

The price may continue to fall for a longer or a shorter time,
depending on the original capacity surplus of the manufacturers and
the position of the demand curve. Assuming that each manufacturer
continues to lower his price while he has surplus capacity, the process of falling prices only ceases when the sales of all the manufacturers have reached the capacity level. At this point prices start
rising. While manufacturers compete for the limited demand before
the turning point, purchasers compete for the limited supply after
that point.

The price rise need not lead to production expansion immediately. First, it may take quite some time before prices exceed the total costs of most manufacturers, and, as long as they are not operating at a profit, they will not consider investment in production expansion attractive. Second, manufacturers that suffered losses in the past will probably not have sufficient capital for investment. Third, devising expansion plans, implementing them, and adjusting them in practice requires time.

However, if the price rise continues, manufacturers will eventually increase their production. As expansion takes place jerkily, total production capacity of the industry will again exceed demand. At that point, the price will cease to rise. Some manufacturers may even be inclined to lower their price again in an effort to increase their sales. The product will probably have been stockpiled by consumers and retailers during the period of rising prices, for although the supply was limited, some consumers and retailers will have purchased more than they directly consumed or sold. As soon as the price manifests a downward trend, the consumers will cease to buy the product in an effort to diminish their stocks, while the retailers will hasten to place their stock on the market. Consequently, a drastic price fall occurs and eventually the process of gradual price falls recommences. L'histoire se repète. Thus, the characteristics of cutthroat competition between the manufacturers of a certain product are constant price oscillations and erratic production expansion.

The development of different enterprises during this market process depends on the type of product. Two cases can be distinguished:

1. If the qualities of the various producers do not differ significantly, prices cannot vary considerably during each period. The manufacturers with low costs will then make the biggest profits during the periods of fierce competition.

2. If the qualities of the various producers differ significantly in the view of purchasers, prices on the market may vary. The manufacturer of a superior brand can either set a higher price than his colleagues with the same ratio between sales and capacity, or he can set the same price as his competitors so that he will sooner reach sales that are equal to his existing capacity. In both cases the manufacturers with the most favorable combination of quality and price will make the largest profits during the period of competition.

Profit differences usually have implications for the development of the market shares of manufacturers. As the strongest manufacturers will either suffer the least losses or make a slight profit during the period of falling prices, they will be in the strongest financial position at the moment when total sales are equal to total capacity. They will also be the first to reach the point at which investment becomes attractive. Manufacturers with relatively low costs will therefore start expanding their production sooner than other manufacturers. It is not probable that manufacturers with high costs will be forced to halt production during the time of falling prices, as depreciation forms a large component of costs in modern industry. However, they will start lagging behind in other respects. The growth of these companies will be hampered as they cannot expand soon enough during the time of rising prices. The point at which prices start sinking again occurs before these manufacturers can dispose of sufficient capital for production expansion. Therefore, market shares eventually shift in favor of the manufacturer with the lowest costs. This trend is reinforced when, after some time (i.e. after various price and investment fluctuations), weak manufacturers are required to renew their production facilities and lack the necessary capital for this investment.

The extent to which the profits of strong enterprises are squeezed and weak enterprises are eventually eliminated over a period of time depends on the rate at which the enterprises can increase their production at a given growth-rate of demand. There are various limits to corporate growth. Usually there must be a period in which expansion plans are made and executed between two production expansions. The length of this period varies in each branch of industry; generally a period of one to five years is required. Moreover, the enterprise cannot attract more than a limited capital supply within a short time, even if the profit outlook is favorable. If the growth rate of strong enterprises is limited by these factors, the period in which the whole branch of industry is operating at full capacity may be lengthened. Then the profits of all the enterprises in the branch will increase and even weak enterprises may manifest some long-term growth.

A final point is that the long-term price level is related to the long-term cost level in a branch of industry. This is clear from consideration of the effect of changes in cost levels on the development of prices. A rise in costs implies that it will take more time before the enterprises are capable of production expansion. Therefore, the price rise continues longer after the point of full employment of the existing capacity and the average long-term price level is increased. A fall in costs implies that manufacturers will be able to increase production sooner after the moment when the industry produces at full capacity, so that the average long-term price level is decreased.

The development of the market in the case of cutthroat competition is shown in Figure 5.2. It has been assumed that demand fluctuates while various demands are possible in each period, depending

FIGURE 5.2

Industry Demand and Sales Under
Cut-Throat Competition

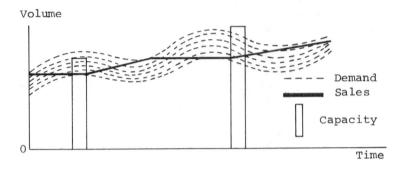

FIGURE 5.3

Cut-Throat Competition: Costs of New Facilities
in Relation to Price

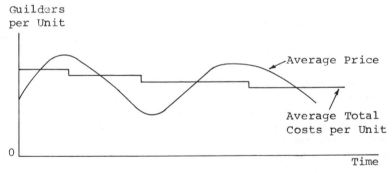

on the price level. The bars indicate the total production capacity
of the whole industry. Production capacities and sales of different
enterprises have not been indicated. In Figure 5.3 it has been assumed
that average costs in the industry fall erratically because of technological progress. In this case, "costs" does not mean the actual costs
of existing production facilities, but the costs of new facilities. The
costs of new facilities determine the point when investment becomes
attractive; the costs of existing facilities are irrelevant for this
purpose.

Agreements between Producers

In order to avoid the constant struggle of cutthroat competition,
manufacturers may make certain agreements to achieve two essential
aims: fixing market shares and fixing prices. In general, none of
the manufacturers in a cartel is prepared to agree to a lower market
share than he could achieve with cutthroat competition; manufacturers
do not relinquish the prospects of long-term growth in favor of short-
term advantages. If any cartel member is convinced that his enterprise would grow more rapidly under free market conditions than
under a set of agreements, he will demand a higher market share.
If his partners refuse to comply with his demand, the cartel may
disintegrate. A condition for a manufacturers' agreement is that
established market shares are considered to reflect true strengths
within the industry. Therefore, in this respect the development of
the market does not deviate from the development of the market with
cutthroat competition.

The development of the average price level in an industry
dominated by cartels ensues from a dynamic process of negotiations.
One of the essential considerations for cartel members during price
negotiations is their total costs. One reason for this is that manufacturers may fear the entry of outsiders when they quote prices
that are considerably higher than their total costs (although there
are various factors preventing outsiders from entering the branch).
A more important reason why total cost is employed as a standard
during price negotiations is that the price level will probably affect
the long-term development of the market shares of the members.
Manufacturers with low costs will object to a high price level as it
promotes the growth of weaker manufacturers, which is in turn
detrimental to their own growth. Weak manufacturers will object
to a low price level as they would suffer short-term losses and be
incapable of long-term growth. The usual result of a continuing
series of price negotiations is that the price level oscillates around
the cost level of the weaker members. Stronger manufacturers then

earn higher returns on their capital investment than they would have by cutthroat competition. These returns are in fact earned at the expense of their long-term growth, but the possibilities of long-term growth are difficult to measure and therefore will not be a factor preventing the stronger manufacturers participating in a cartel. Moreover, they are usually aware that their sales cannot be increased rapidly because of the said limits to corporate growth and, besides, many manufacturers may prefer an uneventful sales development, with reasonable profits, to a struggle for small short-term profits and the chance of higher long-term profits.

A theoretical market development dominated by a cartel is depicted in Figure 5.4 and 5.5. Demand, total production, costs, and prices in various periods are shown as in the previous figures. In Figure 5.5 it is assumed that the cartel aims at such a price regulation (either a uniform price for a uniform quality or a series of prices for various qualities) that a linear increase of total sales in the industry is achieved at an average price that exceeds the average costs. Therefore, the cartel must raise prices in periods of rising demand and lower prices in periods of declining demand. The figure allows adjustment to different assumptions.

Full-Cost Pricing

The third hypothetical development of the market literally means that each manufacturer in a certain branch of industry constantly sets his price equal to his total costs per unit plus the required minimum return on investment. It may be assumed that the manufacturer calculates his total costs per unit according to normal production—i.e. the average production of existing facilities from start up until they are fully depreciated. The minimum return on investment can be defined as the weighted average of interest paid on loans and the required yield on corporate net worth for a feasible financial structure. The sum of total costs and the minimum return on investment is then equal to the proceeds from the finished product required to make investment in new facilities worthwhile. The system of full-cost pricing implies that the manufacturer only changes his price if a change occurs in the corporate cost structure or in the corporate finance structure.

Let us assume that total demand in the industry is larger than total demand for the product. If all manufacturers adjust their prices to total costs plus minimum return on investment, their market shares will develop in accordance with the qualities and the prices of the products. (If the quality does not vary considerably, slight price differences can lead to important shifts in relative sales. The

74

FIGURE 5.4

Industry Demand and Sales Under a Cartel

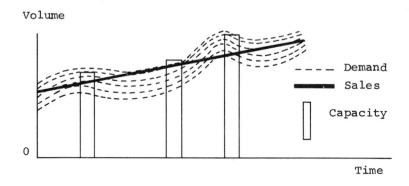

FIGURE 5.5

Cartel: Costs of New Facilities in
Relation to Price

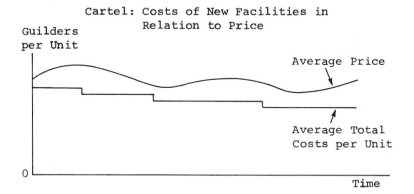

manufacturers may then agree to set a uniform price and, for example, allow manufacturers with low costs to advertize more extensively.) After some time, the capacity of some manufacturers will be fully occupied because of rising total demand. If all the manufacturers initially had a relatively equal surplus capacity, the capacity of the manufacturer with the best combination of quality and price will be fully utilized first. Under the given circumstances, this manufacturer will have sufficient capital to make investment worthwhile. Unless the manufacturer expects a trend break—which is not likely—he will expand, after which corporate growth will continue as before. Meanwhile, the other manufacturers will also produce at full capacity. They also will expand and then resume their previous growth rate. Thus, production in the whole industry expands gradually, not erratically.

So in the long run market shares develop in accordance with quality and price differences. In this respect, market development does not deviate from that under cutthroat competition. Because of price stability, the profit of each manufacturer is determined, first by fluctuations in the general trend of the total demand for the product, second by the manufacturer's production expansion. When a factory has increased its capacity, profits will initially be low or negative as the new equipment is not operating at full capacity. Owing to increasing demand, and in some cases a larger market share, production and consequently profits will increase. In the long run, strong manufacturers will make profits that are entirely in accordance with their desired return on investment. The weaker manufacturers will eventually be eliminated because their sales fall owing to their unfavorable combination of quality and price.

It is clear that a true example of full cost pricing will not be found in practice very frequently. Usually manufacturers adjust their price level to fluctuating supply and demand relations. In that case "full-cost pricing" is no more than a tacit agreement between stronger manufacturers to avoid a large discrepancy between price differences and cost differences. Instead of pricing on the basis of total costs, this system really incorporates pricing in accordance with total costs. In the long run, the market shares of manufacturers develop in approximately the same way as by cutthroat competition, but profits will reach a higher level. A theoretical picture of full cost pricing is shown in Figures 5.6 and 5.7. Costs are again the costs of new production facilities. A basic assumption is that manufacturers change their prices as soon as they discern a change in their costs per unit. Also, it is assumed that demand immediately reacts to price change. If it were assumed that a time lag occurs between a cost change and a price change and between a price change and a demand increase, the diagrams would require slight adjustments.

FIGURE 5.6

Industry Demand and Sales Under
Full-Cost Pricing

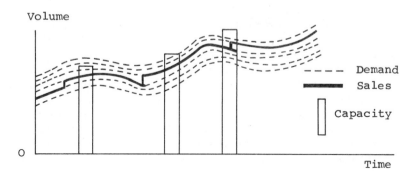

FIGURE 5.7

Full-Cost Pricing: Costs of New Facilities
in Relation to Price

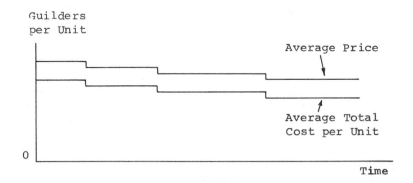

MARKET STRUCTURE

In practice, market development never corresponds entirely to one of the above descriptions. However, it is usually possible to describe most, if not all, market developments on the basis of the three possibilities mentioned.

To illustrate this point, product markets can be divided into three sectors: agricultural products, industrial semifinished products (including mining products), and consumer goods. Constant fluctuations of price and investment are especially discernible in the markets for agricultural products and industrial semifinished products, while price stability is characteristic of the market for consumer goods. This is inherent in the structure of the three markets.

The structure of the agricultural market incorporates a large number of producers, so that negotiations about price harmonization, or stabilization of the average price level, between producers are rare. The supply is frequently sold at agricultural exchanges and auctions, which does not promote adjustment of price differences to the cost differences of the producers. On the contrary, sales at exchanges and auctions imply that all the producers receive the same yield on a certain quality—whatever their cost differences. Nor do these sales techniques reduce price fluctuations; instead they cause the slightest discrepancy between supply and demand to be immediately manifest in a price change. The only way to achieve market development with growth, as under conditions of full-cost pricing, is by government regulation of production and sales. Of course, this is easier said than done, but the problems surrounding regulated agricultural production cannot be discussed within the scope of this chapter.

The number of producers in the market for mining products and industrial semifinished products—coal, iron ore, sulfur, tin, steel, fertilizers, etc.—is not very large. So the supply structure of this market allows full-cost pricing. However, adjustment of price differences to cost differences is frequently prevented by the demand structure. Much of the demand ensues from a limited number of large-size purchasers who negotiate individually with producers. As the agreed prices contained in the contracts are not published, neither party can verify the other's assertions about bids from third parties. Each party must make a subjective evaluation of the other's statements. Various markets for industrial semifinished products show price fluctuations as a result of these subjective evaluations, depending on the total production in the industry in relation to capacity. Given the demand structure mentioned, constant competition can only be prevented by means of agreements between the producers, which explains the great number of cartels in markets for industrial semifinished products.

78

The number of manufacturers in the third type of markets—for consumer products—is usually small, as is the case for semifinished products. However, a significant difference is that the demand for consumer goods is not concentrated in a small number of large consumers; it is spread over a large number of small consumers, which implies that the individual consumer cannot exert pressure on the manufacturer.

Moreover, consumers seldom cooperate to form a pressure group, except over some subordinate point. Demand prices are not determined by way of negotiation; manufacturers announce their prices through widespread advertising. Therefore, the market is fairly transparent for manufacturers. On the whole, markets for consumer goods are characterized by pricing based largely on full costs (including the required minimum return on investment).

SALES FORECASTS

From an analysis of the dynamics of market development, various conclusions might be drawn that are relevant to a sales prognosis as a foundation for long-term corporate planning. It seems that the following steps should be taken for the formation of a sales prognosis:

1. The trend in the future development of total turnover must be estimated with the help of customary statistical methods. (This estimate may require adjustment after step 3.)

2. The future long-term development of the strength of the enterprises in the industry must be determined, which requires primarily analysis of the development of market shares and the factors influencing this development in the past. An estimate must then be made of the possible development of quality and costs of various manufacturers. Moreover, the limits to their growth rate must be ascertained. These estimates assist an enterprise in determining whether developments in corporate market shares in the past will be continued in the future. The trend in aggregate demand can then be multiplied by the trend in the corporate market share to give the trend in the corporate sales development.

3. Next, the trend in the price per unit must be assessed. Long-term price development is determined by cost development in all three forms of competition considered. In order to ascertain the profit margin that is to be added to the estimated costs, future returns on investment in the industry as well as the future corporate position within the industry must be estimated. The average return on investment in the industry in total is largely determined by the growth rate of demand and by the amount of competition. Competition,

in turn, depends predominantly on market structure. The return on investment of a separate firm within the industry is largely determined by the desired future growth of the firm's market share and by the quality and the costs of the firm compared with that of others.

4. Finally, possible deviations from the trends of the sales curve and the price curve must be assessed. An analysis of the sales curve in the past indicates possible fluctuations in future sales volume. By ascertaining whether the market is characterized by cutthroat competition, producers' agreements, or full-cost pricing, possible deviations from the estimated trend of proceeds per unit can be assessed. These deviations can be quantified by an analysis of the price curve in the past.

THE USE OF THE SALES FORECAST
IN INVESTMENT AND FINANCIAL PLANNING

Investment decisions are based on calculations of expected returns on investment. The return on investment is expressed in profitability indexes such as the pay-out period, the average rate of return, or the discounted cash flow rate. Of course the value of these indexes is determined by expected sales volume and prices. The point we want to stress here is that the calculation of profitability indexes must be based primarily on estimated trends in sales volume and prices. As the average of fluctuations around the trends is zero, these fluctuations will not affect the average annual profitability of an investment plan. Only foreseeable deviations from the trend in the near future, which are most significant in the compound interest calculations, will be taken into account. Figures for later periods usually include only the estimated trend curves.

Financial planning requires a wholly different line of thought. If an enterprise wishes to execute an extensive investment plan in order to increase the corporate turnover, the financial prognosis usually contains an increasing shortage of liquid assets during the initial years and a decreasing shortage of liquid assets or cash surpluses in later years. The initial shortage of liquid assets can be offset by enlarging the equity capital or by borrowing. As long as the return on investment is larger than the interest paid on loans—if this is not the case, capital investment is entirely unattractive—borrowing leads to an increase in profits per share and consequently an improved stock exchange quotation. For this reason, most enterprises prefer to borrow rather than to issue new shares. On the other hand, borrowing may lead to difficulties when the need for liquid assets becomes greater than originally estimated. The possibility of these difficulties can be evaluated by an analysis of the relation of owned to borrowed capital over the years according to the financial prognosis. If this relation, which creditors consider an essential criterion for the risk of lending capital, falls below a certain level, an increase in corporate borrowed capital cannot be considered feasible. In this case, the investment plan must be based on an increase in owned capital. The problems inherent in these procedures cannot be discussed here. We only want to remark that it is particularly the minimum sales prognosis that must be employed as the basis for corporate financial planning. The enterprise must beware of making too tight financial plans when corporate expansion is executed. Retaining a surplus of capital in certain years is preferable to halting corporate growth because of lack of money. While trends in future sales volume and prices should be taken into account in the investment plan of an enterprise, the trend minus possible negative deviations should be given special consideration in financial planning.

CONCLUSION

In this chapter the technique of making a financial prognosis, the study of market development as a dynamic process, and the technique of making a sales forecast have been briefly described. We have assumed throughout that total demand for the product considered is increasing in the long run. If the demand were to decrease, profits would manifest a gradual fall in the case of cutthroat competition, producers' agreements, and full-cost pricing. Therefore, the fundamental question in long-term corporate planning is whether the total demand for the goods to be produced in the future will continue to manifest long-term growth. Only if this is the case will enterprises with a favorable combination of quality and costs be assured of reasonable long-term profits. Another fundamental question is whether a specific firm belongs to the group of enterprises with a favorable combination of quality and costs. If the enterprise is not sufficiently capable of quality improvements and/ or cost reductions compared with its competitors, it will not make a sufficient return on its invested capital—even if the short-term outlook is favorable because of a temporary production shortage. The aim of a sales forecast is primarily to find the answers to these questions. Moreover, the sales forecast and the consequent financial prognosis can furnish a picture of possible deviations from the expected trend in long-term corporate development. Thus, the enterprise can determine which financial measures should be taken in order to offset the risks of the market.

6

CENTRALIZATION AND DECENTRALIZATION IN THE MANAGEMENT OF HUNGARIAN ENTERPRISES

Miklos Marosi

INTRODUCTION

In recent years the decentralization of enterprise management has been a much-discussed topic in Hungary. The main concern of these discussions has been to raise the level of democratization of management, but other issues, mainly connected with increased managerial efficiency, have also been brought up. This chapter, however, is not intended to dwell on these debates. Its purpose is to present the results of research done on certain organizational problems connected with the decentralization of management in Hungarian industrial enterprises. Although this research was concerned with Hungarian enterprises only, its findings can be generalized to some extent and may be of interest to a wider audience.

In order to clarify the organizational problems involved, it seems expedient to point to a few characteristics of Hungarian industrial enterprises. In Hungary, as in all socialist countries, the majority of industrial enterprises are stateowned. In the Hungarian economic system the state as the owner of the enterprises controls them in a direct and indirect way. Very important from the point of view of the organization of management are those direct methods by which the state, or more exactly organs of the state such as ministries or town and district councils, exercise control over enterprises. Among other things, it is the exclusive right of these organs to set up or dissolve enterprises. In the present context this means that no enterprise has the right to decentralize management by reorganizing its plants into subsidiaries. On the other hand, the state does not directly dictate to the enterprise what its internal organization of management shall be, i.e., it lies in the power of the enterprise to decide on such questions as the delegation of functions and spheres of authority within the enterprise and on the decentralization of management functions in general. This chapter deals with the organizational activities of enterprises in decentralizing (or centralizing) management; it is not concerned with the organizational activity of the state on the basis of its right to set up or dissolve enterprises.

Another characteristic feature of Hungarian law is that it recognizes only two main forms of state enterprises. The situation described above is typical of the majority of enterprises, but a minority of enterprises are under the management of the so-called trusts. Legally speaking, trusts also qualify as enterprises and not as state organs, but they are invested with the right of direct control over the enterprises under them. Apart from the trusts and a few other exceptions, there is no hierarchical relationship between enterprises. In the following, we shall deal only with enterprises that are not subordinated to trusts.

The structure of Hungarian industry is characterized by the relatively large size of enterprises. In the exercise of their right to form enterprises, state organs carried out a relatively large number of mergers in former times, thus causing the average size of enterprises to be substantially larger than in most other countries. In the 1960s, in particular, the process of organizational concentration of enterprises was much faster than that of industrial concentration of production plant. In 1965, for example, the average labor force of an enterprise in Hungarian industry was 1,183, and 83.4 percent of all industrial workers were in enterprises employing over 1,000 men.[1] As this situation is not fully in accordance with the principles of the new economic system, a number of oversized enterprises were recently reorganized into several smaller ones. Nonetheless, the relative frequency of multiplant enterprises remains typical of Hungarian industry. Hence, the demand for managerial decentralization of management is much stronger than it would be in a system in which the single-plant enterprise was more predominant.

INTERPRETATION AND MEASUREMENT OF DECENTRALIZATION WITHIN THE ENTERPRISE

When certain phenomena are observed in a large number of enterprises, statistical methods must be applied. This in turn requires quantification and the measurement of these phenomena in terms of figures. It is evident that in the case of decentralization we are facing a much more complex phenomenon than, for example, in the case of the span of control. The scope for statistical measurement is, by its very nature, limited in this case, and the accuracy of the results is therefore lower than in economic statistics in general.

For research purposes, the concept of decentralization had to be interpreted in a way that adequately expressed its essence of decentralization, and satisfied the requirement of statistical measurement at the same time. This interpretation is not fully identical with the definitions used in organization theory.

Research workers use the concept of decentralization in two senses. It has been interpreted by them as the delegation of the right of decision-making. This interpretation is fairly old and commonly known. When top management, or its functional or staff apparatus, makes a decision on any question, this is called centralization; when the right of decision-making is delegated to plants, this is called decentralization. In such cases the presence or absence of decentralization is easy to observe. In other cases the situation is more complicated: The act of decision-making itself may be centralized, but in the process of making it, a minor or major role may also be played by the management of plants. As far as decentralization is concerned, it is obviously not indifferent what real part is played in such cases by the management of plants. For example, the annual plan of the enterprise is always approved by the general manager of the enterprise, that is, the act of decision-making is centralized. But the planning process can be organized in a number of ways: It may be the case that the draft plan is prepared by the central planning department of the enterprise, with the plant management only supplying the data. But it is also possible for the management of plants to take an active part in the planning process by defining the plan targets and preparing the draft plans. Very often they work out counter-plans in response to the draft plans of the central planning department. In such cases it is the task of the general manager to adopt an appropriate position, after duly considering divergent views. In both cases the process of decision-making is centralized; yet there is a substantial difference between them: In the first case the process is strongly centralized; in the second there are essential features of decentralization alongside certain features of centralization. When making statistical observations, it is obviously expedient to consider such differences, but the possibility of quantifying them is very limited. To put it in other words, quantification must to some extent be based on subjective evaluation, i.e., on the judgment of the observer.

It must also be noted that the statistical approach can only concentrate on the few most relevant features of the phenomenon under study. In fact the research effort was confined to a narrow range of important "delegating behavior," e.g., standard decisions on planning, engineering, marketing, programming, stock control, or the exercise of employers' rights in the field of personnel management. Outside its purview were left some important fields of decision-making in which the choice between centralization and delegation is severely limited or nonexistent. These included financial measures (which can only be taken centrally in the Hungarian system) and personnel policy, which was centralized in all the enterprises investigated, with one exception.

Another possible interpretation of decentralization hinges on the range of management functions performed by the plant, and that of the functions assigned to its subordinate staff or functional departments. By management functions we generally mean the collection, transmission, and processing of information, the preparation and formulation of actual decisions, the measures taken for their implementation, etc. When examining centralization in management, we must allow for the fact that decentralization is often only partial, i.e., that the division of labor between the center and the plants within the enterprise assigns some management tasks to the former and some to the latter.

It would be an extremely complex and practically impossible task to devise a statistical measure for a division of labor of such a kind. We have therefore simplified our task by identifying "decentralization" with a state of affairs in which any management functions at all are located in plant units below the level of the enterprise. Thus, by saying that the degree of decentralization in Hungarian multiplant enterprises is 29 percent in marketing and 61 percent in planning, we shall mean that 29 and 61 percent of all such enterprises have plant units under them that engage in marketing and planning themselves (and have their own marketing and planning departments).

It is obvious that the figures derived in this way cannot be averaged or used as general measures of decentralization within the enterprise. This is so partly because the scope and importance of different management activities is not uniform, and partly because the division of labor between the center and plant units varies both between enterprises and between different types of activities.

Given the well-known problems of measurement (whose detailed treatment is omitted here), approximate values for the degree of decentralization may be obtained by measuring the size of the functional and staff apparatus within the enterprises, i.e., the percentage of all persons employed (in enterprises) forming part of their decentralized machinery. The following averages were found for Hungarian multiplant enterprises in 1968:

Technical staff	74 percent
Economic-administrative staff	69 percent
Total	71 percent

THE CHARACTER OF PRODUCTION AND
DECENTRALIZATION IN MANAGEMENT

Enterprises of different types organize their management systems in different ways. In other words, enterprises adapt their managerial activities to the specific circumstances in which they find themselves. Socialist authors devote a fair amount of attention to the nature of the link between the characteristics of enterprises and the nature of their management systems: Such analyses are also known to have been made by Western authors.[2] Enterprises of different types are characterized by different spans of control, different ratios of office to production workers, and different forms of management organization. In fact, enterprises of different types decentralize (or centralize) management in different ways. It is easy to demonstrate, for example, that there is a close and unmistakable link between decentralization in management and the size of enterprises or plants. The larger an enterprise, the more rational for its top management to resort to decentralization, and the larger a plant, the greater its ability to maintain an administrative apparatus of sufficient size. There is no need for statistical documentation to prove, for instance, that the management of multiplant enterprises is marked by a higher degree of decentralization than that of single-plant enterprises.

Matters become less obvious when we turn to the relationship between management systems and production methods. If we regard enterprises as integrated systems, we must clearly assume an essential connection between management and production as a controlled process, and no detailed discussion of systems theory is needed to justify this.

It is also evident that a technologically simple production process is associated with a simpler (and a complicated production process with a more complicated) system of management. An important role is also played by the flexibility of the production process, the frequency of changes in production tasks, or the extent to which they are standardized or of a recurring nature. It may be assumed that the more complex and changeable a given production process, the greater the danger of malfunctions, and the greater the instability of the enterprise as an operational system. The elimination or prevention of malfunctions requires an appropriate organization of management, and this organization needs to be more complicated the larger the instability.

This tendency in the organization of management cannot, however, be unambiguously demonstrated in practice. Since the enterprise is an economic system, management organization also presents economic problems. With the increasing complexity and size of the management apparatus, the costs of management increase and its economic efficiency generally decreases. As a result, the technologically determined instability, once it exceeds a certain limit, often brings into play the opposite tendency in the organization of management.

It is generally difficult to measure the complexity and change-ability of the production process by statistical methods. Hungarian research workers have attempted this by means of two index numbers: the index of technical "prefabrication" and that of scale of production. By the degree of prefabrication we mean the extent to which the enterprise is, or is not, ready to satisfy the individual requirements of its customers. To illustrate this by a simple example, the making of custom-tailored suits represents the minimum, and the manufacture of ready-made clothes the maximum, of prefabrication. Enterprises turning out standardized products, or delivering only goods listed in their product catalogues, can be classified unambiguously as belonging to the category of maximal prefabrication. Other enterprises—ship-yards, or enterprises manufacturing custom-built equipment (especially complete factory assemblies), foundries, forging plants, etc.— prepare the technical documentation needed for production and organize the production process according to the individual requirements of their customers. They consequently represent a lower degree of prefabrication. On the basis of detailed investigations conducted throughout the greater part of the Hungarian engineering industry, research workers were able to arrive at approximate measures for the degree of prefabrication.

Examining the decentralization of some important spheres of authority in multiplant enterprises of Hungarian engineering in relation to the degree of prefabrication, it can be stated that the highest levels of decentralization are largely associated with an intermediate (70-90 percent) range of the degree of prefabrication. A more convincing picture can be obtained if we consider the decentralization of the more important management activities, where all ascertainable maxima are associated with this intermediate range (see Table 6.1).

A similar picture is obtained when we adopt the criterion of personnel employed in the management apparatus: The decentralization maximum is again to be associated with the 70-90 percent range in the degree of prefabrication, i.e., where 81 percent of technical employees and 79 percent of economic-administrative employees work in plants, and only 19 and 21 percent of the two categories work in the enterprises' central administrations.

The scale of production is a well-known and important character-istic of the production process. Moreover, it is known that the relationships between the production process and the organization of management can also be analyzed by reference to the typical lot-size

TABLE 6.1

Levels of Decentralization of Management in the
Engineering Industry

Degree of Prefabrication	Up to 50 Percent	50-70 Percent	70-90 Percent	90-100 Percent
Engineering	37	40	66	54
Material procurement	14	54	64	6
Marketing	7	20	33	12
Programming	58	62	70	46
Administration of production, cost accountancy	51	76	83	61

Source: Compiled by the author.

of the enterprise's output (i.e. unit production, small-batch, large-batch, or mass production). The impact of the scale of production on the organization of management can, for instance, be illustrated by the fact that in the Hungarian engineering industry the number of office workers per 1,000 production workers is about twice as high in enterprises engaged in unit production as in those on large-batch or mass production.

A high degree of prefabrication usually results (via standarization) in a large scale of production, and, conversely, a low degree of prefabrication (implying readiness to satisfy the individual requirements of customers) usually calls for unit or small-batch production. Nonetheless, Hungarian experience has brought to light a fair number of exceptions to this. Fully 60 percent of the engineering enterprises producing exclusively standardized products are not large-batch or mass production enterprises, but produce only in small batches (machine tool production, manufacture of specialized vehicles, etc.). Even enterprises manufacturing for export in large batches, or in conditions of mass production, are often ready to satisfy the individual requirements of significant and permanent customers.

Although these exceptions show that scale and degree of prefabrication may be widely divergent, their impact on the decentralization of management is fairly similar. Whether we measure decentralization by reference to the power of decision-making or by reference to the management apparatus and its activities, we invariably find its maximal values associated with the medium ranges of the scale of production, i.e., in enterprises engaged in both unit and batch production, or in batch production only, while the lower degree of decentralization can be found in enterprises at the extremes, i.e., in unit or mass production.

In our view these phenomena can be explained as follows: A high degree of prefabrication and a large scale of production, along with advanced standardization, usually provides the basis for a highly uniform organization of management, for management through detailed instructions, for an accurate and thorough organization of the information system, promoting the technical development of management methods. The simplification and mechanization of management methods in turn opens up new possibilities for centralization, and the evidence seems to support those authors (both in the East and the West) who assert that the recentralizing tendencies observed in the management of enterprises are connected with the increased application of electronic computers.

The data on the Hungarian engineering industry show unmistakably that in the lower ranges of prefabrication and production, decentralization is decreasing (or centralization increasing). Research workers explain this phenomenon by pointing to the fact that low degrees of prefabrication (wide diversity of production) or small scales of production (complexity of production) set a limit to the thoroughness of management organization (the regulation of management activities by detailed instructions) and that, consequently, there is no appropriate organizational basis for increasing decentralization. The operational system of enterprises in this situation is relatively unstable, and the resulting risks lead them to prefer so-called operational management methods in central direction.

It should be noted that as regards the most important functions of decision-making, i.e., annual and long-term planning and personnel management, no necessary link could be established between the decentralization of these functions on the one hand, and the degree of prefabrication and scale of production on the other. The logic of these findings seems to derive from the fact that these functions and spheres of authority are not directly connected with production within the operational system of the enterprises, being mostly independent of production technology.

The picture outlined above is characteristic of most management activities and spheres of authority and, since our coverage of management was complete, we may take it that it is equally characteristic of the Hungarian management system in general.

PRODUCTION ORGANIZATION AND DECENTRALIZATION OF MANAGEMENT

By production organization we mean the organizational forms defining the relationship between plants as the constituent production

units of an enterprise. The terms "horizontal" and "vertical" organization and Florence's concept of "divergent, convergent, and diagonal
organization"[3] (closer to the essence of verticality), have long been
in use in the relevant literature. We hold the view that verticality
means production cooperation between the production units concerned,
and horizontality the lack of such cooperation. Production units may
be in production relationships with each other on the input and the
output side, and their position within the organization of production is
defined by the ratio of their internal turnover (on the input or the output side, i.e., inner cooperation) to the total turnover of the enterprise.
Thus we can derive a simple quantitative expression for the degree
of verticality in the production relations of the enterprise. In practice,
especially in the case of the enterprises of the engineering industry,
divergent and convergent features often coexist, and it is not uncommon
to find flows of deliveries between one production unit and another.

In our computation method, however, we have disregarded the
divergent, convergent, or mutual character of production relations.
We are of the opinion that for management purposes it is primarily
the importance of internal turnover, i.e., the degree of inner cooperation, that matters, since this determines the magnitude of the coordina-
tive tasks of management.

In a few branches of Hungarian industry the distribution of
multiplant enterprises by degree of inner cooperation is as shown in
Table 6.2.

For practical purposes we can classify enterprises of the first
group (with inner cooperation accounting for less than 5 percent of
turnover) as horizontal, those in the last group (90-100 percent) as
vertical, and those in the intermediate groups as more or less of
mixed character.

In earlier Hungarian literature there was a fairly widespread
view that there must be a close negative correlation between
verticality in production organization and decentralization in management. This view was based on the plausible assumption that close
vertical relations between individual production units require the
central coordination of their production, while the absence or weakness
of such relations makes central coordination unnecessary, and management must be decentralized. This apparently plausible notion, however,
is only partly confirmed by empirical evidence.

The lowest degrees of decentralization (i.e. the highest degrees
of centralization) are found in the vertical group of enterprises in all
branches of industry, but the horizontal enterprises (with inner
cooperation below 5 percent) do not exhibit the highest degrees of
decentralization. If we define decentralization with respect to the
delegation of decision-making, the highest degrees of it are found
partly in the 5-20 percent category and partly in the 20-50 percent

TABLE 6.2

Distribution of Multiplant Enterprises
in Selected Industries
(in percents)

Degree of Inner Co-operation	Engineering Industry	Chemical Industry	Building Materials Industry	Textile Industry	Leather and Footwear Industry
0-5	31	33	67	14	29
5-20	36	45	33	9	14
20-50	19	11	-	27	14
50-90	14	11	-	18	14
90-100	-	-	-	32	29

Source: Compiled by the author.

group. If we define it by reference to management activities, only the marketing functions are found to be most highly decentralized in the "horizontal" group, while the other functions achieve this maximum in the 5-20 percent group of enterprises.

This lack of correlation becomes even more pronounced if decentralization is measured by the internal distribution of staffs (i.e., by the percentage of technical and administrative employees working in the management of subordinate plants within the enterprise). It is the engineering industry that appears to provide the most striking proof that not only high verticality, but also high horizontality, can counteract decentralization (see Table 6.3).

We think it is difficult to find a completely satisfactory explanation of this phenomenon. Moreover, lack of data prevented the research team from ascertaining whether this phenomenon was also present in other socialist countries and in the capitalist world, or whether it was something inherent in the specific circumstances of Hungary.

The research team attempted an explanation based on managerial behavior. Enterprise management aims to organize the efficient functioning of the enterprise as an economic system whose unity and effective operation must be based on appropriate relations between its component parts and their coordination in an integrated whole.

If these relations can be established in the field of production, the burden of integration is borne primarily by the production process itself, and the management system must have a structure that corresponds to this.

TABLE 6.3

Relationship Between Decentralization of Management
Personnel and Inner Cooperation in Enterprises
(in percents)

Degree of Inner Co-operation	Decentralization of Management Personnel			
	In Industry		In Engineering Industry	
	Technical Employees	Administrative Employees	Technical Employees	Administrative Employees
0-5	73	74	67	66
5-20	77	74	77	79
20-50	78	77	80	90
50-90	58	70	72	67
90-100	58	35	–	–

Source: Compiled by the author.

If the relations between individual production units are non-existent or unimportant, the burden of integration will of necessity shift to other activities within the field of operations of the enterprise. In other words, the management of the enterprise will attempt to replace the missing relations in the field of production by relations in other fields of the operational system. It is difficult to say whether this behavior should be regarded as economically advantageous or not, as we do not dispose of any methods of cost accounting capable of assessing the efficiency of centralization or decentralization. It remains a fact, however, that in the "horizontal" enterprises of Hungarian industry (where internal production relations are non-existent or insignificant) management relations are fairly strong owing to centralization.

It has been observed, moreover, that among engineering enter-prises the horizontal category shows extremely high concentration ratios in auxiliary activities, such as maintenance and tool-making. In other words, the diagonal relations of maintenance and tool-making replace the vertical relations that are missing in the production process.

NOTES

1. Mrs. Laszlo Tüü, "Industrial Activity and the Concentration of Industrial Organization," Kozgazdasági Szemle, No. 9 (1968).

2. See, for example, B. V. Grigorjev, Upravlenie gosudarstvennim promishlennim predpriyatiem v SSSR (Moscow: Isd. Mos. Universiteta, 1966); V. Ganstak, I. Rozenberg, Puti sovershentsvovaniya upravlenyia promislennim predpriyatiem (Moscow: Gossudarstvennoye Isd. Politycheskoy Lityerturii, 1962); Dr. Sandor Varga, The Inner Management System of Industrial Enterprises (Budapest: Kossuth Publ.H., 1971); J. Woodward, Industrial Organization (London; Oxford University Press, 1965).

3. P. S. Florence, The Logic of British and American Industry (London: Routledge and Regan) 3rd edition, 1972.

7

MARKET STRUCTURE
AND THE FIRM'S
MARKET POWER

Alex Jacquemin

In economics there are certain notions that, though they provide a strong emotional appeal to public opinion, possess a very ambiguous scientific content. One such notion is the concept of "economic power." The gap between its apparent precision for the layman and its ambiguity for the economist is probably a reflection of the fact that the phenomenon is very deeply built into the economic system. It is thus quite difficult to obtain a clear and objective view of the reality of economic power. According to Bertrand Russell, "the fundamental concept in social science is power, in the same sense in which energy is the fundamental concept in physics."[1]

But such a phenomenon never becomes perceptible except through its causes or its effects, and then only in the light of a very broad interdisciplinary approach. "The attempt to isolate any one form of power, more especially, in our days, the economic power, has been, and still is, a source of errors of great practical importance."[2]

Nevertheless, following the general approach of this chapter we should like to distinguish two types of firm's economic power. One may be called the "out-market power" and is made up of the numerous means—social, political, ethical—aimed at transforming the rules of the market game in favor of the holding firm. The firm manipulates its political and social environment in various ways: pressures to obtain favorable tax and subsidy laws, better credit conditions, important governmental contracts, good labor relations. Firms even set themselves up in strong positions as taste setters, style leaders, and social models in our society.

The author would like to thank A. Bergnson, J. Crea, R. Dehem, P. de Wolff, and R. C. O. Matthews for helpful comments and criticisms.

Such a power is economic in character because its scope and its domain lie in economic activity, though its "bases" extend beyond the framework of the market.[3]

The other type may be called the "in-market power" or simply the market power: The firm that owns such power plays the game according to the constraints and the objectives of the markets in which it operates; the scope is the economy and the bases are determined by the working of the market as an institutional frame for the interplay of demand and supply.*

The social scientists who have studied the economic power of the firm may be more or less classified according to a similar distinction. Researchers in sociology and politics have emphasized the first aspect.[4] Economists have concentrated their effort on the second type.[5] Some scholars have tried to offer a synthetic view of the phenomenon, with various degrees of success.[6]

In the limits of this chapter, we should like to propose (1) a static analysis of the firm's market power in its relation to market structure and, (2) the corresponding dynamic analysis based on the Pontryagin Maximum Principle. Finally, the conclusions present some reflections on the connection between the market power and the wider sociopolitical power of the large firm.

STATIC PROFIT MAXIMIZATION AND MARKET STRUCTURE

There exist many possible approaches to a study of the rational firm's policy toward market power. One such general approach includes the numerous oligopoly models that view each firm within a given market structure as recognizing the interdependence between its own actions and the actions of its rivals. Within this line of attack, the theory of games has provided some useful insights, but little development has taken place beyond the two-person situation.[7] Application of the theory of the core of the economy has raised new hopes, yet this promising line of research remains in the very early stages of development.[8]

Our approach is less theoretical and deals with the industrial organisation outlook as developed by E. Mason, J. Bain, R. Caves, and others.[9] Under this approach, analysis focuses on the study of market structure, market conduct, and market performance, and on

---

*There is of course a close connection between the two forms, but as we will see later, it is hard to assert a priori if they are complements or substitutes.

the interdependence of these factors. The main elements of market structure are concentration, product differentiation, and barriers to entry of new firms. Market performance is concerned with the appraisal of the industry's contribution to efficiency, progressiveness, full employment, and the equitable distribution of income in the economy. Market conduct consists of the behavior patterns that firms in an industry exhibit in the market where they sell their product.[10] Such behavior by the firm is generally pictured as aiming at maximum profits within a given market structure. Its conduct is determined by the structure of the industry in which it operates. "The principal frame of reference is the vision of the static economy or the circular flow, in which . . . market structure and behavior are taken as structurally determined."[11]

However, once it is admitted that a more fruitful vision of our modern economy considers the changing contours of business structure and behavior, it becomes clear that market structure may no longer be considered as a "state of nature," as a set of exogenous factors, but as a set of variables open to some manipulation by the firm. For a firm that holds some degree of market power it is possible and profitable to try to increase or at least to sustain the actual degree of concentration through mergers, absorptions, collusion, or loss-leader selling; to try to maintain or to increase the given degree of product differentiation through advertising investments and the various forms of selling costs; to try to sustain or to develop the barriers to entry through the acquisition of patents, retail outlets, scarce resources whose markets are imperfect, in order to impede or to prevent the entry of new firms.[12] Different forms of market conduct have the capacity to produce, either directly or as side effects, gradual changes in the structure of industries. According to such an approach, the more substantial is the market power of a firm, the more the market structure must be viewed as a strategic variable to the individual firm, not as an exogenously determined parameter. In the so-called market structure-conduct-performance pattern, the causal relation can run from conduct to structure to performance.

By analogy with the "prix crié par hasard" of Walras, we may suppose that the powerful firm works on a given structure of industry continuously trying to change it until some kind of equilibrium is reached.[13] Within a limited period of time, the firm will arrive at a position combining a certain level of concentration, of product differentiation, and of barriers to entry, such that the highest level of profit is attained. As P. W. S. Andrews writes: "We can still retain ideas of a firm in balance, a sort of equilibrium; but this would be a balance with its environment, the industrial environment."[14]

This conception implies the existence of what may be called a "structural maximum" for the firm. The expenditures or investments aimed at altering the market structure are assumed to suffer from diseconomies of scale, beyond some level. Indeed it is inconceivable that, in a given time span, a firm will increase its size without being handicapped by problems of budgetary control, decentralization of operation, or reorganization; similarly, the expansion of sales expenditures and the multiplication of barriers to entry will be stopped by various forms of saturation and decreasing efficiency.*

Furthermore, such changes in market structure will be constrained by antitrust legislation. This legislation is usually more concerned with market conduct than directly with market structure or market performance.[15] Among the practices generally condemned are restrictive agreements, price discrimination, exclusive dealing and full-line forcing, resale price maintenance, and so on. It is important to recall that insofar as these practices do arise in conjunction with monopoly, they are more often a symptom of monopoly power than its source.[16]

A worse danger lies in the predatory practices whose aim or effect is to modify the market structure by making the industrial environment less favorable to actual or to potential competition. For example, a strategy of selling below cost may be the best way to drive a competitor out of business by inducing a bankruptcy or by forcing a merger. Equally, monopolistic leverage may be exercised through the institution of tying arrangements: In this case a seller exploits his dominant position in one market to expand his empire into the next.

More fundamentally, horizontal and vertical mergers, pooling of patents, and extensive advertising may be dangerous, not so much as a means of exploiting the actual market power of the firm, but as a means of increasing such power over time through changes in the market structure. The large corporations of the "new industrial state" are not passive economic units that play the game in a given environment. They are actors who try to dominate and to transform in their favor the conditions of their action.

Those considerations may be expressed by a simple model. Let

$$\pi = p(q, s_1)q - c(q, s_2) - (s_1 + s_2)$$

describe the profit function of the firm where:
p = price of the firm's output

---

*However, if a "static" analysis is the appropriate method of exploring the conditions of equilibrium because of a limit to the amount of change any firm can undertake in a given period, there is no reason to assume that there is a limit to its expansion overtime.

c = total variable cost
r = total revenue = p. 9
s_1 = total expenditures for increasing price of the given quantity
s_2 = total expenditures for decreasing cost of the given quantity

Among the expenditures for increasing the price we have the expenditures for increasing size—that is, the degree of concentration in a given market—and the expenditures for intensifying the degree of product differentiation, including every form of selling costs. The large fraction of the expenditures on research and development aimed at "product improvements" may also be classified in that category. Those types are assumed for a given level of output to modify the firm's demand function, by shifting it to the right and by making it less elastic. Indeed, an increase in concentration or in product differentiation is usually viewed as increasing the monopoly power of the firm—that is, heightening the ability to maintain a margin between the price and the cost levels.* Among the expenditures for decreasing cost we have the purchase of patents, the acquisition of retail outlets in a particular market, and the securing of privileged sources of financing. In general, the elevation of entry barriers based on absolute advantages is supposed to affect the cost of the established firm: The acquisition of a patent or of the control of the natural raw material may reduce the cost of production and increase the height of the barrier (the margin between the cost of the established firm and the cost of the potential entrant).[17]

Furthermore, we assume that the favorable effects of changing market structure, on prices and on costs, do not extend beyond some maximum level of s.

Finally, we assume the existence of antitrust legislation that forbids any conduct aimed at changing market structure beyond some predetermined level.

The enterpreneur's problem is then to maximize:

-----

*Let us recall that a higher inelasticity of demand, η, leads to a higher price and to a higher degree of monopoly. This is easily shown in the case of a constant positive marginal cost, mc, where the profit-maximizing price

$$p = \frac{mc.\eta}{1 + \eta} \text{ with } \frac{dp}{d\eta} > 0$$

and by using the Lerner formula

$$L = \frac{p-mc}{p} = \frac{1}{-\eta} \ .$$

$$p(q, s_1)q - c(q, s_2) - s_1 - s_2$$

subject to:

$$s_1^* - s_1 \geq 0 \qquad s_1 \geq 0$$

$$s_2^* - s_2 \geq 0 \qquad s_2 \geq 0$$

$$q \geq 0$$

The Lagrangian function is:

$$\phi(q, s_1, s_2, \lambda_1, \lambda_2) = p(q, s_1)q - c(q, s_2) - s_1 - s_2 + \lambda_1 (s_1^* - s_1)$$

$$+ \lambda_2 (s_2^* - s_2)$$

Assuming the appropriate curvature properties, the Kuhn-Tucker conditions to maximize profit are:

(a) $\dfrac{\partial r}{\partial q} - \dfrac{\partial c}{\partial q} \leq 0$ $\qquad \left(\dfrac{\partial r}{\partial q} - \dfrac{\partial c}{\partial q}\right) q = 0$ $\qquad q \geq 0$

(b) $\dfrac{\partial r}{\partial s_1} - 1 - \lambda_1 = 0$ $\qquad \left(\dfrac{\partial r}{\partial s_1} - 1 - \lambda_1\right) s_1 = 0$ $\qquad s_1 \geq 0$

(c) $-\dfrac{\partial c}{\partial s_2} - 1 - \lambda_2 = 0$ $\qquad \left(\dfrac{\partial c}{\partial s_2} - 1 - \lambda_2\right) s_2 = 0$ $\qquad s_2 \geq 0$

(d) $s_1^* - s_1 \geq 0$ $\qquad \lambda_1(s_1^* - s_1) = 0$ $\qquad \lambda_1 \geq 0$

$\quad\;\; s_2^* - s_2 \geq 0$ $\qquad \lambda_2(s_2^* - s_2) = 0$ $\qquad \lambda_2 \geq 0$

If $q > 0$—that is, if the firm is engaged in production—condition (a) requires the classical equality between marginal cost and marginal revenue. If the legal constraint is not binding—that is, if $0 < s < s^*$, $\lambda = 0$—conditions (b) and (c) imply that:

$$\frac{\partial r}{\partial s_1} = -\frac{\partial c}{\partial s_2} = 1.$$

At the equilibrium position, there is an equality between the contribution of expenditures changing the structure of type 1 to the increase of total revenue, and the contribution of expenditures of type 2 to the reduction of cost. In addition, at any given output, the additional revenue generated must exactly equal the cost of generating that increment.

In terms of elasticity, we have:

$$\frac{\partial p}{\partial s_1} q = 1, \text{ or } \eta_{s1} = \frac{s_1}{p.q}$$

The percentage of revenue, which is allocated to the expenditures aimed at changing market structure, will be, at the equilibrium position, equal to the numerical value of the price elasticity with regard to those expenditures. If the increase in one type of expenditure is considered as having simultaneous consequences for monopoly power and cost savings, as is often the case with mergers, the profit function becomes:

$$\pi = p(q, s_1)q - c(q, s_1) - s_1$$

Condition (b) becomes: $\frac{\partial p}{\partial s_1} \cdot q - \frac{\partial c}{\partial s_1} - 1 = 0$ or

$$\eta_{s1} = \frac{s_1}{pq}(1 + \frac{\partial c}{\partial s_1})$$

With $\frac{\partial c}{\partial s_1} = -1$, the simultaneous increase and decrease in costs due to s_1 will cancel each other out, and s_1 must be raised to the level where $\eta_{s1} = 0$. With $\frac{\partial c}{\partial s_1} < -1$, s_1 must be increased till $\eta_{s_1} < 0$, because such a negative effect on the price will be more than offset by the cost-saving consequence.

Let us consider now the case where the legal constraint is binding: $s_1 = s_1^*$ and $\frac{\partial r}{\partial s_1} = 1 + \lambda_1$. With $\lambda_1 > 0$, we have $\frac{\partial r}{\partial s_1} > 1$. The firm will be unable to change its market structure up to the point at which the addition to total revenue just equals the costs of the change in market structure.

We also have $-\frac{\partial c}{\partial s_2} = 1 + \lambda_2$ and $-\frac{\partial c}{\partial s_2} > 1$. The cost reduction cannot be accomplished to the point required by profit maximization.

In this expression, λ indicates the marginal advantage that would be obtained by the firm in case of a liberalization of the antitrust legislation. Conversely, it measures the maximum price that can be paid, through lobbying, for changing the legislation. When we know the expected monetary value of the penalty of a violation of the anti-trust legislation, we can then determine whether or not the advantage to be gained by violating the law outweighs the expected cost.

DYNAMIC PROFIT MAXIMIZATION AND MARKET STRUCTURE

The preceding analysis has been confined to comparative statics. Yet the interdependence of market conduct, structure, and performance is fundamentally a problem of intertemporal analysis. Time plays two crucial roles. First, it is through the temporal dimension that competitive forces play against the market power of the firm and the imperfections of market structure: a high growth of market demand tends to be associated with a low degree of concentration;[18] industries with rapidly changing technologies "offer strong inducements to entry in the form of opportunities for gains to innovating firms. . . ."[19] Second, the impact of investments aimed at changing market structure is not limited to a given time period, but affects the whole time-path of the firm.

In order to reformulate our model to take account of these phenomena, let $\psi[s(t), I(t), t]$ be the firm's profit function at time t, as a result of having the "inherited" imperfect market structure—i.e., a given level of concentration, of product differentiation, of barriers to entry at that particular date, together with the current expenditures s, aimed at molding market structure.*

The firm attempts to maximize the present value of the stream of profits:

$$(1) \qquad V = \int_0^\infty e^{-\rho t} \, \psi[s(t), I(t), t] \, dt ,$$

where the discount rate ρ=rho is taken to be positive and constant.

While s is a decision variable, I is not a variable subject to choice but a given variable, a function of the market structure at the initial date and the time-path chosen for the decision variable:

$$\dot{I} = f(I, s, t), \text{ with } f'(s) \geq 0, f'(I) \leq 0.$$

More specifically, we suppose that, given the initial market structure $I(0) = I_0$, the set of imperfect market structure depreciates over time. The constant proportional rate of depreciation β expresses the

---

*In econometric studies of the relation between profit rates and market structure, the multiple correlation coefficients show that the structural variables typically account for more than half of total variation in industry profit rates (see note 12).

technological conditions as well as the competitive forces that play, through the temporal dimension, against the market power of the firm and the market imperfections.

On the other hand, the different forms of market conduct have the capacity to produce, not only a direct effect on the firm's current profit, but also gradual changes in the structure of industries. For example, advertising investments, besides their direct impact on the quantity demanded, have the indirect long-run effect of changing the given degree of product differentiation in the industry. Let us express this assumption in the following differential equation:

(3) $$\dot{I} = \alpha s - \beta I, \text{ with } \beta \geq 0, \alpha \geq 0$$

The coefficient α implies that the "marginal cost" of the rate of change in market structure is itself constant: there are no diminishing returns to the rate of change of the industrial environment.

The problem is then to select the control-path $s*(t)$ so as to maximize V, subject to (3) and to the initial condition, and taking into account the effect of the choice of s on both the instantaneous rate of profit and the future market structure. It may be solved by using the Pontryagin Maximum Principle.[20]

We construct the Hamiltonian function:

(4) $$H = e^{-\rho t}[\psi(s, I, t) + \lambda(t)(\alpha s - \beta I)]$$

where the auxiliary variable is defined such that $e^{-\rho t}\lambda(t) = \dfrac{\partial V*}{\partial I}$; $V*$ is the value of V that would result from the optimal feasible control-path $s*(t)$. Hence $e^{-\rho t}\lambda(t)$ is a shadow price—that is, the value, at time zero, of the marginal unit of imperfect market structure at time t.

To obtain the necessary conditions for a maximum, let us set the partial derivative of (4) with respect to s equal to zero:

(5) $$\psi'(s) + \lambda(t) f'(s) = \psi'(s) + \lambda(t)\alpha = 0$$

Furthermore, the function $\lambda(t)$ must satisfy the differential equation:

(6) $$-\dot{\lambda} = \psi'(I) - \lambda(t)\beta - \rho\lambda.$$
or
(7) $$\lambda(\rho + \beta) = \psi'(I) + \dot{\lambda}.$$

If max H is concave in I for given λ and t, then a market conduct aimed at changing market structure, satisfying (3), (5), and (6), and the transversality conditions

102

$$\lim_{t \to \infty} e^{-\rho t} \lambda(t) = 0, \quad \lim_{t \to \infty} e^{-\rho t} \lambda(t) I(t) = 0$$

is optimal, if the optimal path exists.

To interpret equations (5) and (6) and (7), we assume some plausible specifications about signs of partial derivatives:

(a) $\qquad\qquad\qquad \psi'(I) > 0, \quad \psi''(I) < 0$

(b) $\qquad\qquad\qquad \psi'(s) \gtreqless 0, \quad \psi''(s) < 0.$

Condition (a) asserts that, ceteris paribus, the higher the concentration, the product differentiation, or the barriers to entry, the more profitable are the firm's operations, but at a decreasing rate.

Condition (b) says that a higher level of s first increases the instantaneous total profit but decreases it beyond a certain level. Furthermore, the marginal profit is decreasing.

If we write $\psi'(s) = \acute{R}(s) - \acute{c}(s)$, where R and c are respectively the revenue and the cost generated by s, we may conclude from (5) that along the optimal control path of the decision variable, at any time t, a positive shadow price associated with imperfect market structure would imply that the marginal revenue generated by s is less than the marginal cost equally generated by s. For achieving the highest overall reward, the firm has to sacrifice some current profit. This result may be compared with the previous static model where $\lambda = 0$.

Furthermore, we may interpret in (6) $-\lambda$ as the loss to be incurred if a (unitary) change in market structure were postponed for a short time: Once the optimal time-path is followed, that loss in the contribution of the unitary increase in market structure imperfections to the profit realized during the interval, net of the marginal value of the investment to offset decay and of the interest.

According to (7) we may also state that the marginal opportunity cost of investment in changing market structure should equal the sum of the marginal profit from increased imperfections and the capital gain in market imperfections: This corresponds to the equilibrium relation for investment in capital goods.[21]

To define the optimal policy, let us now eliminate $\lambda(t)$ and $\dot{\lambda}$. Differentiating (5) with respect to time, we have:

(8) $\qquad\qquad\qquad \dot{\lambda} = \dfrac{-\dot{s}\, \psi''(s)}{\alpha}$

Substituting by their values λ and $\dot{\lambda}$ into equation (6), we obtain the following system of differential equations:

(9)
$$\dot{s} = (\rho + \beta)\left[\frac{\psi'(s)}{\psi''(s)}\right] + \alpha\left[\frac{\psi'(I)}{\psi''(s)}\right]$$

(3)
$$\dot{I} = \alpha s - \beta I$$

$$\dot{I} = 0 \quad \text{for } s = \frac{\beta}{\alpha} I$$

$$\dot{s} = 0 \quad \text{for } (\rho + \beta)\left[\frac{\psi'(s)}{\psi''(s)}\right] + \alpha\left[\frac{\psi'(I)}{\psi''(s)}\right] = 0$$

Equations (9) and (3) permit a simple two-dimensional analysis of the path of the system.

On the one hand, the slope of the curve for a stationary I, ($\dot{I} = 0$), is positive: $\left.\dfrac{dI}{ds}\right|_{\dot{I}=0} = \dfrac{\alpha}{\beta} > 0.$

On the other hand, the slope of the curve for a stationary s, ($\dot{s} = 0$), is negative: $\left.\dfrac{ds}{dI}\right|_{\dot{s}=0} = -\dfrac{\alpha}{(\rho + \beta)}\dfrac{\psi''(I)}{\psi''(s)} < 0.$

If the long-run equilibrium where both s and I are equal to zero is a saddle point,* there are two stable trajectories that describe the unique optimum path for $I_0 \neq I^*$ where I^* and s^* correspond to the saddle point.

Furthermore, $\dfrac{\partial \dot{I}}{\partial s} = \alpha > o$, for a given I

and $\dfrac{\partial \dot{s}}{\partial I} = \alpha\left[\dfrac{\psi''(I)}{\psi''(s)}\right] > 0$, for a given s.

Hence, for points above the curve $\dot{I} = 0$, $\dot{I} > 0$, and for points to the left of the curve $\dot{s} = o$, $\dot{s} < o$. Then, as long as $I_0 < I^*$, the optimal strategy of a firm that has the power to mold market structure is to use most of its power in the initial period to reduce the effort as I_0 approaches its equilibrium value I^*.

CONCLUSIONS

To conclude, it seems possible and useful to construct models according to which the firm's strategy will include efforts to mold

---

*To prove that (s^*, I^*) is a saddle, we have to expand linearly (9) and (3) around this point. From the obtained system, we compute the characteristic roots: if the roots are real and opposite in sign, market structure in order to maximize its objective function. The use of Optimal Control Theory seems particularly valuable for developing the dynamic analysis of industrial organization, especially because the control variables may be completely distinct from the given variables.

Yet, such an analysis calls for further developments and is no more than an introduction to a difficult problem. One possible extension would specify the various functions in order to build a system of simultaneous equations that can then be tested.[22] Another possible contribution would be a model recognizing explicitly the presence of uncertainty that affects the relevant functions and parameters.*

(s*, I*) is a stationary point of long-run equilibrium. But this computation requires us to specify the form of our equations.

*As a first step in this direction, one could assume that there are several possible states of the world for the firm, i.e., a monopolistic market structure and a competitive market structure. Subjective probabilities are attached to the occurrence of each possible state and these probabilities are viewed as being subject to influence by the firm's strategy. The firm maximizes its expected profit:

(1) $$E[\pi] = \gamma(s)\pi_m + [1s-\gamma(s)]\pi_c$$

where $\pi_m = P_m(q)q - c(q)-s$ is the monopoly profit, and $\pi_c = P_c q - c(q)-s$ is the competitive profit. In (1), γ, the probability of having a monopoly profit, is assumed to be an increasing, continuously differentiable and concave function of s, where s is the expenditures aimed at molding market structure.
The first-order condition for a maximum with respect to s, states that:

(2) $$\frac{\partial \gamma}{\partial s} = \frac{I}{\pi_m - \pi_c}$$

For a given γ, s is simply determined by the difference between π_m and π_c: The higher this difference, the more will be spent on s, and the less will be the marginal effect of s on γ.
The corresponding dynamic model would imply that the monopoly profit could be obtained at time t and that $\dot{\gamma} = f(s)$, with $f'(s) \geq 0$.
Then the Hamiltonian is:

$$H = e^{-\rho t}[(1-\gamma)\pi_c + \gamma\pi_m] + \lambda(t)f.$$

105

Finally, it is necessary to point out that power in the marketplace is but one facet of the firm's economic power. In addition, the firm possesses what we have called "out-market power," which is made up of the numerous means (social and political) aimed at transforming the rules of the game in favor of the firm.

It is possible to consider that there exists a complementary relation between out-market and market power. The powerful firm will try to mold in its favor, not only the market structure, but its political, social, and institutional structure as well. "The branch manager of the company whose plant is the largest employer in a town or the vice-president of the firm proposing to build a plant which will become the largest employer in a small state treats with local government not as a citizen but as a quasi-sovereign power. Taxes, zoning laws, roads, and the like become matters of negotiation as much as matters of legislation."[23]

In this sense, an increase in the underlying power of firms in the markets in which they operate would lead to a corresponding increase in their social and political power. But the inverse is not necessarily true: An increase in political or social power may be obtained at the expense of market power. The giant firm, socially important because of the number of people it influences directly as employees, suppliers, and customers, may be, from an economic point of view, "without muscle" or inefficient. In other words, "the corporation is the vehicle through which power comes to be held and exercised. . . . Power increases with the size of the firm. Here lies an important explanation of the tendency of many large firms to become larger, even if sometimes the profitability of such an expansion is open to serious question."[24]

In conclusion, the various forms of power are clearly connected in the hands of the firm but the sign of this connection is somewhat ambiguous. What must at least be emphasized is that today out-market power is probably much more important than market power. This situation comes from the increasing institutionalization of the market economy. Everyone now admits that our system is no longer a delicate self-regulating mechanism but a set of institutions open to manipulation by the participants. In this view, the powerful corporation becomes more and more a "body politic," a "rationalized system for the accumulation, control and administration of power."[25]

Such an evolution is also manifest in Eastern countries and shows us that the power of big organizations and its control are universal problems that have to be solved in any economic system.

NOTES

1. Bertrand Russell, Power, A New Social Analysis (London: Allen and Unwin, 1946), p. 10.

2. Ibid., p. 12.

3. According to A. Kaplan, "When we have specified what scope a power has, on what base it rests, over what domain and with what weight it is exercised, then we can say that we have described a distinctive form of power." In R. L. Kahn and E. Boulding, Power and Conflicts in Organizations (New York: Basic Books, 1964), p. 16.

4. See, for example, R. L. Kahn, op.cit.; D. Cartwright, A Field Theoretical Conception of Power, Studies in Social Power (Ann Arbor: University of Michigan Press, 1959); H. D. Lasswell and A. Kaplan, Power and Society (New Haven: Yale University Press, 1950); M. Crozier, "Pouvoir et Organisation," Archives Européennes de Sociologie, T.V. 1964, No. 1.; for a general synthesis, see A. Jacquemin, L'entreprise et son pouvoir de marché (Paris: Presses Universitaires de France, 1967), pp. 25-35.

5. See, for example, F. Machlup, The Political Economy of Monopoly (Baltimore: John Hopkins Press, 1952); E. Mason, Economic Concentration and the Monopoly Problem (Cambridge, Mass.: Harvard University Press, 1957); J. Houssiaux, Le Pouvoir de Monopole (Paris: Sirey, 1958).

6. See, for example, A. Berle, Power without Property (New York: Harcourt, Brace, 1959); C. Kaysen, "The Corporation: How Much Power? What Scope?," in E. Mason, ed., The Corporation in Modern Society (New York: Atheneum, 1966); J. Lhomme, Pouvoir et Société économique (Paris: Cujas, 1966); F. Perroux, L'Economie du XXe siècle (Paris: Presses Universitaires de France, 1961).

7. See M. Shubik, Strategy and Market Structure (New York: John Wiley, 1959).

8. This theory, originally based on the Edgeworth box, defines the core of the economy as being the set of possible resource allocations that are admissible in the sense that no coalition can block any of these allocations. The coalitions that lead to the allocations in the core may be said to hold economic power. See J. Gabszewicz, "Théorie du noyau et de la concurrence imparfaite," Recherches Economiques de Louvain, July, 1970.

9. E. Mason, Economic Concentration and The Monopoly Problem (Cambridge, Mass.: Harvard University Press, 1957); J. Bain, Industrial Organization (New York: John Wiley, 1967), and Barriers to New Competition (Cambridge, Mass.: Harvard University Press, 1956); and R. Caves, American Industry: Structure, Conduct, Performance (Englewood Cliffs, N.J.: Prentice-Hall, 1967).

10. Caves, op.cit.

11. J. P. Miller in National Bureau of Economic Research, Business Concentration and Price Policy (Princeton: Princeton University Press, 1955), p. 135.

12. Empirical studies confirm the existence of a positive statistically significant relationship between market shares of the largest firms in the industry and the price-cost margin in that industry (N. Collins and L. Preston, "Price-Cost Margin and industry Structure," Review of Economics and Statistics, August, 1969); between advertising outlays in the industry and profit rate (W. Comonor and T. Wilson, "Advertising, Market Structure and Performance," Review of Economics and Statistics, November, 1967); between barriers to entry controlled by the dominant firms of the industry and profit rate (H. Mann, "Seller Concentration, Barriers to Entry and Rates of Return in Thirty Industries," Review of Economics and Statistics, August, 1966).

13. See P. Sylos-Labini, Oligopoly and Technical Progress (Cambridge, Mass.: Harvard University Press, 1962), p. 36.

14. P. W. S. Andrews, On Competition in Economic Theory (London: Macmillan, 1964), p. 91.

15. See A. Jacquemin, "The Criterion of Economic Performance in the Antitrust Policies of the United States and the E.E.C.," Common Market Law Review, No. 2. (April, 1970).

16. L. Telser, "Abusive Trade Practices: An Economic Analysis," Law and Contemporary Problems, No. 3. (Summer, 1965).

17. See F. Modigliani, "New Developments on the Oligopoly Front," Journal of Political Economy, June, 1958.

18. R. L. Nelson, Concentration in the Manufacturing Industries of the U.S. (New Haven, Yale University Press, 1963).

19. M. Gort, Diversification and Integration in American Industry, National Bureau of Economic Research (Princeton: Princeton University Press, 1962), p. 105.

20. L. S. Pontryagin, V. G. Boltyanskii, R. S. Gramkrelidze, and E. F. Mischenko, The Mathematical Theory of Optimal Processes (New York: John Wiley, 1962).

21. K. Arrow, "Applications of Control Theory to Economic Growth," Lectures in Applied Mathematics, Vol. 12. (1968), Stanford Institute for Mathematical Studies in the Social Sciences; see also M. Albouy and A. Breton, "Interprétation économique du principe du maximum," Revue Française de Recherche Opérationnelle, No. 14. (1968).

22. For such an application, see A. Jacquemin, Product Differentiation and Optimal Advertising Policy: A Dynamic Analysis (Louvain: Institute des Sciences Economiques, 1971) (mimeographed).

23. Kaysen, op.cit., p. 100.

24. R. A. Gordon, <u>Business Leadership in the Large Corporation</u>, 2nd ed. (Berkeley, University of California Press, 1961), p. 306. In our static model it means that management will maximize its utility function where s as such becomes an objective:

$$U = U(\Pi, s), \text{ with } \Pi = p(q,s)q - c(q) - s.$$

At the equilibrium position, $\dfrac{\partial r}{\partial s} = 1 - \dfrac{\partial U}{\partial s} \Big/ \dfrac{\partial U}{\partial \pi}$.

With $\dfrac{\partial U}{\partial s} \Big/ \dfrac{\partial U}{\partial \pi} > 0$, we have $\dfrac{\partial r}{\partial s} < 1$, or $\eta_{s_1} < \dfrac{s_1}{\rho q}$.

The level of expenditures for increasing concentration or size will be such that the incremental expenditures add less to total revenue than they add to total cost.

25. E. Latham, "The Body Politic of the Corporation," in Mason, op.cit., p. 220.

8

THE RELATION BETWEEN ENTERPRISE MANAGEMENT AND CENTRAL CONTROL: THE HUNGARIAN EXPERIENCE

Béla Rabi

The socialist economy is of necessity an economy based on central planning. Social ownership of the means of production creates both the preconditions and the need for a planned approach to development, which in turn requires central management and control. These are the classical theses that lie at the root of the system of management and control in all socialist states. The concept of planned development, however, differs from one country to another, in accordance with the model each one has chosen to adopt.

In certain systems of management and control, planned development may mean that central organs specify for each enterprise what tasks it has to fulfill and what means shall be at its disposal to fulfill them. This is usually called the "centralized model." In these conditions the autonomy of an enterprise reduces to the search for the best possible combination and adaptation of means and ends within the constraints specified by central authority.

Since January 1, 1968, however, the system of economic control and management operative in Hungary has involved a different concept of planned development, at once broader and more sophisticated. The central plan marks out the major directions of development and the main proportions of the economy, ensuring dynamic equilibrium without prescribing detailed tasks for individual producers. In such a model planned development is said to be achieved if these major objectives of the central plan are realized in a harmonious way. This happens not through direct orders, but basically through the use of economic levers. Under such a system the autonomy of the enterprise covers a wider area: the choice of aims, the selection of means, and the choice of the general direction of development—all are basically brought within the purview of its own decision-making powers.

DIVISION OF POWER IN DECISION-MAKING

The present Hungarian system of economic management and control is based on a new division of powers between the center and the periphery that maintains consistency in the overall process of decision-making.

The following powers of decision are reserved for the center: the main directions and proportions to be followed in national economic development (i.e., major investment projects to be directly selected by government); aggregative limits on credit in accordance with the structural shifts in the economy foreseen by the plan; the division of national income into consumption and investment; the growth rate of personal incomes (and hence of consumption); problems relating to the standard of living, prices of staple goods, cultural, educational, and social problems of prime importance, etc.

While the central plan ensures the dynamic equilibrium of the economy as a whole, partial equilibria are ensured through the use of the market aided by decentralized decisions. The enterprises themselves have scope for choice within the spheres assigned to them by the state, and their autonomy extends to everything within that, subject only to the constraints imposed by the limitations of their own resources. This covers the whole process from the drafting of plans to the use of sales receipts and profits earned from production and sales. In this way enterprises are transformed from mere organs of execution into genuine units of economic choice.

The autonomous decisions of enterprises are influenced by measures of economic regulation under the national plan. Their decisions will harmonize with economic policy at the national level provided their interests, and those of their work force, run parallel with those of the national economy—at least in general direction. This parallelism must be safeguarded by the regulatory system in force.

CHARACTERISTIC FEATURES OF ENTERPRISE AUTONOMY

The state enterprise is of course the property of the whole nation. Yet it has been separated out by the state as an economic organ intended to follow its own independent interests.

Enterprises have wide scope for autonomous choice. They decide independently on problems of current production, and generally also on those involving investment. Their choice is only marginally constrained by direct instructions of an explicit sort, but they are guided by the economic parameters set for them by the regulatory actions of the state under the central economic plan.

The decisions of enterprises are subject to a system of incentives, both of a collective and of a personal nature. These incentives are partly moral and partly material. Enterprises and their managers strive to fulfill their potential not exclusively in order to exploit material advantage, but also under the influence of moral incentive, e.g., social esteem, recognition of achievement, etc. Nonetheless, material incentives are of great importance, particularly as they must be relied upon to secure the implementation of decisions taken. There can be no question of widening the scope of enterprise autonomy without the creation of a proper system of material incentives.

The basic ingredient in the system of material incentives is the total profit realized. The purpose of all operations of socialist enterprises is to satisfy social demands and social needs. Given a proper economic system, the objective of an enterprise (increased profits) will be conducive to the achievement of the social objectives (the satisfaction of needs), since the enterprise is driven to rationalize production and to produce what is backed by monetary demand. Apart from increasing personal incomes, a greater volume of profits will facilitate the expansion and modernization of capacity, thus enabling the state to improve its services to society as a whole.

METHODS AND INSTRUMENTS OF CENTRAL CONTROL

The main instrument of central control is the national economic plan. From the point of view of operational control it is the medium-term (5 year) plans that are the most fundamental. The long-term (10 to 15-year) plan is a projection of major trends into a more distant future and as such is not suited to serve as an instrument of operational control. For that purpose it lacks the necessary articulation and consistency of detail. Yet long-term plans are of great importance as a basis on which the 5-year plans are formulated. Annual plans are unsuitable as instruments for the implementation of economic policy because of the shortness of their time horizon. They provide a check and an analysis on the progress of the 5-year plan and the means of remaining on course under changing economic conditions with the aid of short-term measures.

Medium-term plans are drawn up in an integrated way and checked for consistency both aggregatively and in a breakdown of 13 to 39 sectors. The plans include as an integral part the regulatory measures that "transmit the intentions" of central authority and ensure the realization of the main objectives without specifying the targets for individual executants. The fundamental aim of the medium-term national economic plan is to ensure the dynamic equilibrium of the economy and to regulate the market with the aid of economic levers.

This form of planned control does not imply the complete abandonment of administrative measures (i.e., specific instructions). The state, as the repository of national ownership rights, cannot and does not renounce the exercise of these rights. It institutes and liquidates enterprises; it appoints and dismisses enterprise executives and calls them to account when necessary. The state defines the limits of enterprise autonomy. In case of need the state also interferes directly with the operation of enterprises through the controlling ministries and checks on their activities in a regulatory manner.

The instruments of economic control are the following: the price system and price policy, the credit system and interest policy, the tax system, foreign exchange control, commercial policy, and the system of material incentives. Measures in these fields operate as an organic part of the plan and are subordinate to its main objectives, but they also generate feedbacks on the plan itself. These measures must be coordinated in order to preserve the parallelism of interests between enterprises and the nation, at least in general direction, thus influencing enterprise decisions in the same direction.

The Price System and Price Policy

A characteristic feature of the price system is the threefold subdivision of prices according to stringency of control: centrally determined (fixed) prices, prices subject to limits, and free prices. The centrally fixed prices are set for consumer goods of decisive importance to the cost of living and for the most important raw materials. These and the limit prices will also have an influence on free prices.

The price system has a threefold role within the mechanism of management and control:

1. Prices are tools of economic calculation. Enterprises make their decisions on the basis of calculations that use prices. In this way prices are economic signaling devices of the first importance.

2. Prices influence and regulate the magnitude of production and consumption (to the extent that they determine the net revenues of enterprises).

3. Prices affect the distribution and redistribution of the personal incomes of the population.

It will be seen from this that the level of prices, their structure, and relative magnitudes have an extremely important guiding role in the harmonization of the interests of enterprises with those of the national economy, in the mutual adaptation of production and consumption, and in the determination of living standards. The direct or indirect regulation of prices and the action of the price mechanism are thus one of the most important regulators and the basic precondition for the realization of the aims of central authority. At the same time the absolute and relative levels of prices are extremely important signaling devices in the process of planning. In a flexible price system they transmit the value judgments of the market to the decision-makers, central and peripheral alike. In this way prices, as an embodiment of the laws of the market, also provide a feedback mechanism for the objectives and decisions formulated in the plan. This is of particular importance in the case of an open economy, such as that of Hungary, where economic relations with the outside world are of crucial importance.

The Credit System and Interest Policy

Credit and interest policy are closely linked with other elements of the financial system. From the point of view of economic administration, the function of the credit system is a dual one: On the one hand it is one of the means for the fulfillment of the national plan, on the other hand it is one of the safeguards of equilibrium in the circular flow of goods and money and guarantees the value of the national currency.

Every year the government issues directives for credit policy as an organic part of the national economic plan. These directives define the total volume of credit to be available to the national economy, with a fairly flexible breakdown into economic sectors, and also specify the priorities arising from the main objectives of the plan. The sum total of credits depends on the capacity of enterprises for credit absorption, i.e., on the foreseen effective demand of the market, and on the supply of credit that seems justified on the basis of the plans. As an operational regulator of the economy, the volume of credit is an annual plan indicator, although general directives for credit creation are also included in the 5-year plans. Nevertheless the regulations specifying the conditions, limits, and priorities under which credit is to be available are determined on an annual basis. At present enterprises can make use of credits for two purposes: for purposes of investment for which long-term and medium credits are available, and for working capital, which is covered by medium- and short-term credits. In this way credit creation can affect the whole circle of economic activities undertaken by enterprises and enables the state to exert its influence indirectly through the credit system. A similar method of regulation is used in connection with interest policy. The main purpose of interest policy is to steer economic activity into the direction corresponding to the intentions of government, mainly by its general control over basic rate of interest. In formulating interest policy great importance attaches to the principle of priority, i.e., to the support and preferential treatment accorded to specific branches of the economy and specific enterprises, or in certain circumstances to the limitation of the economic activities of other branches and enterprises. The regulatory role of credit policy is realized in the main through selectiveness in the granting of credits. The banks intervene in the economic life of the country in accordance with the economic policy and directives of the government by expanding or limiting their selective grants of credit.

The Tax System

One of the most important indirect regulators of the economy is the system of rules relating to enterprise revenues. This system exerts influence in two directions: on the one hand through various taxes and deductions flowing into the state budget, and on the other hand through state contributions to enterprise funds and various subsidies flowing to enterprises (based on the guidelines of the plan). The following taxes and other charges can be distinguished:

1. The capital charge. This is one of the channels through which the new income created by enterprises is tapped. It expresses a particular aspect of the mutual relationship between state and enterprises, i.e., the state's demand for a minimal share of the net income arising from the resources utilized by enterprises. This demand has the additional effect of creating incentives for the economical use of fixed and working capital and for their maintenance at the best possible level. At the same time, the charge enters the prices of finished products and thereby provides guidance to the user of these products on the resources used up in their production. As a rule the capital charge is fixed at 5 percent of the gross value of fixed capital. In a number of branches of the economy, however, it is levied at a different rate, and in some subbranches or enterprises it is waived altogether.

2. Charges on net income geared to wage payments. A part of the net income of society is withdrawn from enterprises in proportion to their wage bills. The greater the number of productive workers in an enterprise the higher the net income it can produce. But direct payments for productive work, i.e., the wage cost included in normal cost calculations, do not exhaust the true social costs connected with the use of current labor. A charge proportional to the wage bill makes

it possible to incorporate into prices all personal transfer payments paid out over and above direct wages (e.g., the cost of social insurance subsidies, pensions, etc.). Finally it should be noted that charges proportional to the wage bill will also stimulate the saving of labor. These charges are, as a rule, 25 percent of the total wage bill of an enterprise. They are at present deducted in two different ways: as social insurance contributions and as a payroll tax. For certain enterprises the charges are levied at other rates.

3. The turnover tax. In certain cases the state must use prices as an instrument of economic policy by interposing a turnover tax that raises the level of consumer prices above the level of wholesale prices. In this way the turnover tax, which is in essence an excise tax, provides a means of giving effect to the conscious preferences of the state. Shifts in the level of consumer and wholesale prices can be motivated by considerations of productive efficiency, or by the requirements of culture, social welfare, or hygiene. In addition to its role as a regulator of supply and demand, the turnover tax may be used to establish equilibrium between them. As a deduction from enterprise revenues, the role of the turnover tax is insignificant; it is above all a means of regulating prices.

4. The production tax on enterprises. The profits of enterprises may show such divergence that proportional taxation in a uniform manner must be excluded. The production tax does not affect the portion of profit that is due to the enterprise's own performance; it is levied only on those portions that accrue owing to certain (at present irremovable) shortcomings in the price structure or to movements in export prices abroad. It is precisely to mitigate such economically unjustified differences in profits that the production tax is used. In fixing the rates of the production tax, great attention must be paid to the need for preserving the incentives of enterprises. Specific rates of production tax are fixed for each enterprise, or for each product.

5. The tax on profits and on enterprise funds created out of profits. In the system of enterprise charges the form and extent of enterprise taxation in relation to the material incentives of the labor force occupies a place of central importance. An especially important role falls to profits since in the final analysis this is an indicator that is affected by all aspects of the economic activities of an enterprise. The absolute profit reflects not only the outlays on labor and other inputs but also other charges on revenue. The economic activity of enterprises is aimed at achieving as much profit as possible. High profits are not merely advantageous from the point of view of the enterprise but, given certain conditions in the economic system, are also indicative of economic performance that benefits the national economy. In this way the interests of the enterprise lie

in a direction that approaches national interests in the best possible way.

In connection with the charges on enterprise profits and the preservation of their material incentives we must fulfill two conditions: on the one hand we must secure to the state budget sufficient deductions to enable it to fulfill those of its financial tasks that are a charge on central funds, and at the same time we must secure to enterprises sufficient retentions out of profit to safeguard their independent financial operation. Simultaneously, the material interest in achieving profit must motivate enterprises to utilize their own resources and develop their independent economic activities to the fullest possible extent. For this reason the portion of profits retained by enterprises may be used to form a fund for personal incentives to workers, a fund for the further development of the enterprise, and a reserve fund.

In accordance with these objectives the profits retained in the enterprise are channeled into the profit-participation-fund to increase personal incentives; the development fund of the enterprise to serve as a source of finance for further development; and, the reserve fund to put the economic activities of the enterprise on a secure basis.

The taxation of profit is also an important element in the whole system of income regulation because it simultaneously serves several different purposes: the magnitude and structure of profit taxation and the resulting incentives must correspond to the directives of the medium-term plan (the requirements of a balanced budget, the need for self-administered resources within the enterprise, the projected growth in personal incomes); it must also preserve the motivation of enterprises toward an increase in profits; and it must be an integrated system, i.e., it must ensure that all enterprises operating under similar economic conditions and earning equal profits should be able to form incentive funds of equal size.

In principle the system of profit taxation works in the following way: The profit of each enterprise is divided into two parts according to uniform and generally applicable principles. The division depends on the total wage bill and the capital output-ratio of each enterprise. The division does not depend on absolute figures but proceeds in accordance with a formula involving different weightings of the basic factors (i.e., an enterprise must divide its profit into two portions, standing to each other in the same ratio, for example, as double the annual wage bill to the annual average value of the capital stock). In this way the division is made to reflect the particular circumstances of the enterprise, its need for a wage fund and for capital stock. The importance of regulating this division in a uniform manner will be evident. One of the two parts, from which the profit participation fund is to be fed, is taxed in a manner appropriate to this purpose, while the other part, from which the development fund is to be created, is subject to tax according to special tax tables.

The centralized regulation of incomes does not merely take the form of various deductions from net income. In particular cases the state may also contribute financial resources to the enterprise. The basic forms of state subsidies are subsidies to cover deficits, price supports, state support for the development of production, and export subsidies.

Price supports are an adjustment to the price level similar to the turnover tax but with the opposite sign. If for any reason the state decides to fix the consumer price of a given product at a lower level than its production cost, the enterprise affected by this measure is given a support price. Subsidies to cover deficits are normally granted to enterprises when losses arise through the introduction of new capacity or techniques and where production costs either exceed the selling price of the products or are too high to assure an appropriate profit. In a number of circumstances the state supports the development of the enterprise. The relevant subsidies may be divided into two basic groups: the so-called direct and indirect forms of support. Direct support is given in the form of direct financial subsidies from the state budget for the development of the enterprise. Indirect support is usually given in the form of tax remissions or preferential taxation. Export subsidies are given to enable an enterprise to produce exports that are important for the national economy but unprofitable for the enterprise itself. The subsidies influence both the price of the product and the profit disposable by the enterprise.

Foreign Exchange Control and Commercial Policy

These two instruments regulate exports and imports. The foreign currency received for exports must be paid into the central bank and the currency needed for imports is issued by the central bank in accordance with a licensing system. Foreign currency is converted into Hungarian forints by means of a single conversion coefficient so that the producing enterprises acquire an interest in the foreign prices paid for their products. The foreign trade organizations act as agencies working on commission in the great majority of cases, and in this way productive enterprises carry the risks and feel the direct effects of their activities in export markets.

THE NATURE OF INDEPENDENT PLANNING BY ENTERPRISES AND THE LINKS BETWEEN PLANS AT ENTERPRISE AND NATIONAL LEVELS

It will be generally known that the system of economic administration at present operative in Hungary does not oblige enterprises to draw up plans for themselves, nor does it impose on them obligatory performance indicators deriving from a breakdown of the national targets. Nevertheless, every enterprise must of necessity have some independent program. The considerable widening of the decision-making powers of enterprises did not mean that their development and general economic activities could proceed without any direction; on the contrary, it required a strengthening of the principle of planned development at a higher level. Enterprise plans must in the first instance permit the correct organization of work and raise the level of managerial efficiency. The enterprise plan ensures the undisturbed operation of simple reproduction (current production) and opens up the possibility of purposeful development for the enterprise.

With the abolition of obligatory plan indicators and direct instructions the enterprises have to take responsibility for discovering sales outlets themselves. Having found these, they can work out sales plans and base their plans of production on the latter. At the same time, however, the production plan must be safeguarded from the supply side as far as the factors of production are concerned. Sales possibilities depend to a great extent on the up-to-date character of the output to be sold. There is also a close link between the modernization and the development of the enterprise, particularly since the resources for capital investment do not accrue to the enterprise gratuitously but must be created by it through economic activity, i.e., capital investment must be made to pay for itself. One can only take account of all these links and ensure their consistency with material incentives by means of an integrated plan for the enterprise.

In addition, it is only the enterprise plan that can guarantee that sufficient finance will be available. It is an important hallmark of management and control through economic levers that the earlier system of automatic financing on the basis of planned targets has been abolished, and the scope for free choice in economic transactions now flows from the money earnings of the enterprise. In this way, the flow of monetary resources does not automatically follow from the flow of output, and each economic unit must make provision for the financial means necessary to realize its economic decisions. This in turn requires foresight in all directions, i.e., planning.

It follows that under present conditions enterprises must work out a plan, not because this is prescribed by higher authority, but because this is required by their own interests and by the need to link their programs with the national economic plan. Since the enterprise plan is not ratified, the indicators of which it is made up are not obligatory and no report on their fulfillment is required; therefore, the work of the enterprise is not judged on the basis of plan fulfillment. Furthermore, the abolition of planned directives has also eliminated the practice of "planning with reference to previous achievement (in the base period)" and thereby the previous practice of "bargaining for plan indicators." The enterprises no longer have an interest in concealing their reserves; on the contrary, full disclosure of their reserves can now lead to fuller allocations of necessary material and financial resources and therefore all enterprises have an incentive to make their plans as realistic as possible. After all, plans can only fulfill their organizational functions properly to the extent that they are realistic.

What, then, is the link between the plan at the enterprise and at the national level? As a rule the national plan does not regulate the relations between enterprises. These relations should establish themselves in the interests of efficiency and expediency in reaching established goals. What matters from the point of view of society is a high degree of efficiency in economic activity, and not the nature of the decisions that ensure this efficiency in particular instances. In this way attention is concentrated on the achievement of the final goals, and the ways and means of this achievement can be left to be decided by the dictates of efficiency. This is all the more valuable since a higher degree of efficiency will open up the possibility for the setting and implementation of more ambitious goals.

None of this, however, means that enterprise plans are not closely linked to the national plan. The decisions and resource allocations foreseen in the central plan for the regulation of the market and the economic levers used on enterprises to a large extent determine the scope and limits for enterprise plans. Enterprises that do not take account of these constraints can find themselves working out unrealistic and unrealizable plans, as a result of which they can be plunged into financial difficulties.

The national plan is of help to enterprises in the working out of their own plans, partly directly and partly in an indirect way. Enterprises receive documentary information that allows them to come to direct of indirect conclusions.

The investment chapter of the central plan imparts direct information for the development plans of enterprises and—in the case of capital goods producers—also for current production plans. In this chapter both industrial and social investment projects of major importance are specified by name and location. This tells enterprises in what branches and in what enterprises expansion and development programs will be taking place on the basis of central decisions. In this way it becomes possible to estimate the inputs necessary for the implementation of these investments. With the knowledge of the gestation periods and completion dates of these central projects it is possible to estimate their probable output, the approximate growth in supply, and their requirements of raw materials and manpower. Information on noncentralized investment may also be derived, though somewhat less directly. This is because the central plan defines the proportion of depreciation funds to be left with individual enterprises and also the sectoral limits on bank credit. It is possible on the basis of this, taking account of the profit allocations to the development funds of enterprises, to plan the capital projects which are financed from the enterprise's own resources.

Direct information may also be derived from the system of income regulation that is ratified and announced simultaneously with the national plan. The system of regulators worked out in accordance with the national plan contains all the conditions and links that form the integrated system of regulatory tools. It gives the enterprises very important indications on their future economic environment and on the direction their own plans should most appropriately take in the light of the possibilities open to them under this system. Apart from the document on the plan as legally ratified, the enterprises receive important worksheets used in the calculations underlying the plan. This supporting material contains, among other things, projections on the development of production, the manpower situation, the position regarding material supplies, production efficiencies, and foreign trade links. This information does not of course bind anyone, but nonetheless provides enterprises with valuable guidelines.

The national plan also contains information on administrative measures, e.g., input quotas of particular materials or other constraints and possibly certain indications relating to foreign trade and international agreements. This also provides concrete and direct information.

The central plan, whether taken as a whole or in its detail, indicates the general directions for the working out of enterprise plans even though it does not contain direct instructions to enterprises. If we further take into account that the plan also regulates the market and thus provides the enterprises with a nonanarchic and foreseeable environment, we have ample grounds for the assertion that the national economic plan is indeed the basic tool of central management and control.

**DECISION-MAKING BY
WORKERS AND MANAGEMENT:
THE ELECTRIC POWER
INDUSTRY IN CROATIA**
Jadranko Bendeković

INTRODUCTION

Since the electric power industry operates in an imperfect market and is likely to behave as a monopoly, it will not achieve in its operation and development the objectives desired by society. Some substitute for competition as a control mechanism therefore has to be introduced. The necessity of introducing such a mechanism was recognized a long time ago, and different institutional frameworks have been set up in various countries. The essence of these solutions is a set of laws and regulations imposing efficient behavior on the electric power industry. This has been done in Yugoslavia also, but one can question whether this solution has the necessary control mechanism, and, in addition, whether self-management has anything to offer in this respect.

This chapter deals with the problem of setting up a self-management framework that might lead to a decision-making process able to ensure the optimal operation and development of the electric power industry from the point of view of society. The problem is discussed in terms of a model of the power industry in Croatia.* In

---

*Yugoslavia consists of six republics: Bosnia and Herzegovina, Croatia, Macedonia, Montenegro, Serbia, and Slovenia.

The author is indebted to Rikard Lang and Zeljko Paukovic of the Economic Institute, Zagreb, for very valuable comments on an early draft of this contribution. However, all responsibility for any inconsistency and misinterpretation is exclusively the author's.

other words, this chapter takes the example of the power industry in Croatia to discuss a more general problem of multilevel decision-making, under conditions of self-management, in an industry where externalities are present.

First, existing conditions for the operation and development of the power industry in Croatia are presented. Then, we sketch the relevant characteristics of the industry given these conditions. Finally, a new model of decision-making is discussed. A solution has been sought along the lines of the participation by consumers and socio-political units in decision-making at every level of the electric power industry's organizational structure.

EXISTING CONDITIONS IN THE ELECTRIC POWER INDUSTRY IN CROATIA

Electric power in Croatia is supplied by a power pool consisting of three power systems, each identified as an individual enterprise: Rijeka, Split, and Zagreb.* The operation and development of the pool is strongly influenced by the structure of generating units—by the structure of production, as well as by the characteristics of their consumers—by the structure of power consumption in the area the system supplies. Its operation and development are also subject to an institutional framework. The structure of production, the structure of consumption, and the institutional framework are therefore the main determinants of the pool's behavior.

The structure of production involves the participation of hydroelectric and thermal power stations. At the moment neither tidal nor nuclear plants are in existence in this pool. Thus, Table 9.1, showing the structure of production, refers to hydroelectric plants and oil- or coal-burning thermal plants.

One speaks of the structure of consumption since all consumers do not have the same time-pattern and intensity of power consumption. Some of them show very typical behavior: The quantity of the power

---

*A "pool" refers to a group of interconnected electric power systems, each under a separate management, that are planned and operated according to a formal pooling agreement designed to supply power at lower cost and with increased service reliability. A "system" comprises a number of interconnected power generating plants and power distribution networks. At present four enterprises (systems) are in existence in Croatia. The fourth, Slavonija, was founded in February, 1971 and therefore is not relevant to our analysis, since it had no impact on the industry's behavior in the period studied.

TABLE 9.1

The Structure of Electricity Production in 1970

	Hydroelectric				Thermal				Total	
	Capacity		Production		Capacity		Production		Capacity	Production
	MW*	Percent of system's total capacity	GWh**	Percent of system's total production	MW	Percent of system's total capacity	GWh	Percent of system's total production	MW	GWh
Rijeka	325	77.8	1,188	87.2	93	22.2	175	12.8	418	1,363
Split	290	100.0	1,811	100.0	-	-	-	-	290	1,811
Zagreb	108	29.3	625	56.9	260	70.7	473	43.1	368	1,098
	723	67.2	3,624	84.8	353	32,8	648	15.2	1,076	4,272

*MW = Megawatts
**GWH = Thousand kilowatt hours

Source: Monthly Report for January, 1971, IEPIC (Integrated Electric Power Industry of Croatia), Zagreb, February, 1971.

they demand, as well as the time and pattern of their consumption, can be anticipated with a high level of certainty. Hence, they do not put any unexpected demands on the power system, and the power supply can be regulated ahead of time. These consumers usually take large quantities of power and are called "big consumers." Other consumers do not exhibit such standard behavior. In particular, the hours of consumption vary over time (see Table 9.2).

The basic institutional features of the power industry in Yugoslavia were laid down in 1965,[1] but later a number of laws were passed in each republic to reinforce the principles introduced at the federal level. The two fundamental elements of the institutional framework are the organizational structure and the decision-making process (see Figure 9.1).

TABLE 9.2

The Structure of Electricity Consumption in 1970

	Rijeka		Split		Zagreb	
	GWh*	Per-cent of system's total consump-tion	GWh	Per-cent of system's total consump-tion	GWh	Per-cent of system's total consump-tion
Big consumers	44	5.3	625	42.4	420	14.0
Others	785	94.7	850	57.6	2,584	86.0
Total consumption	829	100.0	1,475	100.0	3,004	100.0

*GWH = Thousand kilowatt hours.

Source: Monthly Report for January, 1971, IEPIC, Zagreb, February, 1971.

The Integrated Electric Power Industry of Croatia (IEPIC), the central bureau of the industry, is in charge of the coordination of the activities of the three enterprises. It represents them in their contacts with the federal and the republic's administration, and with the electric power industry's representatives in other republics. It also conducts technical and economic research for the enterprises. It has no power of decision-making, but acts as an advisory body. Therefore, the decisions to be made by the power industry are made by the enterprises. Figure 9.1 covers the organization of the power industry in Croatia only, but the situation is analogous in other republics, and the model for Croatia will be sufficient for our analysis. Consequently, there is no need to consider the whole power industry of Yugoslavia in presenting the general outline of a self-management decision-making model in this industry.

The decision-making process was defined by a series of laws and regulations passed at the republic level to complete the Basic Law and bring its principles to bear at the operational level. However, the price of electric power was uniformly determined for the whole territory of Yugoslavia by the Federal Executive Council, i.e., at the federal level. It was set up as a maximum price, and the only possible

FIGURE 9.1

The Organizational Structure of the
Electricity Pool

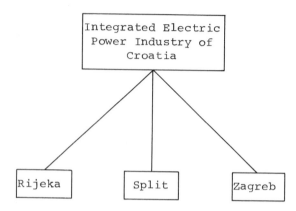

independent action left to the members of the pool regarding price
was the possibility of setting a lower price than the maximum allowed,
which actually did not occur. All other decisions were left to the
administrations of the republics.

The first important decision made (in 1966) by the administration
of the republic of Croatia was to choose the power plants and transport
lines to be built by 1970.* In order to accumulate funds for financing
these investments a law was passed forcing all investors in the rest
of Croatia to contribute 2 percent of all capital invested for any purpose
in the period 1966-70.[2] This capital was given to the electric power
industry in the form of a loan.

However, in the following years the situation differed from that
expected. First, power consumption did not increase at the rate
anticipated, but more slowly. Second, the funds raised by the compulsory contributions of investors were less than expected. Third,
costs of construction greatly exceeded those planned. As a consequence,
the administration of the republic of Croatia revised the choice of
facilities to be constructed in order to make the plan feasible. A new
program on a smaller scale was proposed by IEPIC and approved by

---

*This was done by accepting the "Program for the Construction
of Electric Power Facilities until 1970" proposed by the Integrated
Electric Power Industry of Croatia. Udružena elektroprivreda SRH,
Zagreb, 1966.

126

the administration of the republic in 1968.[3] The need for additional
funds called for the passing of a new law introducing an additional
compulsory contribution of 2.5 percent of all capital invested.[4]
Forced taxation for this purpose therefore amounted to 4.5 percent
of the investment outlays made by the economy of Croatia.

Finally, one has to point out that electric power was supplied
in the absence of laid-down terms of sale and technical conditions of
delivery. The Basic Law introduced the possibility of imposing these
constraints on the electric power industry at the federal or republic
level, but regulations of this kind were not put into force.

Summarizing existing conditions for the operation and development
of the power industry in Croatia, the following conclusions may be
drawn:

1. Two systems in the pool (Rijeka and Split) supply a substantial
part of the power to consumers from their own plants, with the exception
of some power bought externally for supply in peak-load periods; the
third system (Zagreb) has to rely on the other power systems for
roughly two-thirds of the power needed.

2. There are two levels in the organizational structure of the
power industry in Croatia: the level of the enterprise, corresponding
to a region in Croatia, and the level of the pool, covering the whole
territory of Croatia,

3. The vital decisions are taken by the federal government
(fixing the maximum price) or by the republic government (investment
decisions and financing). The enterprises have a narrow scope for
independent action, comprising mostly decisions of minor importance.
In supplying power, enterprises are not restricted by any formal
regulations concerning the manner and conditions of supply.

The institutional framework for the operation and development
of the power industry in Croatia follows the generally accepted pattern
for the regulation of the public utility sector. Its basic feature is that
the influence of society is introduced at the top level of the power
industry's organizational structure, regulating the whole industry as
one homogeneous unit. The question is: Does this secure a social
optimum? In order to answer this question we need to survey the
actual behavior of the three power systems in Croatia.

THE CHARACTERISTIC BEHAVIOR OF THE
POWER INDUSTRY IN CROATIA

The institutional framework just presented did not set up the
power systems in Croatia as independent economic agents, since the
vital decisions were taken with little reference to them. This held
especially for the years immediately after the introduction of the new

institutional framework in 1965. Before this, the power industry of Yugoslavia was organized on a purely functional basis, with decision-making in the hands of the federal administration, since functional organization required a high degree of centralized decision-making. The basic features of this decision-making process on the management side were:

1. A reduced number of criteria were taken into account in decision-making, since decisions had to be taken to satisfy all pools in the power industry.* This was relevant especially for those investment decisions that considered only a limited number of the social costs and benefits involved in the construction of a new plant.

2. Functional organization also was present in the operation of the power industry. This was normal, since operating decisions did not involve externalities. However, the benefits of a high level of functionalism and centralization were outweighed by the complications involved in coordination, mostly because of the constraints imposed by technology and the number of people involved in the decision-making process.[5]

3. Only a small number of units in the electric power industry had mutual contact in the decision-making process. The result of this was the creation of an increasing number of levels in this structure, i.e., a widening of the gap between the lowest and the highest level. By the same token, decision-making was removed from the consumer preferences that should be respected when making decisions, and the problem of transmitting preferences to the level at which decisions were made was constantly present.

4. A high level of centralization provoked lack of adaptability to changes brought about by technological progress or by lower-level needs that did not match the standard pattern. The substitution of liquid fuel for coal, demanded by new technology, disturbed the whole

---

*For instance, in making a choice of new plants to be built, only costs to the power industry were taken into account. Some social costs were introduced into the appraisal of projects by requiring the coal-burning plants to be built near the coal mines. This was done in order to help coal production, but the problem was too complex to be solved by such a one-sided criterion. Also, the technical data taken into account were very simplified and could not secure the optimal choice even from a technical point of view, since they simply could not cover the needs of all pools in Yugoslavia. For a detailed discussion of this problem see Gorupić-Bendeković-Pauković, "Economic Relationships in the Electric Power Industry," Ekonomski Institut Zagreb, 1969, pp. 109-16.

structure of the power industry, causing strong resistance even to the rate of substitution acceptable in the light of the capital requirements involved. Thus, the economy was confronted at the start with low productivity in the coal industry, and the effects of this were spread throughout the whole economy.

Apart from the consequences for management, the high level of centralization in the institutional framework led to a misallocation of resources. Two points are important here:

1. There was irresponsibility on the part of investors, as a result of the method of investment financing. All capital outlays were financed from central funds, and two distinctive phases were identified in the process of financing. First, in order to be competitive at the investment auctions, investors tried to show lower costs for the construction of the facilities they wanted. Second, when carrying out projects, they did not make adequate efforts to economize, since all additional costs were covered from central funds. This was because sunk costs were too large for the project to be given up. In this way the whole of Yugoslavia bore the consequences of this inefficiency, and an investor had no real incentive to behave rationally.[6]

2. There was a single price for electric power in the whole of Yugoslavia, even though the costs of power supply differed considerably. Since this price was established as an average, some systems in the power industry made a surplus and others a loss. The problem was solved simply by taking from the first and giving to the second. This again did not stimulate efforts to minimize costs. Furthermore, consumers, charged a price lower than costs, were led to take unjustifiably large amounts of power, while others whose price was higher than costs were deprived of the power they had paid for. This is why consumption of power increased at a very fast rate in some parts of Yugoslavia.

If one can arrive at a general conclusion concerning the behavior of the power industry before 1965, one can say that there was a strong tendency for it to develop along the lines of its own, mostly technical, logic. This meant that the power industry's development was not fully geared to overall socioeconomic development, but was oriented to a certain degree in directions imposed by the aspirations of the people employed in the industry.*

The period after 1965 was influenced to a large extent by all the features just mentioned, in spite of the fact that the new institutional

---

*One of the consequences was a considerable surplus of generating capacity in Bosnia and Herzegovina over a period of several years. Also, interconnections were built mainly in a south-north direction with insufficient lines from east to west, thus reducing the possibility of exchanging reserve capacities.[7]

framework made provision for stronger influence from society. This was made possible by an increase in the role of the administrations of the republics.

The process of decision-making was decentralized in the sense that an increasingly important role had been given to the administrations of the republics. Again only two participants were present in taking the vital decisions: the administration of the republic and the power industry.

The control mechanism over the power industry actually consisted of approving prices and passing laws to raise capital for financing development. This was now done at the republic instead of the federal level, and there is no doubt that decisions were made that took into account a larger number of criteria, both technical and economic. However, the question is whether this was enough to guarantee the optimal behavior of the power industry.

Confronted with a given price, the power industry of Croatia tried to find a way to maximize income in other directions. Their efforts were directed toward lowering costs of operation through (2) supplying electric power of an inferior quality, i.e., of an unacceptably low voltage and frequency, and/or (2) offering inferior reliability by not assuring in advance the necessary reserve capacity in each system in Croatia.

Income maximization under the constraint of a given price was therefore carried out by giving lower quality service in order to reduce costs of operation instead of improving the efficiency of the power industry to lower costs. In this way the inefficiency of the power industry was thrown onto the consumers of electric power, i.e., the institutional framework did not act as a pressure for efficiency. One might argue that this problem can be solved easily by passing a few regulations that would force the power industry to meet the aspirations of society. However, the best answer to this was the remark of an engineer concerning the problem of finding the real source of inefficiency. His words were: "Only our conscience knows the troubles for which we are responsible. Nobody else can find out." The occurrence of long arguments, which have led in some cases to throwing the blame back and forth, seems to support this view.

It turns out that each of the three systems in Croatia tried to promote its own interests at the expense of its consumers or, more broadly, of the region the system had been supplying and of the other regions in Croatia.

At the same time, their efforts were directed toward increasing prices, and most of the contacts between society and the power industry concerned the efforts of the first to lower price, and the second to increase it. So, figuratively speaking, the power industry and society were opponents instead of partners. This was especially obvious in the case of the Zagreb system, which needed a higher price to accumulate capital for financing the construction of the plants it desired. The price set as an average for Croatia covered the capital needs of the Split and Rijeka systems, but was not high enough to secure the capital for satisfying the rapidly growing demand in the Zagreb region.

The institutional framework tried to establish a control mechanism for the electric power industry by limiting the price of electric power only. But mere fixing of the price was not sufficient to guarantee that the electric power industry would behave in an optimal socioeconomic way. Obviously a more subtle and diversified mechanism was needed.

The development of the power industry in Croatia after 1965 gave some hints of a general outline for a solution. In spite of the short-comings of the institutional framework, each of the three systems had established a closer link with its consumers than ever before, in this way more fully respecting the territorial interests of the regions in Croatia. The first emphasis on territorial interest began to appear immediately after the Basic Law was passed in 1965. Indeed, the increasing demand for decentralization in the electric power industry in Yugoslavia, which led to the Basic Law, was a result of efforts to respect regional preferences in the course of economic development. For instance, the Split power system set the price of electric power below the maximum level determined by the administration of Croatia, and only when a new program for building additional facilities was initiated and later accepted did the price rise to the limit.* This decision was made by both the power industry and the consumers, even though there was no institutional requirement of this kind. The original reason for the joint action was the plan of the Split region to develop the aluminum industry. This industry needed additional electric power, and the price was increased by general agreement to accumulate the capital required. Similar close coordination between the development of the region and the power industry also was es-tablished in Rijeka and Zagreb, although to a lesser degree.

This close cooperation in investment planning seems to be absolutely necessary, since the power industry does not have the capital at its disposal for financing this development, but the ex-perience also was similar in operating the power industry. Reductions and even interruptions of supply were quite common until 1968, but practically eliminated afterward, in spite of the fact that hydrological conditions were exceptionally bad.

---

*From July 1, 1965 to September 1, 1966 the price for the consumers in the region of Split was lower than that in Rijeka and Zagreb.

One of the outstanding examples of this kind is the supply of power to the Dugi Rat carbide factory in the Split region, with a loss for the Split power system, but with a gain for the whole region.*

In addition to all this, in spite of the lack of a formal agreement regulating their relationships among the three systems in Croatia, cooperation within the pool did not experience major difficulties. This dispelled the fear that decentralization and self-management, as generally accepted in Yugoslav society, were not applicable to such an "unsuitable" industry as the electric power industry since it would lead to inefficiency. In fact, recent developments have shown that the introduction of territorial decision-making can be an effective control mechanism and can exercise the necessary pressure for efficiency.

The basic reason for this is the increased responsibility of the power system to its consumers as a result of the closer links between them. When the electric power industry was organized strictly on a functional basis, the highest organizational level was responsible for the industry's activity, and a power system having direct contact with consumers would hold its own pool and other pools responsible for any inefficiency. The location of responsibility was far away from that of power supply, and the responsibility of the power industry to the consumer became a very abstract notion. All this was necessary, it was argued, because of the high degree of functional integration demanded by technology. By the same logic, any decentralization, and therefore the introduction of territorial decision-making, would hinder the efficiency of the power industry.

The empirical evidence in Croatia does not support such a general conclusion. Furthermore, it seems that territorial decision-making puts a bigger responsibility on the electric power industry, with the result that the control mechanism is more efficient. The increased responsibility is in various ways forcing the power system to promote functional integration within the pool in order to offer better quality and more reliable service. Thus the integration of interests is the best basis for the functional integration of the power industry.

This is why, in spite of the fact that the institutional framework for the power industry in Croatia was not all that it should have been, the power industry of Croatia respected socioeconomic needs in the period after 1965 to a greater extent than ever before. The introduction of a new institutional framework is made necessary now by the shortcomings of the existing system, but also, at the same time, by the

---

*Some reductions of power supply took place in 1967 and 1969 in order to deliver power to Dugi Rat so as not to stop the exports of carbide to Great Britain, since foreign exchange was a limited resource. These reductions were decided upon jointly by the Split system and its consumers.

need to institutionalize the control mechanism that has been emerging during the last few years and to remove any roadblocks slowing down its development.

The solution has been sought along the lines of participation by consumer and sociopolitical units in decision-making, not only at the top level of the structure of the power industry, but at every level. This means that participation needs to be introduced at the level of the system, and at the level of the pool. Speaking in terms of territorial coverage, participation appears at the regional level and then at the level of the republic. Further integration of the power industry beyond the limits of the republic, or beyond the limits of power pools, is carried out by the power industry alone. The next step is to set forth a model of such participation.

A MODEL OF DECISION-MAKING IN THE
ELECTRIC POWER INDUSTRY
UNDER SELF-MANAGEMENT

The purpose of the new institutional framework is to establish an efficient control mechanism for the operation and development of the power industry. This is done through decentralization or—which comes to the same thing—bringing elements of territorial decision-making into the power industry.

Therefore, the first step is to identify the decisions to be made in the power industry. They can be classified into two groups: (1) those decisions that do not involve important externalities affecting economic agents outside the power industry (they mainly refer to decisions concerning the operation of the power industry); and (2) those decisions causing considerable externalities (these decisions have to be taken mainly in the process of developing the power industry).

Since operating decisions are determined by technology and do not give rise to externalities, they can be controlled by a set of regulations determining the general pattern and conditions of power supply. This part of the control mechanism therefore consists of these regulations, and the power industry can be left to make operating decisions by itself within these constraints. The second group of decisions calls for the participation of the economic agents affected by the decisions, and this participation forms the second part of the control mechanism. The group covers four different categories of decisions: (1) planning decisions, or the projection of consumption and production, and the projection of new facilities, if needed; (2) investment decisions, or the appraisal of feasible projects for the construction of new plants, setting up the criteria for making a choice, determining the share of the participants in financing the investment, and defining the obligations and rights emerging from participation in financing; (3) price decisions, or the price level for electric power, the price structure and the intended purpose of each element of the price structure; and (4) decisions concerning treatment of electric power consumers or general conditions of power supply.

The next step is to identify the participants in decision-making. A very general classification gives the following groups of participants: the electric power industry itself; other industries in the energy sector; other sectors of the economy; and the sociopolitical units— communes, republics, and the federation—representing households and other consumers.

All of these appear in the process of decision-making if decisions involving externalities are to be taken, i.e., they participate in the formulation and acceptance of regulations designed to control the operation of the power industry, and also in decisions concerning the development of the power industry. They can show up at different levels of the organizational structure of the power industry. These levels are the fundamental level, which is that of an electric power system covering a region, and the level of coordination corresponding to the electric power pool, and the level of coordination among pools, covering the territory of a republic and of the whole of Yugoslavia respectively.

At the fundamental level, only the participants from the region in question will take part in decision-making. At the next level they will represent the territory supplied by the pool. We can now construct a table illustrating decision-making at each level. Table 9.3 contains the information concerning decision-making at the fundamental level.

Briefly, at the fundamental level all the participants take part in all four groups of decisions. This is the level at which territorial interests are introduced, and hence self-management in the power industry has to include economic agents outside the system itself. Thus, this is the level at which preferences concerning the social optimum are revealed directly, and the decisions made reflect the optimum for the region.

The close functional integration of the power industry imposed by technology, and the fact that the decisions made at the fundamental level of the region have effects outside the region, impose a need for coordination in decision-making with other power systems in the pool. This is done at the level of the pool. Since the pool covers the territory of a republic, each of the participants will represent one of four groups of participants, but this time from the entire republic. Table 9.4 shows decision-making at the level of the pool.

The principal difference between Table 9.3 and Table 9.4 is that, in the latter, price decisions are not included.

TABLE 9.3

Decision-Making at the Fundamental Level

| Participants | Type of Decision | | | |
	Planning Decisions	Investment Decisions	Price Decisions	Treatment of Consumers
Electric power system	x	x	x	x
Energy sector	x	x	x	x
Other sectors of the economy	x	x	x	x
Communes or association of communes	x	x	x	x

X = the presence of a participant in the making of a specific group of decisions.

This is because the price is derived from a combination of costs of financing and costs of development. These differ among regions (or power systems), and hence cannot be uniformly determined for the whole republic (or power pool).

Coordination does not stop at the level of the pool, since functional integration exists between pools and externalities may affect more than one power pool. This is why there is always a need for coordination between pools. Two types of coordination between pools can be identified. The first is when there are important external affects, and the second when they are absent. The former is shown in Table 9.5.

In this case, coordination between pools is reduced to investment decisions, such as those relating to generating plants and even more to high-voltage interconnection lines needed to maintain the necessary degree of reliability. All participants take part in decision-making because externalities are present, and therefore this coordination is substantially the same, at least from the managerial point of view, as that within the pool. The other types of decision do not appear at the level of interpool coordination, since they are made at the level of the pool.

TABLE 9.4

Decision-Making at the Level of the Pool

Parti-cipants	Types of Decisions			
	Planning Decisions	Investment Decisions	Price Decisions	Treatment of Consumers
Electric power pool or all the systems in a republic	x	x	0	x
Energy sector of a republic	x	x	0	x
Other sectors of the economy in a republic	x	x	0	x
Administration of a republic	x	x	0	x

X indicates that a participant is taking part in the making of a decision and 0 indicates that he is not.

The second type of coordination, when externalities are not present, simply takes the form of business transactions by the pool—for example, the purchase of reserve capacity and/or the exchange of energy flows. These decisions relate to the operation of the pool, and are taken by the pool itself with no outside participation, since there is no need for a social control mechanism.

The fundamental feature of the decision-making process in the electric power industry under conditions of self-management is therefore the introduction of territorial autonomy in the first instance, at the level of the power system, in order to attain the social optimum. But the functional integration demanded by technology, and the considerable external effects that are a feature of the industry, require a coordination with other power systems (thus forming a pool), and further coordination among pools. Thus the introduction of territorial autonomy does not hinder functional integration, but actually helps it, since the power system seeks to promote the interests of its territory via cooperation with other systems. The power system always remains the fundamental level for decision-making, since all decisions

TABLE 9.5

Coordination between Pools, with Externalities Present

Parti- cipants	Planning Decisions	Investment Decisions	Price Decisions	Treatment of Consumers
Two or more power pools	0	x	0	0
Energy sector of the territory covered by these pools	0	x	0	0
Other sectors of the economy in the same area	0	x	0	0
Administrations of the republics affected by coordination	0	x	0	0

have to be accepted at this level, but this does not mean that these decisions are taken without coordination with the pool. In this way two simultaneous processes are taking place: first, raising the level of coordination to get the necessary degree of functional integration, and second, widening it to meet the aspirations of society.

A very important question is: What is the optimal level for taking a decision to achieve these aspiration? One answer to this question has been known for a long time: A decision should be taken at the level associated with a minimum of external effects, i.e.,

$$(1) \qquad \sum_{i=1}^{n} E_i = \text{min.}$$

where E_i stands for the i-th external effect.

This consideration requires the taking of decisions at higher and higher levels of the organizational structure of the power industry in order to take externalities into account. But this results in a reduction of the number of criteria relevant to the taking of decisions, and to this extent deviates from the aspirations of the people.

Simply to pay attention to the aspirations of the people, on the other hand, leads to decision-making at lower and lower levels of the structure, in order to increase the number of criteria, n, i.e.,

$$(2) \qquad\qquad n \longrightarrow \infty$$

Such a policy would neglect the requirements imposed by functional and technical efficiency in the power industry, and would increase the number of criteria so much that they would be too heterogeneous to allow the taking of any decision.

This is why it seems that the optimal level for taking a decision has to be decided on the basis of a compromise between criterion (1) and criterion (2). Starting from the fundamental level associated with a power system, decision-making should climb up the organizational structure to the level of coordination at which the number of criteria is reduced to an acceptable minimum. Depending on the nature of the decision, territorial criteria are introduced at each of these levels in order to respect the aspirations of society. The need for this is greater the more heterogeneous are the interests and aspirations of the people.

NECESSARY CONDITIONS FOR IMPLEMENTATION OF THE MODEL

Three conditions, as a minimum, seem to be of vital importance for the successful implementation of the model just presented. First, the short- and long-term aspirations of each of the participants in decision-making have to be defined. This is the same thing as saying that the short-and long-term plan for socioeconomic development has to be formulated to give to each participant the necessary information for rational decision-making.

Second, the aspirations of each participant have to be met within an acceptable period of time. To do this in the short run is frequently impossible owing to limited resources. Therefore, the manner in which decisions are taken has to be such as to eliminate any domination by one participant over the others.

Third, a mechanism for compensation has to be set up. Limited resources do not permit realization of all aspirations in the short run, and some participants have to modify their aspirations to fit in with the common long-term interest. In giving up or modifying these aspirations, they have to be sure that their aspirations will be met in the

138

future or in some other place. Hence, the temporal and territorial compensations arrived at in the process of decision-making assure each participant that his interests will be respected in an acceptable manner.

The model in this chapter has been worked out for the case of the electric power industry, since this industry possesses general characteristics relevant to this model, i.e., a high level of functional integration requiring multilevel decision-making, as well as the presence of important externalities. However, worker and managerial self-management decision-making under conditions of this type is not confined to the electric power industry. It is present in the whole infrastructure, as well as in industries having a high level of concentration. Thus the views expressed here, at least in their most general sense, represent current attitudes in Yugoslavia toward multilevel decision-making, in the presence of externalities, in a self-managed society.

NOTES

1. "Basic Law of the Electric Power Industry" Official Gazette, No. 17, 1965.

2. See "Law on Construction and Financing Electric Power Facilities until 1970," Official Gazette, No. 28, 1966.

3. "Program for Construction of Electric Power Facilities in SR Croatia until 1970 (revised version)," Udruzena elecktroprivreda SRH, Zagreb, 1968.

4. "Law on Construction and Financing Electric Power Facilities until 1970" Official Gazette No. 17, 1968.

5. See "The Position and Role of the Electric Power Industry and the Mechanism of its Functioning and Reproduction in Our Self-management Socioeconomic System," IEPIC, Zagreb, 1970, Appendix 1.

6. Proposition for the Integration of the Yugoslav Electric Power System, Sarajevo, 1969 pp. 31-38.

7. See Proposal for the Development of a 380 KV Network in Yugoslavia, JUCEL, Belgrade, 1970. A report for the Tenth Congress of CICRA, Dubrovnik, 1970.

10

RECENT EXPERIENCE
WITH MODELS IN
INDUSTRY
Bertil Näslund

During the past 20 years, many new quantitative methods, which require the construction of a model, have been developed in order to improve decision-making in organizations. To a large extent this work has been done at universities where these models are taught primarily to students of engineering and business. Relatively little is known about the extent and nature of the models actually used, the characteristics of the firms that use them, and the major problems of implementation.

In order to explore these latter problems, several studies have been made in different countries, coordinated by M. Radnor at Northwestern University in the United States. The Swedish studies were at the Department of Business Administration, Stockholm University. In this chapter some of the Swedish results will be summarized and related to results obtained in other countries. (For other presentations of the Swedish results, see Lonnstedt, Bark-Holst and Welinder, Bratt and Henriksson, Nicander and Silvander, and Näslund.)[1] A study has been made of the industrial applications of models reported in Management Science, Operations Research, and Operational Research Quarterly during the past five years and the models used in these applications have been examined in various ways. In a concluding section the problem of implementation will be discussed.

THE MODELS MOST FREQUENTLY
USED IN INDUSTRY

The increase in the use of models in industry exhibits a similar pattern in various countries. Figure 10.1 shows the development in Sweden, compared with the way in which Swedish industry has increased

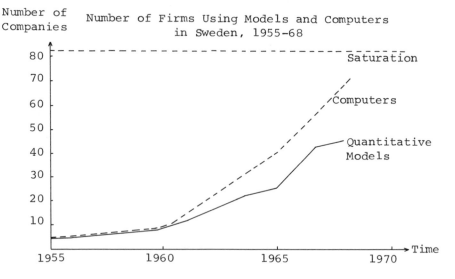

FIGURE 10.1

Number of Firms Using Models and Computers
in Sweden, 1955-68

Source: L. Lonnstedt, Operationsanalys i Borsnoterade
Foretag (Stockholm: Bonniers, 1971).

its use of computers: the number of firms using computers and
mathematical models has increased rapidly during the past decade,
but the use of computers has increased more rapidly.

A similar increase in the use of mathematical models seems
to have taken place in many countries. Current surveys based on
slightly different approaches provide the following figures about the
percentage of firms using quantitative models in different countries:
Sweden—55 percent,[2] Norway—41 percent,[3] United States—66-75
percent.[4]

Various studies have been made to determine which models
and quantitative methods are most frequently used. These studies
have been carried out somewhat differently and therefore the results
shown in Table 10.1 must be interpreted with caution. The most
frequently used methods seem to be simulation, linear programming,
and inventory models. (It is not always clear what some authors
mean by inventory models, but they probably refer to techniques that
have been developed specifically for inventory problems, without
utilizing simulation or linear programming.) In the table, the number
1 has been assigned to the method that is used most frequently, etc.
The scores are summarized in the last column.

As can be seen from Table 10.1, simulation models seem to be
the ones that are used most frequently.

TABLE 10.1

Quantitative Methods Used in Industry
in Various Countries, Ordered
According to Frequency

Technique	Canada	Great Britain	Den-Mark	Norway	Japan	Sweden	Sum-mary
Simulation	1	1	2	1	1	1	7
Linear Program-ming	3	3	1	3	2	2	14
Inventory Models	2	2	3	2	3	3	15

Sources: For Canada: J. Abrams, Progress Report on Investigation of Operational Research in Canada (Toronto: University of Toronto Press, 1969).

For Great Britain: S. Eilon, S. J. Hough, and R. J. Beets, "Profile of Current Members of the Operational Research Society," Operational Research Quarterly, June, 1966.

For Denmark: T. Bak-Jensen, "Operationsanalysens anvendelse i en rad danska foretag," T. Bak-Jensen A/S, 1969.

For Norway: H. M. Blegen "Nagra Norska Industriforetags anvandande av Operationsanalys," Opublicerad Arbetsrapport Norges Tekniska Hogskola, Trondheim, 1969.

For Japan: T. Kawase "Perspective on Management Science in Japan," Tokyo: Keio University, 1969.

For Sweden: L. Lonnstedt, Operationsanalys i Borsnoterade Foretag (Stockholm: Bonniers, 1971).

Another way of determining the models that industry finds most useful is to see which models are used in the industrial applications reported in the leading professional journals.

In order to study this aspect, Management Science, Operations Research, and Operational Research Quarterly were covered from 1966 to 1970.* It is sometimes not completely clear whether the models reported were really applied. Sometimes the models used

---

*The author is grateful to O. Hogberg, who assisted him in this work.

cannot easily be classified and more than one model was used in one instance. The main findings are summarized in Table 10.2.

The main results of this study confirm the findings in Table 10.1 (In Table 10.2 we have tried to distinguish simulation from heuristic methods; this was not always easy, since the definitions of the two terms are ambiguous.) Some attention should be drawn to the fact that the journals investigated deal primarily with problems of a general and theoretical nature. Since both simulation and heuristic methods are often specific to a certain problem, industrial applications of these models might be of greater interest to these journals than, say, applications of mathematical programming.

In order to investigate the relationship between some characteristics of firms and the extent to which models were used, 83 firms listed on the Swedish stock exchange were investigated.[5] (Since it was not possible to use statistical methods in a satisfactory way, no formal hypothesis testing has been done.)

The main findings of that study were that larger firms were more likely to use formal models than small firms, that the line of business that a firm is in is of importance (manufacturing firms being the most likely to use models), and that the higher the level of education of its employees, the more probable it is that a firm will use models.

HOW FIRMS ARE USING MODELS AND SOME EVALUATION OF THE RESULTS

Different functional areas in firms tend to use models to a different extent. The above-mentioned study by Lonnstedt shows that models are used most frequently in production, sales, and finance, in

TABLE 10.2

Quantitative Models Used in Industry and
Reported in Three Leading Journals

Method	Number of Reported Cases
Simulation	11
Heuristic methods	10
Mathematical programming	7
Others	9
Total	37

that order. The problem areas in which models are most frequently used are: (1) planning—37 percent (mostly pert-planning and related methods),(2) production—22 percent, (3) inventory—19 percent, (4) others—22 percent.

Studies in Sweden, the United States, and the United Kingdom[6] indicate that, as a rule, the models used in industry do not cover the whole firm, but are restricted to certain departments or more limited problem areas.

The firms using models allocate an average of $60,000 per year to this activity and the models usually require less than four man-months for completion.

It seems difficult to estimate the savings obtained from using mathematical models. The applications studies in Management Science, Operations Research, and Operational Research Quarterly usually do not report the savings achieved by models, but the eight instances in which savings were indicated ranged between $20,000 and $180,000 annually. (Even if the savings appear to be of a certain annual magnitude, it should be observed that they will not stay that way for ever; therefore, besides determining the current savings, one has the very difficult task of determining for how long they will continue before new methods make them obsolete.)

Several authors who have studied the use of mathematical models in industry have surveyed industry's arguments both for and against the use of such models.[7] Some of these arguments are the following:

1. The reasons most frequently mentioned for not using models in industry:

(a) Sometimes important and crucial nonmonetary considerations cannot be built into the analysis.

(b) Important decisions might be delayed while waiting for the model to be completed and implemented.

(c) Secret data and other considerations might have to be brought into the open.

Some of these negative factors arise because people do not yet have the appropriate education to work with models. Furthermore, the data required by the models are often not available. But if an organization starts using models it needs a supply of data that will probably be useful for other models as well.

2. The principal benefits of models are that they:

(a) require formal thinking about central elements of a decision;

(b) bring hidden assumptions and goals and their implications into the open;

(c) probably simplify group discussion, since key factors are made explicit.

One argument that I have often heard from businessmen is that the use of formal models might lead the whole industry in the wrong direction. If everyone uses approximately the same model for long-run decisions and finds that a particular course of action is the correct one, this might lead to unnecessary overcapacity in the selected section of the industry.

This problem has to do with the interaction of many models in the market both when competing firms use similar models and when one firm transfers costs to another by using a model (e.g., when a firm uses an inventory model it might transfer costs to the seller, which might in turn lead to a higher purchasing price that offsets the cost reductions from using the model).

Both of these problems require the use of higher-level models that explicitly consider the actions of other independent firms. The development and utilization of these models (probably of a game theoretical nature) are important areas for current theoretical and applied research.

THE PROBLEM OF IMPLEMENTATION

It is quite natural that all models constructed are not actually implemented. The main reason for this is that it is often not clear in advance what the model will look like when it is completed and what profits one can obtain by using it. In particular, circumstances might have changed, so that when the model is ready to be used, it is no longer adequate.

In order to investigate if there are some circumstances that might make implementation easier, Lonnstedt studied 107 projects involving the formulation of quantitative models in 12 firms.[8]

It is of interest to observe in connection with our first section that, although simulation is frequently used, it is not necessarily an easy method to implement. In Table 10.3 it is shown that 27 percent of all the models developed, including 41 percent of the simulation models, were not implemented.

In the above-mentioned study by Lonnstedt, various properties of the model, the organization, and the user were studied to see if some of these properties could explain why some models were implemented and others were not.*

The main findings were:

1. If the user had previous experience of quantitative models, implementation was more likely to occur.

---

*The design of the research was such that conventional statistical methods could not be used to generalize the results. Therefore, the findings can be seen only as indications of possible explanations.

148

TABLE 10.3

Percentage of Models not Implemented

Method	Percent Not Implemented	Number Studied
Linear programming	35	17
Simulation	41	29
Pert planning	17	40
Others	29	21
Total	27	107

Source: L. Lonnstedt, Operationsanalys i Borsnoterade Foretag (Stockholm: Bonniers, 1971).

2. The potential value of using the models, as well as the measurability and uncertainty of that value, played an important role in deciding on implementation, as one might expect.

3. The possibility of exactly specifying the scope of the problem and the ability to quantify the variables and gain easy access to data were important.

In order to overcome the difficulty associated with implementation, corporations have initiated liaison groups and/or coordination policy committees for the implementation of their models. This is done partly to overcome a rapid, unplanned transition from one phase to another.

These transitions often take place in industrial work where it is often possible to distinguish research→development→engineering →tooling→production→marketing. As soon as one such phase is completed, the problem of implementation arises.

When a firm intends to solve a problem with the use of models, the first phase involves development of the model and the second phase the attempt to put it to effective use.

This problem is discussed further by Radnor, Rubinstein, and Transik[9] who state the following main conditions as important for successful implementation:

1. Assurance that there is a clear and recognized need for the results at the time the project is undertaken.

2. Involvement of the ultimate user of the results early in the process and maintenance of communication throughout the project.

3. Direction of the project to be concentrated in an individual or small group that can review progress and make decisions about changes in direction or level of effort.

4. Ensuring top management's support and enthusiasm.

5. Allowing or encouraging researchers to follow projects through in their application, and to make careers in this area if they so desire.

Knowledge concerning implementation is very incomplete and much more research is necessary. It seems important, however, not to leave the problem of implementation to the end of different phases of industrial work such as development of the model or putting the model to effective use, but rather to involve the ultimate user early in the previous phase and let, for example, some member of the team developing a model participate in the operative use of it.

Furthermore, it seems important that when developing quantitative models it should be possible to specify and demarcate the problem clearly, and to quantify the parameters relatively easily from the point of view of data collection.

CONCLUSIONS

The use of models in industry has increased rapidly during the past ten years in most countries. Some companies even require that certain decisions should be based on at least some formal model. Thus it is reported that at General Electric all investment decisions of more than $500,000 must be based partly on probability assessments of the rate of return.[10]

The models are most frequently used in large firms within the manufacturing industry. They do not cover the whole organization and they are most frequently used in production.

Implementation of the models is reported to be a problem. But this can be partly overcome by starting "implementation" early in the development of the model and involving the ultimate user in the formulation of the model and in work on its construction.

NOTES

1. L. Lonnstedt, Operationsanalys i Borsnoterade Foretag, (Stockholm: Bonniers, 1971); "Innovationsteorier och operationsanalysens intrangandeforlopp i foretagen," Department of Business Administration, Stockholm University, 1969; "Akademisk utbildning av operationsanalytiker," Research Report 40, Department of Business Administration, Stockholm University, 1970; K. Bark-Holst and H. Welinder, "Undersokningar av operationsanalysavdelningar i tre industriforetag-case studier," Department of Business Administration, Stockholm University, 1969; P. Bratt and G. Henriksson, "Kartlaggningar

av operations analysavdelningar i de statliga foretagen," Department of Business Administration, Stockholm University, 1969; U. Nicander and L.-B. Silvander, "Kartlaggning av operationsanalysens utbredning i svenska borsnoterade foretag," Department of Business Administration, Stockholm University, 1969; B. Naslund, "Hur utnyttjar vara svenska foretag OA," Ekonomen, September 1969; "Simulering i vara foretag," Ekonomen, October, 1971; "Recent Experiences with Models in Industry," Research Report 63, Department of Business Administration, Stockholm University, 1971.

2. Lonnstedt, Operationsanalys i Borsnoterade Foretag, op. cit.

3. H. M. Blegen, "Nagra Norska Industriforetags anvandande av Operationsanalys," Opublicerad Arbetsrapport Norges Tekniska Hogskola, Trondheim, 1969.

4. C. Schumacher and B. A. Smith, "A Sample Survey of Industrial Operations Research Activities," Operations Research, November-December, 1965; W. Vatter, "The Use of Operations Research in American Companies," Accounting Review, October, 1967.

5. Lonnstedt, Operationsanalys i Borsnoterade Foretag, op. cit.

6. Ibid. M. Radnor, A. H. Rubinstein, and A. S. Bean, "Integration and Utilization of of Management Science Activities in Organizations," Operational Research Quarterly, June, 1968. B. D. P. Rivett, "A Survey of Operational Research in British Industry," Operational Research Quarterly, December, 1959.

7. R. V. Brown, "Do Managers Find Decision Theory Useful," Harvard Business Review, May-June, 1970.

8. Lonnstedt, Operationsanalys i Borsnoterade Foretag, op. cit.

9. M. Radnor, A. Rubinstein, and D. A. Transik, "Implementation in Operations Research and R & D in Government and Business Organization," Operations Research, November-December, 1970.

10. Brown, op. cit.

11

THE USE OF MODERN
COMPUTER TECHNIQUES IN
SOVIET INDUSTRIAL MANAGEMENT
N. V. Machrov

The introduction of modern computer techniques into industrial management marked an important stage in the large-scale program for the further improvement of the planning and management of the country's economy. By now electronic computers are in operational use at all levels of economic management, helping to regulate all aspects of economic development. The bulk of the machines are used directly for production management at the level of individual enterprises or associations of enterprises, and experience shows that they greatly contribute to improved performance in that sphere. Their effect is demonstrated by the higher general level of output and performance indicators for enterprises and their associations and by the general reduction in administrative costs.

The improved output and performance indicators are the result of the increased precision and promptness with which decisions can be taken, lower inventory-output ratios, fuller utilization of equipment and other resources (human and material), and speedier completion of orders.

In our experience electronic computers can reduce inventory requirements by 15-25 percent and production time by 20-30 percent, while improving the utilization coefficients of equipment by up to 7 percent. All this has beneficial effects on the general performance of individual enterprises and their associations. At the same time, administrative expenses are reduced, particularly through the release of highly qualified personnel from routine work of an inappropriate kind.

Computers find their most frequent uses in the economy as parts of fully automated management systems, at the level of individual enterprises, enterprise-associations, and whole industrial branches. With their aid the automated management system (AMS) becomes the basis of organized management for all subdivisions of the national economy.

At the present time AMSs are being designed and introduced in industrial and agricultural enterprises; in associations of industrial enterprises; in organs of internal trade, industrial supply, transport and communications; in institutes devoted to research, culture, health and education, universities, etc.; in municipal service enterprises and public utilities; in finance and credit institutions and savings banks.

In sum, the electronic computer, within its system of automated management, finds practical application in all the primary units of which the economy is composed.

The ministries and departments of the USSR are the basic organs of operational management for enterprises, institutions, and organizations. At the same time, however, a given ministry or department may have jurisdiction over enterprises belonging to different branches of the economy, and thereby act as an integrated organ of diversified multibranch character.

The AMSs of enterprises, institutions, and other organs are coordinated and integrated into an overall branchwide automated management system (BAMS) in accordance with the established structure of economic administration. At the present time BAMSs are being set up in industrial ministries and departments, in the State Supply Committee of the Council of Ministers, in agricultural ministries, and in the various welfare and service ministries. A BAMS mutually coordinates and integrates the AMSs of constituent enterprises, institutions, and organizations within the framework of the state system of economic management and on the basis of unified methodologies of planning, informational flows and data processing, and specialized training systems.

At the highest level of the planning apparatus (in the State Planning Commissions of the Soviet Union and the Union Republics) work is proceeding on the construction and application of an automatic system of "ex ante accounts" (ASEA), which is intended to facilitate the mechanization and automation of forecasting procedures for medium-term and short-term plans of economic development.

Integrated AMSs are also being set up at the national level: in the Central Statistical Administration, the All-Union Ministry of Finance, the All-Union State Bank, and in a variety of other functional organs.

When the ASEA of the State Planning Commission is integrated with the AMSs of functional government organs and BAMSs, the basis will have been laid for a system of information flows and a network of computer stations at the national level. In this way they form the building blocks for a unified informational system for the country as a whole that will combine the pursuance of the centralized objectives of economic planning with the economic autonomy of individual enterprises, in accordance with the current economic reform.

The introduction of these various systems in the Soviet Union is accompanied by the ever-wider application of mathematical methods in economics, particularly those of optimization. Among the models that have found the widest application at the present time are the following: (1) models of economic forecasting; (2) models of medium-term economic planning; (3) input-output models at national and regional levels; (4) optimizing models of development and location; (5) optimizing models of specialization and subcontracting among enterprises; (6) optimizing models of assignment (supplier to user); (7) optimizing models of medium- and short-term planning for industrial branches; (8) optimizing models of product mix within branches; (9) optimizing models of production programming within enterprises; (10) optimizing models of manpower distribution within branches and enterprises; (11) optimizing models of capacity utilization; (12) optimizing models fulfilling production orders within a complex network of operations.

The use of mathematical methods in economics and of electronic computers is a powerful instrument for improving the effectiveness of economic planning, the performance of individual sectors, and of strengthening links within the socialist economy.

In our experience, the use of mathematical methods and computers at the national level can yield the following savings compared with the traditional methods applied in planning decisions:

1. optimizing development and location—10-15 percent;

2. optimizing assignment of suppliers to users—10-12 percent;

3. optimizing medium- and short-term plans for industrial branches—8-10 percent;

4. optimizing utilization of productive capacity—7-8 percent;

5. optimizing the time profile for the fulfillment of special orders or other operations—up to 25 percent.

These examples show that in the solution of these problems the creation of management systems is fully justified on economic grounds. Owing to the greater effectiveness of mathematical methods and computers at higher levels of economic administration, the primary aim must be their application in the State Planning Commissions, the Planning Commissions of Union Republics, in ministries and departments. Thus greater impetus is given to the introduction of automated management systems at the highest levels of economic administration.

The designing and setting up of these systems on such a broad front demands the carefully planned use of qualified human and technical resources as well as a rational time profile for the introduction of automated systems into various ministries and departments.

Similar requirements must be fulfilled at the level of enterprises, institutions, and organizations.

Two measures were of particular importance in the setting up of automated management systems within ministries and departments: (1) the drafting of a national timetable for the creation of management systems, which also defined the concrete objectives to be achieved by their introduction; and (2) the elaboration of unified methodologies for the design and introduction of branch systems of automated production management.

The following objectives were pursued in the general standardized methodology for the setting up of management systems of information flows at the level of ministries and departments:

1. a unified time-profile for the formulation of projects;

2. the compilation of project data in various ministries and departments with a view to facilitating their mutual cooperation and access to each other's results;

3. a unified procedure for the mutual "tie-in" of ministerial and departmental management systems with the systems used at the highest echelons of planning and management in the country;

4. certain general guidelines for all ministries and departments (the organization of specialist teams for the evaluation of projects, standardized documentation, network and critical path analysis, etc.).

The introduction of a general methodology for informational flows promoted speedier completion of work and led to a saving of economic resources. Thanks to these methodologies, ministries and departments and their teams of experts were able, without additional research effort, to work out organizational forms and time-profiles for the introduction of management systems, to make modifications suited to their specific requirements, and to organize the required interchange of information.

Apart from this, standard methodologies were used to define the mutual responsibilities linking the teams of experts with the top management of ministries and departments, and this was instrumental in drawing wider sections of the administrative apparatus into the practical work of setting up management systems.

At the level of the nation as a whole, the introduction of a general methodology led to a time saving of one to two years in the work of the main ministries and departments. By these means the rhythm of work could be made more regular and smooth.

The program for the setting up of management systems on the branch level follows the methodology of the larger management systems set up at the higher level, with full regard to the peculiarities of each branch and to its special needs during the transition to an optimal regimen of work.

The crucial requirements that flow from the creation of systems of management and information at ministerial and departmental levels are the formulation of integrated criteria for the performance of these organs; the definition of the parameters that are to guide their interactions with other echelons in the national economy and with the higher tiers in the hierarchy of planning and management; the selection of a mathematical model for the optimal organizational structure of production of ministries and departments under the new system; the definition of data flows; and the specification of the composition and structure of the technological apparatus on which the new management systems is to be based. All these aspects are closely interrelated and make special demands on the time-profile and the nature of the program.

Whatever the apparatus used, the building of particular models must be based on a systematic analysis of the concrete conditions within which the ministries have to work, and this must be carried out in the earliest stages of the research concerned with the establishment of management systems.

The development of systems of management and information at the ministerial level is closely bound up with the interaction of these systems with those at the higher echelons of the planning apparatus and with the development of a national network of computing centers.

The strict coordination of research and development work on management systems at the ministerial level with that proceeding at the level of the higher planning and management organs leads to cost-saving in the implementation of both.

The creation and development of automatic management systems in the Soviet Union runs parallel with the establishment of a national network of computer centers. This will provide the technological basis for an integrated system of information flows at the national level, and later on for a system of optimal planning and management in the socialist economy.

12

AN INPUT-OUTPUT
FORECASTING MODEL
FOR BUSINESS PLANNING
Clopper Almon

If we hope to shape the future to human aspirations rather than leaving it to the unbridled working of egotism and special interests, we must have a vision of that future. And if the vision is to be shared— not to remain the dream of an individual until it is realized or forgotten—then it must be expressed somehow in words, numbers, or pictures. The interindustry forecasting model described in this chapter is meant to aid in making visions of the future shareable by expressing part of them—that part which concerns production, employment, and investment by the industries in the economy—in carefully balanced, well-controlled numbers and graphs. It fills in these concrete details in visions of the future that would otherwise remain vague. It can examine the difference in output, employment, and investment in each industry that would be caused by:

1. a low defense budget instead of a high one;
2. quotas on international trade instead of a liberal trade policy;
3. fluctuations instead of steady growth;
4. strong antipollution measures and incentives for recycling of materials, instead of lax controls and no such incentives;
5. slow growth in productivity instead of a continuation of the historical rate.

A model that can examine such questions can serve two purposes: (1) it can aid in rational public discussion of these issues, and (2) it can help individual businesses form a realistic view of the future, one not excessively colored by the successes or frustrations of the moment or by a subjective refusal to consider certain obvious possibilities.

The model we have developed at the University of Maryland has been used in both of these ways. In this chapter, we will describe first what the model shows, then explain briefly how it works, and

TABLE 12.1

Comparison of Normalcy, Imports Quotas, and Disarmament
Seller 106 Machine Tools, Metal Cutting

BUYER	1969	1975NRM	1980NRM	1980QTA	1975DIS	69-75	69-80	QUOTA	DISARM
106 Machine tools, metal cutti	57.4	68.7	80.5	77.9	61.6	3.0	3.1	2.8	1.2
20 Complete missiles	1.2	1.0	1.0	1.0	.8	-2.4	-1.3	-1.3	-6.1
21 Ammunition	3.6	2.2	2.2	2.2	1.8	-8.2	-4.2	-4.3	-11.3
22 Other ordnance	1.7	1.5	1.6	1.6	1.3	-2.3	-.5	-.6	-4.5
83 Steel	4.4	5.2	5.9	6.2	5.1	2.8	2.8	3.1	2.6
92 Metal cans	1.0	1.3	1.5	1.6	1.3	4.4	4.2	4.4	4.5
95 Structural metal products	2.9	3.5	4.1	4.1	3.5	3.4	3.3	3.2	3.4
96 Screw machine products	4.2	5.6	7.0	7.0	5.5	4.7	4.6	4.6	4.3
98 Cutlery, hand tools and ha	2.1	2.8	3.5	3.6	2.8	4.8	4.7	4.8	4.8
100 Valves, pipe fittings, and	9.5	12.3	14.9	14.5	12.1	4.3	4.0	3.8	3.9
102 Engines and turbines	10.9	14.8	17.9	16.9	14.4	5.1	4.5	4.0	4.7
103 Farm machinery	4.4	6.5	7.4	7.3	6.5	6.3	4.6	4.5	6.3
104 Construction, mining, and	11.5	14.5	16.8	15.9	14.4	3.8	3.4	2.9	3.7
105 Materials handling machine	3.0	3.7	4.4	4.3	3.6	3.6	3.4	3.2	3.0
107 Machine tools, metal formi	3.1	3.8	4.4	4.3	3.4	3.5	3.3	2.9	1.9
108 Other metal working machin	39.9	51.3	62.4	61.7	49.5	4.2	4.1	4.0	3.6
109 Special industrial machine	18.7	24.4	29.1	28.8	24.2	4.5	4.0	3.9	4.3
110 Pumps, compressors, blower	5.6	7.3	8.7	8.2	7.1	4.4	4.0	3.4	4.0
111 Ball and roller bearings	1.3	1.7	2.0	2.0	1.6	4.4	4.2	4.1	3.9
112 Power Transmission equipme	6.1	8.1	9.7	9.1	7.9	4.7	4.2	3.7	4.3
113 Industrial patterns	2.0	2.5	2.9	3.1	2.4	3.7	3.5	3.9	3.1
115 Other office machinery	1.4	1.9	2.3	2.3	1.8	4.8	4.5	4.4	3.9
116 Service industry machinery	3.6	4.7	5.7	5.4	4.6	4.7	4.3	3.8	4.3
117 Machine shop products	18.8	25.7	33.4	32.8	24.7	5.3	5.2	5.1	4.6
118 Electrical measuring instr	1.0	1.2	1.5	1.3	1.2	3.3	3.4	2.4	2.3
119 Transformers and switchgea	1.1	1.4	1.6	1.5	1.3	4.3	3.6	3.4	2.8
120 Motors and generators	3.9	5.0	6.1	5.9	4.8	4.2	4.2	3.8	3.5
121 Industrial controls	1.1	1.4	1.7	1.6	1.3	4.4	4.2	3.6	3.7
123 Household appliances	1.3	1.9	2.3	2.3	1.9	5.7	5.0	5.1	5.8
124 Electric lighting and wiri	1.7	2.2	2.6	2.8	2.2	4.2	4.1	4.4	4.1
127 Communication equipment	4.7	4.8	5.5	5.2	4.3	.5	1.5	1.0	-1.3
128 Electronic components	5.9	7.6	9.7	9.8	7.2	4.1	4.6	4.6	3.4
133 Motor vehicles and parts	17.7	22.4	28.1	28.9	22.4	3.9	4.2	4.5	3.9
134 Aircraft	4.5	4.6	5.3	4.6	4.1	.2	1.5	.1	-1.8
135 Aircraft engines and parts	6.5	6.1	6.8	6.4	5.4	-1.1	.4	-.2	-3.1
136 Aircraft equipment, nec	8.6	8.6	9.6	8.3	7.7	.1	1.0	-.3	-1.8
137 Ship and boat building and	2.2	2.9	3.4	3.4	2.7	4.8	3.8	3.9	3.2
138 Railroad equipment	1.1	1.7	2.1	2.0	1.6	7.5	6.0	5.7	6.5
141 Engineering and scientific 1	1.9	2.1	2.4	2.2	2.0	1.9	2.4	1.5	.7
142 Mechanical measuring devic	2.2	2.7	3.2	2.8	2.6	3.8	3.7	2.5	3.3
151 Railroads	1.6	2.0	2.4	2.4	2.0	4.0	3.8	3.7	3.9
171 Business services	4.0	5.1	6.1	6.1	5.0	4.0	3.8	3.8	3.9
184 Unimportant industry	1.9	2.5	3.0	3.0	2.4	4.3	4.0	4.2	4.1
Sum of intermediate flows	297.0	369.3	443.3	432.3	352.1				

TABLE 12.1 (continued)

Sales To Capital Equipment Buyers

BUYERS	1969	1975NRM	1980NRM	1980QTA	1975DIS	69-75	69-80	QUOTA	DISARM
5 Ordnance	16.1	13.4	9.7	9.7	13.1	-3.1	-4.6	-4.6	-3.4
25 Household and office furn	6.2	9.1	10.7	11.0	9.3	6.4	4.9	5.2	6.8
46 Iron and steel	32.8	36.8	39.2	41.3	36.3	1.9	1.6	2.1	1.7
47 Non-ferrous metals	10.1	14.4	16.7	17.1	13.7	6.0	4.6	4.8	1.7
48 Metal containers	47.9	65.5	83.2	84.2	66.0	5.2	5.0	5.1	5.3
49 Plumbing and heating	8.3	16.7	16.9	14.7	11.3	11.7	6.5	5.2	5.2
50 Structural metal products	35.9	51.7	61.0	57.9	47.4	6.1	4.8	4.3	4.6
51 Stampings	92.2	121.3	148.9	136.8	99.2	4.6	4.4	3.6	1.2
52 Hardware, plating, wire pl	47.0	70.8	88.4	81.4	58.5	6.8	5.7	5.0	3.7
53 Engine and turbines	49.4	66.4	79.7	75.3	62.1	4.9	4.3	3.8	3.8
54 Farm machinery	8.2	11.6	11.7	12.5	11.6	5.8	3.2	3.8	5.8
55 Construction, mining, mater.	45.7	56.2	63.6	58.0	48.0	3.4	3.0	2.2	.8
56 Metalworking machinery an	145.0	202.9	230.5	217.2	171.0	5.6	4.2	3.7	2.7
57 Special industrial machin	49.3	73.4	81.7	77.0	68.2	6.6	4.6	4.1	5.4
58 General industrial machin	75.5	107.5	126.5	119.5	94.4	5.9	4.7	4.2	3.7
59 Misc. machinery and shops	129.9	162.0	203.4	178.7	130.1	3.7	4.1	2.9	-.0
60 Office and computing mach	31.8	36.8	46.0	38.1	30.0	2.5	3.4	1.7	-1.0
61 Service industry machiner	17.9	29.2	35.6	32.3	23.8	8.1	6.2	5.4	4.8
62 Electric measuring, trans	22.4	25.0	25.4	23.7	23.6	1.8	1.2	.5	.9
63 Electric apparatus and mo	44.1	52.5	62.3	55.5	44.6	2.9	3.1	2.1	.2
64 Household appliances	15.3	18.9	20.4	17.9	15.2	3.5	2.6	1.4	-.1
65 Electric lighting and wir	41.4	60.3	72.2	69.6	50.8	6.3	5.1	4.7	3.4
66 Radio-, TV-sets and phono	4.9	7.0	8.9	8.9	6.6	6.0	5.5	5.5	5.1
67 Communication equipment	59.0	77.8	90.2	86.5	69.6	4.6	3.9	3.5	2.7
68 Electronic components	59.0	81.5	104.3	95.5	69.1	5.4	5.2	4.4	2.6
69 Batteries, x-rays and eng	13.0	15.0	16.3	14.3	10.5	2.3	2.0	.9	-3.6
70 Motor vehicles and parts	221.0	180.1	207.8	187.5	150.3	-3.4	-.6	-1.5	-6.4
71 Aircraft and parts	162.4	127.3	150.5	134.8	111.2	-4.1	-.7	-1.7	-6.3
72 Ships and boats	4.0	6.0	6.1	6.1	5.1	6.6	3.7	3.7	4.0
73 Locomotives, railroads an	2.3	2.6	2.2	2.1	2.4	2.1	-.4	-.9	.6
75 Engr. and scient. instrum	8.3	11.0	13.0	11.7	10.0	4.7	4.0	3.1	3.1
76 Mech. measuring devices a	15.9	20.0	21.5	18.0	15.2	3.8	2.7	1.1	-.8
77 Surgical and medical inst	12.3	16.3	18.9	17.2	14.0	4.7	3.9	3.1	2.2
78 Optical and photographic	39.5	63.3	78.5	80.2	59.4	7.9	6.2	6.4	6.8
79 Misc. manufactured produc	49.5	69.9	82.2	84.0	60.1	5.8	4.6	4.8	3.2
Sum of sales to equipment	1623.6	1979.8	2334.1	2176.3	1712.0				

Sales To Final Demand

BUYERS	1969	1975NRM	1980NRM	1980QTA	1975DIS	69-75	69-80	QUOTA	DISARM
186 Personal consumption expen	47.6	74.7	99.7	99.5	75.4	7.5	6.7	6.7	7.7
187 Defense expenditures	55.4	41.6	41.6	41.6	33.3	-4.8	-2.6	-2.6	-8.5
188 Non-defense federal expend	62.9	85.9	104.8	104.8	85.9	5.2	4.6	4.6	5.2
189 Education	28.7	36.6	43.5	43.5	36.6	4.0	3.8	3.8	4.0
190 Health, welfare, and sanit	.7	.9	1.1	1.1	.9	4.6	4.2	4.2	4.6
192 General state and local go	8.4	10.8	12.6	12.6	10.8	4.2	3.7	3.7	4.2
193 Change in inventories	62.5	35.6	27.3	12.0	33.1	-9.4	-7.5	-15.0	-10.6
194 Exports	199.1	217.6	234.0	197.4	216.8	1.5	1.5	-.1	1.4
195 Imports	-226.5	-270.6	-317.1	-193.4	-241.6	3.0	3.1	-1.4	1.1
Sum of sales to final demand	238.7	233.1	247.5	319.1	251.1				
Total	2159.4	2582.2	3024.9	2927.7	2315.2	3.0	3.1	2.8	1.2

illustrate its application in both analysis of public policy and in individual business forecasting.

WHAT THE MODEL SHOWS

The forecasts start from an input-output flow table that shows, for 1967, the sales of each of 185 product classes (which cover the entire economy) to their various uses. These uses are of several parts. First come the uses in the production of each of those same 185 products. These entries show only sales for use on current expense account, not capital account. Another block of uses shows the sales on capital account of each of these products to 94 industries, aggregates of the 185, as purchasers of capital equipment. Then follows the sale of each product to each of 28 types of construction, to inventory accumulation, to household consumption, to six categories of government expenditures, and to exports.

The U.S. Department of Commerce prepared such a table for the year 1963. At comparatively little cost, we made a 1967 table, keeping it as close as we could to the technology of the 1963 table but requiring agreement with all the data in the preliminary reports of the 1967 Census of Manufacturing and other 1967 data. We will soon similarly prepare a 1969 table, starting from our 1967 table.

The forecasts show, quite simply, a table of just this sort for each future year up to 1980 or 1985. It would be most awkward, however, to have to compare two of these tables. Therefore, we have had the computer arrange the numbers in more digestable ways. Three are shown in Table 12.1 and Figures 12.1 and 12.2. Table 12.1 displays the sales of machine tools to each buyer. Each line shows the name of a buyer and his purchases in 1967, 1975, and 1980 (1975 and 1980 under alternative assumptions to be explained below). It also shows growth rates between pairs of years. This display makes it easy to analyze what is happening to the market for a particular commodity to see which segments are growing or declining.

One of the attractions of an input-output model is that it allows one to go behind the forecasts for the particular market segments and to ask what is causing them to grow as they do. For example, the largest customer of machine tool builders, other than themselves, is the automobile industry, and Table 12.1 shows that the automobile industry's demand is growing faster than the industry average (4.2 percent per year against 3.5). To see why, we need to look at the connection between automobile equipment investment and the demand for automobiles.

Figure 12.1 shows the history and forecast of this relation. It also gives the employment in this industry. All three series are

plotted on the same scale with the 1967 value equal to 100. The plot
shows a strong rise in output, somewhat above the trend of the last
six or seven years. After a few years to digest the heavy capital
spending of 1964-66, the industry's capital needs should push spending
above the 1966 level by 1975. But why is output rising faster than
it would on the trend of the last ten years? Figure 12.2 shows another
graph for the automobile industry that gives the history and forecast
of output, consumption, exports, and imports for automobiles. From
it we see that consumption is forecast to rise about on or a little
below trend, but that imports slacken their growth and gradually
loose a little in market share. Thus, the good growth in the sales
of machine tools to automobiles turns out to depend in part on the
assumption of moderate auto imports. How much machine tool demand
would be affected by, say, doubling auto imports by 1980 could easily
be found by another run of the model.

Plots like Figure 12.2 and listings like Table 12.1 are available
for all 185 industries. Plots like Figure 12.1 are available for the
94 industries into which the 185 are grouped as buyers of capital
equipment. Graphs of construction by type—residential, commercial,
industrial, hospital, etc.—are also produced, as are graphs of gross
national product and its principal components. Such, then, is the
form of the output from the model. But the content of the output
depends of course on what we put into it. The next section discusses
the workings of the model.

HOW THE MODEL WORKS

Any one set of forecasts made by the model is the result of a
three-step process.

Step 1. Specify structural relationships, such as: how much
plastic will be used per automobile in 1980? what fraction of newspapers will be reprocessed into paper in 1980? how will consumers
divide each dollar of additional income among the various consumer
goods? what fraction of the increase in demand will be supplied by
imports? how much investment will each industry need for each
million dollars of expansion in its output? how rapidly will productivity
change in each industry?

Note that the answers to these questions do not determine the
size of the economy, but only its proportions, its shape, or structure.
To determine the absolute size, we go to step 2.

Step 2. Project overall controls, such as population, labor force,
employment, number of households, government spending by category,
and defense spending by product. This step also includes projections
of interest rates, depreciation rates, and, at present, relative prices.

FIGURE 12.1

Motor Vehicles

70 Motor Vehicles and Parts

Output58$ (●)	20429.7	25692.5	29336.9	25404.5
	45812.8	48660.9	43743.7	49295.1
	71049.1	74316.0	77474.7	
Employment(■)	594.1	696.0	726.6	623.9
	906.0	916.0	776.6	819.9
	913.8	920.3	924.0	
Investment(0)	313.3	353.1	418.8	359.8
	615.3	1101.1	784.6	724.6
	960.1	998.1	1035.2	
	+	+	+	+

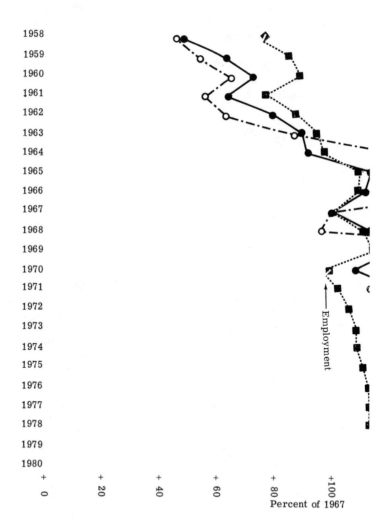

1958
1959
1960
1961
1962
1963
1964
1965
1966
1967
1968
1969
1970
1971
1972
1973
1974
1975
1976
1977
1978
1979
1980

+0   +20   +40   +60   +80   +100

Employment

Percent of 1967

162

31889.3	36091.1	37079.8	45614.4	44820.7	40141.1
52837.6	55852.7	58772.2	61745.8	64907.7	67845.0
716.3	769.1	786.4	897.3	891.7	809.0
851.2	867.7	879.5	889.7	900.3	906.6
407.9	571.9	789.2	971.9	948.6	643.0
804.7	856.7	877.2	897.4	960.3	924.0

+   +   +   +   +   +   +

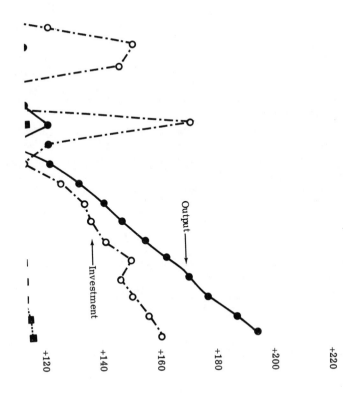

Output

Investment

+120   +140   +160   +180   +200   +220

The first two steps involve a great deal of discretion and econometric analysis, but judgment has the last word before proceeding to the final step, which is done entirely inside the computer.

Step 3. Calculate the forecasts by combining the overall controls with the structure. The basic logic here is to determine the course of after-tax consumer income, which, together with the specified government demand, yields the specified level of employment.

Note one important implication of the logic of the calculations: the model is either a full-employment growth model or a cyclical model according to what employment level it is required to reach. It has no prognostication of its own about whether 1976 will find us with 8 percent unemployment or 3 percent. The user has to provide that figure. For five- and ten-year forecasting, we believe that it is probably more reasonable to say that Congress will adjust tax rates to achieve an acceptable level of unemployment than it is to say that existing tax rates will continue in force. We are attempting, however, to calculate what tax rates would be necessary to attain the specified level of employment.

Let us now examine a little more closely how each of the three steps has been taken.

Structural Forecasts

Consumption expenditure per capita by product has been related to income per capita, rate of change of this income, relative prices, time, and, in some cases, the proportions of the population in specific age groups. In finding this relationship, we used a comparison of households of different incomes to determine the long-term response, or elasticity, of expenditures on various products to changes in income levels. Then we imposed this income elasticity in a historical or time-series study that uses income and the other variables mentioned above to explain the actual growth of consumption expenditure. This analysis was done for each of the 126 (out of 185) products consumers buy.

Equipment investment equations were derived from a time-series analysis of the investment behavior of the 94 industries[*] into which the 185 products were grouped. The basic assumption of the equations is that the capital desired by an industry, K^*, depends on the output, Q, of that industry and the cost of capital, r, as follows

$$K^* = aQr^{-\sigma}.$$

---

[*]The grouping was necessary because investment data are not available in the 185-product detail.

Here a and σ are constants. Actual capital stock, however, is not always—indeed, is scarcely ever—equal to desired stock. Firms invest to bring the stock up to the desired level and to replace worn-out or obsolete machines. Our equations allow for the spreading, over up to six years, of the spending necessary to bring capital up to the desired level. How much of the total needed is spent in the first year in which it is needed, and how much in the second, and so on, is determined separately for each of the industries. (The technique used is the polynomial interpolation or "Almon" distributed lag.) Into the calculation of r, the real cost of capital, go the real interest rate (the nominal rate minus the rate of inflation), the physical depreciation rate, the depreciation rate for tax purposes, the tax rate, and the investment tax credit. In selecting the forecasting equation, we combine a priori expectations with the desire for a good fit to historical data. We expect that the life of capital is about what is legally allowed and that an increase in output should eventually lead to the same percentage increase in capital, provided that r does not change. We have found that if we ignore these expectations in the process of curve-fitting, we will often find them violated in the results. But on the other hand, we can often make the equations conform closely to them at very little cost to the closeness of the fit to the historical data. Thus, our equations are not just the outcome of a curve-fitting exercise, but they have some economic sensibility built into them.

Imports are related to the domestic demand for the product, and exports are related to the total imports of the previous year. These relations are not necessarily proportional, and they can be easily replaced by specific projections.

Employment is calculated by multiplying output by labor productivity, and labor productivity is forecast from a cyclical variable— the rate of change of output—and a trend variable—either time, or more commonly, the average installation date of the capital equipment in the industry. The use of this last variable is the outcome of many attempts to try to make labor productivity depend on capital investment. After a number of unsuccessful tries to explain productivity with the quantity of capital, perhaps adjusted by some factor for its vintage, we found that this measure of the newness of capital works much better.

The hardest part of the structural forecasting is to project the technical coefficients: the plastics per car, the machine tools per dollar of investment by the aircraft industry, the lumber per dollar of residential construction, and so on. The first point that must be made is that at the 185-sector level there is not as much change as one might expect, and it is not always where expected. Between 1963 and 1967, the kind of electronic components going into computers

FIGURE 12.2

Motor Vehicles and Parts

133 Motor Vehicles and Parts				
Output (●)	21462.8	26951.2	30909.8	26701.4
	48098.7	51040.4	45732.1	51505.4
	74360.3	77793.5	81119.7	
Consumption(■)	9308.5	11861.9	13987.3	11841.1
	22499.0	23744.0	21736.5	23508.6
	34224.7	35829.4	37419.3	
Imports (0)	-640.5	-952.3	-711.3	-440.6
	-4598.7	-5184.6	-4877.4	-5197.4
	-6372.8	-6549.6	-6720.9	
Exports(▲)	1132.8	1064.9	1118.3	1017.7
	2735.6	3212.6	3489.7	3445.2
	4929.0	5147.2	5360.2	

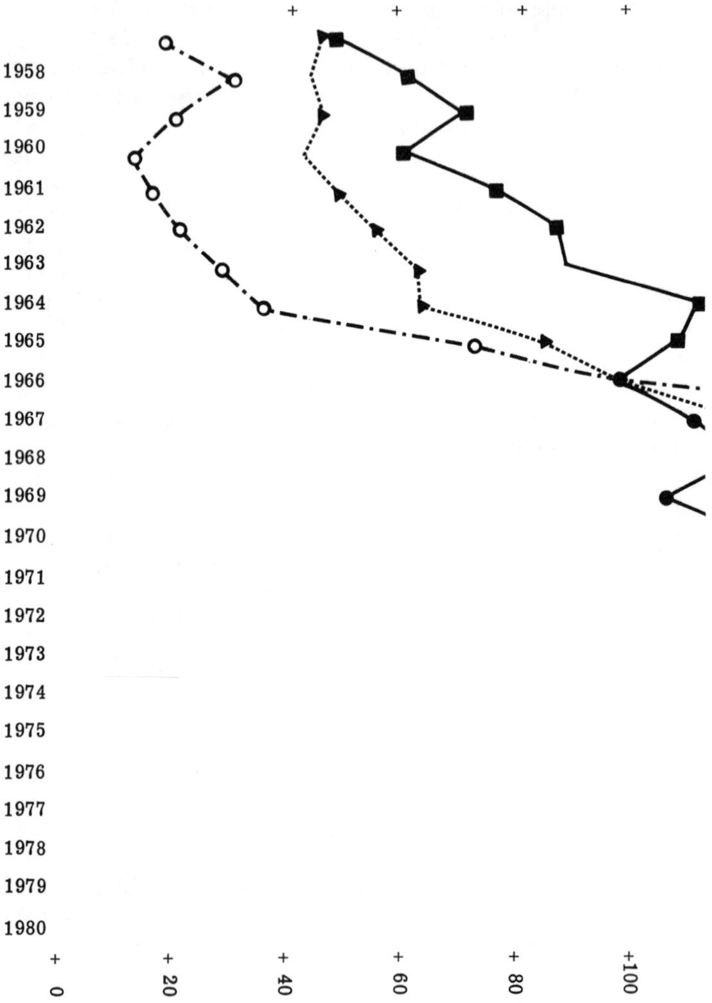

1958
1959
1960
1961
1962
1963
1964
1965
1966
1967
1968
1969
1970
1971
1972
1973
1974
1975
1976
1977
1978
1979
1980

+0   +20   +40   +60   +80   +100

33431.7	38017.7	38934.0	48017.3	46867.2	41958.4
55198.9	58356.6	61429.3	64552.6	67867.7	70999.7
15008.3	16870.8	17283.3	21588.6	20838.0	18772.2
25084.9	26570.7	28037.1	29526.1	31056.1	32626.7
-597.9	-670.0	-888.4	-1074.9	-2143.7	-2853.0
-5383.7	-5546.1	-5704.0	-5865.1	-6036.7	-6197.7
1168.5	1297.8	1474.9	1511.6	1965.5	2258.7
3751.5	3956.4	4158.1	4352.8	4547.1	4752.7

+   +   +   +   +   +   +

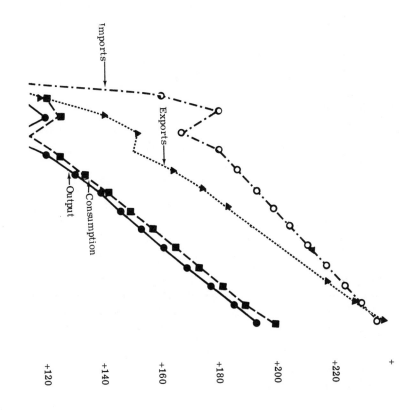

changed radically and made possible the development of the "third generation" machines. Nevertheless, the value of electronic components per dollar of computer changed hardly at all. Meanwhile, the input of glass bottles per dollar of soft drink production increased 35 percent! That dramatic change was caused by nothing more remarkable than the replacement of returnable bottles by nonreturnable ones. Likewise, there was a huge increase in the coefficient of knit fabric into apparel, apparently solely for stylistic reasons. Note that neither of these two big changes involved any significant new technology or capital investment by the using industry. Coefficient forecasting is clearly not the same thing as technological forecasting.

We began our study of coefficient change by comparing the 1963 coefficients with our 1967 coefficients. Out of some 11,000 coefficients, only 500 both (1) amounted to 1 percent or more of their column and row and (2) changed by more than 2 percent between 1967 and 1969. We then began examining these coefficient changes. Some of them were spurious, caused by a strike or other unusual market condition. Some, such as those mentioned above, were of short-term duration and had largely run their course by 1967. They were toned down considerably. All coefficient changes of more than 3 percent per year were reduced by half of the excess over 3 percent for forecasting.

In particular cells where we have annual time-series information, we have used it in place of the two-point comparisons. The list of such cells includes the major uses of steel and copper, manufacturing use of electricity, rail transportation, and some uses of plastics. It will soon include most cells in the paper and paperbox markets. Across-the-board changes in machine tool and computer rental markets are also made.

It is disappointing that in only one case—the use of nuclear energy in electric power production—were we able to use technical knowledge in forecasting the coefficients. No doubt part of the blame for this failure must be laid to our ignorance and lack of aptitude in that area. But the more fundamental difficulty is that a forecast of the technology that will be available in the future is just a first step toward forecasting input-output coefficients. The crucial questions are: What will be the market for the new product or process? How much of it will be sold? To what extent does it just replace another product of the same industry, causing no coefficient change, and to what extent does it replace products of some other industry and thereby change two coefficients? Those are tough questions. Market researchers all over the country are puzzling over them. It seems highly unlikely that our small group of academic economists could make a substantial contribution to answering them. Rather, we have built a tool for the analysis of the consequences of alternative answers to those questions. We have hoped that users would provide us with such alternative expectations about coefficient changes. We are still hoping.

Forecasts of the Overall Controls

These forecasts are not distinctive features of our model. We use the Census Bureau's projection of population (Series C) and household formation,[1] and the Bureau of Labor Statistics's projection of the labor force.[2] Projections of the real cost of capital have been made under a variety of assumptions. The relative prices used in the consumption equations are at present projected by trends. In the near future, we hope to replace them with forecasts derived from the model.

Calculations

In the first year of the forecast, investment and construction have already been determined by the growth of output in previous years. Therefore, we need only to make a first guess at disposable income, calculate from it consumer spending on each product, add that to government and investment spending and exports to get total final demand. Then we work the final demand back through the inter-industry structure, decomposing automobiles into steel, plastic, tires, batteries, etc., and then decomposing steel into iron ore, coal, electricity, and so on. In the end, we find the total output of each of the 185 products. From the outputs, we calculate employment by industry (the same 94 industries that were used for equipment spending), and then sum the employment over all industries. If the total differs from the assumed employment, we revise our guess of disposable income and repeat all the calculations, a task that requires two seconds of computer time. In the end, disposable income is determined to achieve a prespecified level of employment.

With the first year of the forecast thus determined, we can proceed on to the second, because investment in that second year is determined by the growth in output in the first and preceding years. Then, knowing the second, we climb on to the third, and so on. Actually, that description oversimplifies the process slightly, because investment this year does, to some slight extent, depend upon growth in output this year. The first time that we calculate investment for, say, 1975, we assume that the growth in output between 1974 and 1975 will be the same as it was between 1973 and 1974. From those

169

TABLE 12.2

Total Outputs—Comparison of Normalcy, Imports Quotas, and Disarmament

	BUYER	1969	1975NRM	1980NRM	1980QTA	1975DIS	69-75	69-80	QUOTA	DISARM
1	Dairy farm products	5572.4	6125.2	6563.5	6559.8	6159.7	1.6	1.5	1.5	1.7
2	Poultry and eggs	3380.4	3677.8	3936.6	3983.0	3697.5	1.4	1.4	1.5	1.5
3	Meat, animals and misc liv	20648.1	26481.5	31443.9	32028.1	26665.6	4.1	3.8	4.0	4.3
4	Cotton	1332.5	1644.4	1711.1	1832.9	1660.7	3.5	2.3	2.9	3.7
5	Grains	15929.7	18100.3	20141.6	18498.9	18139.6	2.1	2.1	1.4	2.2
6	Tobacco	1231.4	1554.2	1725.2	1660.0	1566.0	3.9	3.1	2.7	4.0
7	Fruits, vegetables, and ot	8446.5	11034.9	13219.8	13459.3	11133.2	4.5	5.7	4.2	4.6
8	Forestry and fishery produ	1113.3	1619.2	2075.5	2205.0	1642.6	6.2	5.7	6.2	6.5
9	Agricultural, forestry and	1729.4	2091.9	2400.1	2387.1	2100.2	3.2	3.0	2.9	3.2
10	Iron ores	871.2	1032.9	1162.1	1443.4	1018.5	2.8	2.6	4.6	2.6
11	Copper ore	1659.5	1795.7	2115.3	1994.6	1768.6	1.3	2.2	1.7	1.1
12	Other non-ferrous metal or	614.5	804.5	1032.6	1181.2	751.4	4.5	4.7	5.9	3.4
13	Coal mining	3529.8	4545.1	5567.1	5493.8	4533.5	4.2	4.7	4.0	4.2
14	Crude petroleum and natura	13152.4	17420.9	21014.5	22233.2	17419.4	4.7	4.3	4.8	4.7
15	Stone and clay mining	2601.0	3586.6	4540.5	4766.4	3590.8	5.4	5.1	5.5	5.4
16	Chemical fertilizer mining	649.9	971.5	1282.4	1438.7	965.5	6.7	6.1	7.2	6.6
17	New construction	28624.0	35498.7	41757.1	41697.1	35780.0	3.6	3.4	3.4	3.7
18	Maintenance and repair con	30213.9	39268.6	47180.7	47190.9	39285.7	4.4	4.1	4.1	4.4
19	Complete guided missiles	5340.0	4630.3	4629.8	4628.0	3692.3	-2.4	-1.3	-1.3	-6.1
20	Ammunition	4990.0	3044.3	3128.6	3108.4	2526.4	-8.2	-4.2	-4.3	-11.3
21	Other ordnance	1372.0	1194.6	1293.8	1281.3	1048.8	-2.3	-.5	-.6	-4.5
22	Meat products	23288.5	29592.1	35301.1	36154.9	29774.9	4.0	3.8	4.0	4.1
23	Dairy products	12854.6	14502.2	15937.1	15987.4	14573.2	2.0	2.0	2.0	2.1
24	Canned and frozen foods	8934.8	11914.9	14545.3	14754.0	12024.1	4.8	4.4	4.6	4.9
25	Grain mill products	10635.4	13248.2	15661.1	15500.8	13293.9	3.7	3.5	3.4	3.7
26	Bakery products	6650.4	7308.4	7747.9	7749.4	7380.8	1.6	1.4	1.4	1.7
27	Sugar	1847.5	2065.9	2316.4	2262.9	2080.1	1.9	2.1	1.8	2.0
28	Confectionery products	2975.4	3489.9	4180.2	4201.7	3478.9	2.7	3.1	3.1	2.6
29	Alcoholic Beverages	8209.5	11517.7	14181.2	15026.2	11736.9	5.6	5.0	5.5	6.0
30	Soft drinks and flavorings	4526.4	5884.6	7329.3	7321.9	5891.7	4.4	4.4	4.4	4.4
31	Fats and oils	5187.7	6416.8	7719.8	7572.0	6409.3	3.5	3.6	3.4	3.5
32	Misc food products	4748.3	5546.0	6222.6	6185.3	5591.7	2.6	2.5	2.4	2.7
33	Tobacco products	7114.9	8744.9	9712.4	9441.7	8807.1	3.4	2.8	2.6	3.6
34	Broad and narrow fabrics	14249.4	19717.5	24157.2	26048.6	19987.4	5.4	4.8	5.5	5.6
35	Floor coverings	1936.1	2740.1	3549.0	3527.6	2765.0	5.8	5.5	5.5	5.9
36	Misc textiles	2196.3	2715.9	3199.4	3434.9	2728.9	3.5	3.4	4.1	3.6
37	Knitting	4692.8	7422.4	9755.4	10004.5	7540.4	7.6	6.7	6.9	7.9
38	Apparel	16970.7	23536.6	28680.0	30196.0	23929.6	5.5	4.8	5.2	5.7
39	Household textiles	4524.3	6394.2	8124.7	8225.4	6445.7	5.8	5.3	5.4	5.9
40	Lumber and wood products	7571.8	10177.4	12498.7	12684.3	10214.8	4.9	4.6	4.7	5.0
41	Veneer and plywood	1571.2	2111.8	2557.8	2843.9	2121.7	4.9	4.4	5.4	5.0
42	Millwork and wood products	3506.7	4716.2	5797.4	5951.5	4753.0	4.9	4.6	4.8	5.1
43	Wooden containers	475.4	593.2	701.3	707.9	591.1	3.7	3.5	3.6	3.6
44	Household furniture	5168.6	6731.0	7767.6	7777.2	6859.1	4.4	3.7	3.6	4.7

(continued)

TABLE 12.2 (continued)

		1969	1975NRM	1980NRM	1980QTA	1975DIS	69-75	69-80	QUOTA	DISARM
46	Other furniture	2719.4	3589.4	4255.0	4112.7	3432.4	4.6	4.1	3.8	3.9
47	Pulp mills	1084.2	1463.0	1834.9	2249.3	1462.2	5.0	4.8	6.6	5.0
48	Paper and paperboard mills	8231.0	10298.3	12107.7	12184.1	10321.3	3.7	3.5	3.6	3.8
49	Paper products, nec	5815.0	7415.4	8808.5	8780.6	7443.8	4.1	3.8	3.7	4.1
50	Wall and building paper	400.1	475.7	547.0	548.9	477.7	2.9	2.8	2.9	3.0
51	Paperboard containers	6291.9	8327.9	10247.3	10345.6	8341.9	4.7	4.4	4.5	4.7
52	Newspapers	6038.7	8084.3	9953.2	9974.7	8136.1	4.9	4.5	4.6	5.0
53	Books, periodicals, and mi	6300.7	8553.3	10451.7	10447.8	8630.1	5.1	4.6	4.6	5.2
54	Other printing and service	6702.0	8611.1	10363.7	10344.6	8618.7	4.2	4.0	3.9	4.2
55	Industrial chemicals	16019.3	21225.7	26220.2	25524.0	20998.8	4.7	4.5	4.2	4.5
59	Fertilizers	1859.3	2496.7	3054.2	2757.5	2506.8	4.9	4.5	3.6	5.0
60	Pesticides and other agric	977.8	1446.9	1830.4	1740.4	1454.5	6.5	5.7	5.2	6.6
61	Misc chemical products	3317.2	4089.1	4859.8	4939.0	4060.9	3.5	3.5	3.6	3.4
62	Plastic materials and resi	4134.6	5486.2	6801.2	6534.9	5453.4	4.7	4.5	4.2	4.6
63	Synthetic rubber	1129.9	1393.7	1674.0	1711.5	1390.1	3.5	3.6	3.8	3.5
64	Cellulosic fibers	703.9	994.1	1245.5	1353.3	1005.7	5.8	5.2	5.9	5.9
65	Non-cellulosic fibers	2206.9	3602.5	4898.6	5259.3	3640.4	8.2	7.2	7.9	8.3
66	Drugs	5639.9	6134.6	6878.3	6798.3	6183.9	1.4	1.8	1.7	1.5
67	Cleaning and toilet prepar	7142.8	9627.6	11847.3	11798.9	9674.2	5.0	4.6	4.6	5.1
68	Paints	2875.5	3433.9	3925.8	3906.4	3427.6	3.0	2.8	2.8	2.9
69	Petroleum refining and rel	23191.4	30391.1	36127.7	36923.8	30348.4	4.5	4.0	4.2	4.5
71	Paving and Asphalt	1341.9	1747.0	2127.9	2125.2	1751.9	4.4	4.2	4.2	4.4
72	Tires and inner tubes	4178.6	5064.0	6062.9	6220.4	5077.5	3.2	3.4	3.6	3.2
73	Rubber products	3548.9	4440.9	5267.1	5354.0	4407.5	3.7	3.6	3.7	3.6
74	Misc plastic products	6394.6	9201.8	11937.9	12123.9	9150.4	6.1	5.7	5.8	6.0
75	Leather tanning and indust	891.0	995.6	1093.2	1192.5	1009.0	1.8	1.9	2.6	2.1
76	Leather footwear	2980.5	3295.3	3673.4	4111.9	3351.7	1.7	1.9	2.9	2.0
77	Other leather products	756.2	1023.5	1232.4	1463.5	1040.6	5.0	4.4	6.0	5.3
78	Glass	4090.8	5648.3	7182.4	7327.5	5656.7	5.4	5.1	5.3	5.4
79	Structural clay products	962.7	1183.3	1387.4	1456.4	1190.4	3.4	3.3	3.8	3.5
80	Pottery	389.6	517.4	615.3	731.2	519.6	4.7	4.2	5.7	4.8
81	Cement, concrete, and gyps	6416.6	8023.4	9450.9	9455.4	8076.5	3.7	3.5	3.5	3.8
82	Other stone and clay produ	3402.4	4238.4	5032.3	5011.6	4217.4	3.7	3.6	3.5	3.6
83	Steel	28291.0	33434.7	38346.1	39810.8	33034.7	2.8	2.8	3.1	2.6
84	Copper	4990.1	6226.9	7707.9	7678.8	6111.7	3.7	4.0	3.9	3.4
85	Lead	541.4	635.9	750.4	747.2	621.7	2.7	3.0	2.9	2.3
86	Zinc	283.0	337.5	387.4	454.1	331.0	2.9	2.9	4.3	2.6
87	Aluminum	6006.3	7855.1	9675.1	9707.3	7685.3	4.5	4.3	4.4	4.1
88	Primary non-ferrous metals	650.3	1011.0	1344.2	1417.2	985.7	7.4	6.6	7.1	6.9
89	Non-ferrous rolling and dr	1033.1	1271.3	1522.9	1431.1	1231.7	3.5	3.5	3.0	2.9
90	Non-ferrous wire drawing a	4109.5	5018.4	6188.1	6183.6	4948.0	3.3	3.7	3.7	3.1
91	Non-ferrous castings and f	974.9	1399.3	1850.3	1800.2	1352.4	6.0	5.8	5.6	5.5
92	Metal cans	2656.2	3460.0	4219.1	4289.4	3485.7	4.4	4.2	4.4	4.5
93	Metal barrels, drums and p	393.3	530.2	659.9	657.9	528.1	5.0	4.7	4.7	4.9
94	Plumbing and heating equip	1838.1	2286.5	2687.7	2664.3	2301.9	3.6	3.5	3.4	3.7

(continued)

TABLE 12.2 (continued)

		1969	1975NRM	1980NRM	1980QTA	1975DIS	69-75	69-80	QUOTA	DISARM
95	Structural metal products	11093.5	13637.2	15872.8	15780.0	13581.6	3.4	3.3	3.2	3.4
96	Screw machine products	3003.2	3984.0	5006.0	5003.2	3888.4	4.7	4.6	4.6	4.3
97	Metal stampings	3701.1	4626.9	5560.6	5336.1	4592.8	3.7	3.7	3.3	3.6
98	Cutlery, hand tools and ha	3748.3	5005.2	6257.5	6379.4	4999.4	3.7	4.7	4.3	4.8
99	Misc fabricated wire produ	2078.6	2646.5	3185.6	3193.7	2635.3	4.0	3.9	4.0	4.0
100	Valves, pipe fittings, and	2884.7	3731.5	4503.0	4379.7	3655.4	4.3	4.0	3.8	3.9
101	Other fabricated metal pro	3368.4	4540.3	5712.2	5871.6	4481.2	5.0	4.8	5.1	4.8
102	Engines and turbines	3945.2	5354.1	6492.8	6124.8	5215.6	5.1	4.5	4.0	4.7
103	Farm machinery	4572.7	6680.5	7595.3	7463.0	6664.7	6.3	4.5	4.5	6.3
104	Construction, mining, and	5987.9	7531.5	8718.0	8245.4	7457.0	3.8	3.4	2.9	3.7
105	Materials handling machine	2396.2	2975.8	3488.4	3403.0	2863.6	3.8	3.4	3.2	3.0
106	Machine tools, metal cutti	2159.4	2582.2	3024.9	2927.7	2315.2	3.0	3.1	2.8	1.2
107	Machine tools, metal formi	765.9	944.1	1103.1	1056.9	857.2	3.5	3.3	2.9	1.9
108	Other metal working machin	5307.1	6826.2	8309.1	8212.5	6584.7	4.2	4.1	4.0	3.6
109	Special industrial machine	5092.9	6651.8	7911.2	7827.1	6597.2	4.5	4.0	3.9	4.3
110	Pumps, compressors, blower	2743.1	3567.9	4238.1	3980.7	3480.5	4.4	4.0	3.4	4.0
111	Ball and roller bearings	1477.4	1918.1	2333.6	2311.0	1869.8	4.4	4.2	4.1	3.9
112	Power transmission equipme	1452.0	1928.7	2300.1	2170.0	1883.5	4.7	4.2	3.7	4.3
113	Industrial patterns	1736.5	2172.1	2550.1	2680.2	2088.1	3.7	3.5	3.9	3.1
114	Computers and related mach	5126.0	8243.0	11130.5	10164.8	8064.7	7.9	7.0	6.2	7.6
115	Other office machinery	1206.5	1605.1	1974.4	1963.7	1522.6	4.8	4.5	4.4	3.9
116	Service industry machinery	5522.4	7305.9	8873.9	8414.7	7129.3	4.7	4.3	3.8	4.3
117	Machine shop products	4142.8	5681.3	7377.7	7238.8	5454.9	5.3	5.2	5.1	4.6
118	Electrical measuring instr	1412.2	1719.1	2062.8	1849.0	1625.4	3.3	3.4	2.4	2.3
119	Transformers and switchgea	3042.8	3928.5	4534.3	4413.9	3827.8	4.3	3.6	3.4	3.8
120	Motors and generators	2779.7	3566.0	4413.2	4244.2	3437.3	4.2	4.2	3.8	3.5
121	Industrial controls	1255.4	1631.3	2001.4	1869.8	1569.7	4.4	4.2	3.6	3.7
122	Welding apparatus and grap	1353.6	1759.2	2161.2	2170.7	1713.6	4.4	4.3	4.3	3.9
123	Household appliances	5075.6	7141.4	8749.7	8914.1	7201.5	5.7	5.0	5.1	5.8
124	Electric lighting and wiri	4416.6	5680.3	6898.6	7182.2	5663.0	4.2	4.1	4.4	4.1
125	Radio and TV receiving	4352.7	5585.4	6887.0	7372.2	5587.1	4.2	4.2	4.8	4.2
126	Phonograph records	317.2	443.8	550.5	542.9	450.0	5.6	5.0	4.9	5.8
127	Communication equipment	10562.0	10858.4	12452.1	11799.7	9786.8	.5	1.5	1.0	-1.3
128	Electronic components	8074.1	10340.9	13333.0	13361.5	9882.1	4.1	4.6	4.6	3.4
129	Batteries	971.0	1223.0	1453.1	1438.8	1203.8	3.8	3.7	3.6	3.6
130	Engine electrical equipmen	1432.1	1893.2	2369.7	2393.7	1874.9	4.7	4.6	4.7	4.5
131	X-ray equipment and electr	550.4	763.6	940.0	879.0	755.0	5.5	4.9	4.3	5.3
132	Truck, bus, and trailer bo	1459.9	2064.8	2467.7	2347.9	1986.8	5.8	4.8	4.3	5.1
133	Motor vehicles and parts	51040.4	64552.6	81119.7	83276.7	64587.6	3.9	4.2	4.5	3.9
134	Aircraft	9381.2	9515.6	11068.6	9510.6	8424.4	.2	1.5	.1	-1.8
135	Aircraft engines and parts	3940.9	3690.3	4095.7	3848.7	3279.6	-1.1	.4	- .2	-3.1
136	Aircraft equipment, nec	4898.3	4921.2	5462.0	4752.9	4386.6	.1	1.0	- .3	-1.8
137	Ship and boat building and	2426.5	3230.2	3698.2	3721.4	2940.8	4.8	3.8	3.9	3.2
138	railroad equipment	2057.8	3226.7	3998.4	3845.8	3033.1	7.5	6.0	5.7	6.5
139	Cycles and parts, transpor	499.5	781.2	983.2	1662.5	783.0	7.5	6.2	10.9	7.5

(continued)

172

TABLE 12.2 (continued)

		1969	1975NRM	1980NRM	1980QTA	1975DIS	69-75	69-80	QUOTA	DISARM
140	Trailer coaches	1485.1	2290.7	3013.7	2986.4	2305.6	7.2	6.4	6.4	7.3
141	Engineering and scientific	1185.0	1327.5	1548.0	1390.2	1237.5	1.9	2.4	1.5	.7
142	Mechanical measuring devic	2260.2	2830.7	3385.2	2966.0	2757.5	3.8	3.7	2.5	3.3
143	Optical and opthalmic goo	1181.3	1493.9	2225.4	2469.5	1461.9	3.9	5.8	6.7	3.6
144	Medical and surgical instr	1531.3	2101.8	2535.5	2506.5	2092.3	5.3	4.6	4.5	5.2
145	Photographic equipment	3705.3	5330.5	6796.2	6513.9	5297.7	6.1	5.5	5.1	6.0
146	Watches, clocks, and parts	499.1	766.1	983.3	1345.5	776.8	7.1	6.2	9.0	7.4
147	Jewelry and silverware	1817.3	2680.2	3383.1	3280.2	2730.6	6.5	5.6	5.4	6.8
148	Toys, sporting goods, musi	2393.1	3236.7	3913.4	4585.8	3259.6	5.0	4.5	5.9	5.2
149	Office supplies	767.9	1000.8	1205.1	1205.5	1005.5	4.4	4.1	4.1	5.2
150	Misc manufacturing, nec	2812.1	3719.7	4466.1	5152.9	3725.4	4.7	4.2	5.5	4.7
151	Railroads	13196.6	16750.7	20052.6	19850.8	16673.4	4.0	3.8	3.7	3.9
152	Busses	3390.7	4439.9	5161.1	5153.7	4444.9	4.5	3.8	3.8	4.5
153	Trucking	17682.9	22664.1	27281.3	27144.8	22530.0	4.1	3.9	3.9	4.0
154	Water transportation	2197.6	2653.1	3151.2	3247.6	2573.4	3.1	3.3	3.6	2.6
155	Airlines	4256.4	5788.6	7556.1	7584.8	5697.9	5.1	5.2	5.3	4.9
156	Pipelines	1267.6	1656.8	1984.9	2068.2	1651.5	4.5	4.1	4.5	4.4
157	Freight forwarding	314.4	416.2	512.4	513.1	414.6	4.7	4.4	4.5	4.6
158	Telephone and telegraph	19889.7	26148.9	32493.8	32326.6	26131.0	4.6	4.5	4.4	4.5
159	Radio and TV broadcasting	2661.2	3495.3	4240.8	4252.0	3511.4	4.5	4.2	4.3	4.6
160	Electric utilities	21256.7	27563.8	33767.8	33763.9	27681.3	4.3	4.2	4.2	4.4
161	Natural gas	14946.9	19313.4	23367.4	23381.7	19427.3	4.3	4.1	4.1	4.4
162	Water and sewer services	3723.1	4964.8	5959.9	5952.6	5003.3	4.8	4.3	4.3	4.9
163	Wholesale trade	63812.9	82631.4	99534.5	97914.1	82550.9	4.3	4.0	3.9	4.3
164	Retail trade	91931.6	121114.4	146835.4	146335.1	122145.9	4.6	4.3	4.2	4.7
165	Credit agencies and broker	24461.7	34618.6	43890.0	43802.4	34983.5	5.8	5.3	5.3	6.0
166	Insurance and broker's age	24631.2	33898.5	41826.9	41700.6	34364.8	5.3	4.8	4.8	5.6
167	Owner-occupied dwellings	53207.3	73336.2	89996.6	89763.0	74575.8	5.3	4.8	4.8	5.6
168	Real estate	59371.0	79590.9	96878.7	96862.8	80331.3	4.9	4.5	4.4	5.0
169	Hotel and lodging places	5254.7	7248.3	8950.2	8915.6	7315.6	5.4	4.8	4.8	5.5
170	Personal and repair servic	15675.9	21348.1	26632.2	26525.6	21674.9	5.1	4.8	4.8	5.4
171	Business services	34109.1	43271.3	51766.4	51604.6	42795.5	4.0	3.8	3.8	3.8
172	Advertising	17389.8	22816.4	27674.0	27750.2	22918.6	4.5	4.2	4.2	4.6
173	Auto repair	13877.8	17762.6	21058.3	20996.8	17980.4	4.1	3.8	3.8	4.3
174	Motion pictures and amusem	7968.3	9877.8	11045.9	10967.7	10228.8	3.6	3.0	2.9	4.2
175	Medical services	31750.1	42079.1	51357.7	51281.6	42431.7	4.7	4.4	4.4	4.8
176	Private schools and nonpro	21437.3	32450.2	41428.9	41242.4	33146.3	6.9	6.0	5.9	7.3
177	Post office	6227.7	8282.9	10204.5	10186.3	8286.7	4.8	4.5	4.5	4.8
178	Federal gov. enterprises	635.0	879.0	1092.0	1090.2	889.7	5.4	4.9	4.9	5.6
180	State and local electric u	2146.1	2955.6	3677.2	3674.2	2965.3	5.4	4.9	4.9	5.4
181	Directly allocated imports	8932.2	10280.4	11916.9	11949.6	9862.6	2.3	2.6	2.6	1.7
182	Business travel	11051.0	14344.0	17381.5	17323.8	14293.5	4.3	4.1	4.1	4.3
183	Office supplies	3303.7	4323.5	5242.9	5228.7	4316.3	4.5	4.1	4.1	4.5
184	Unimportant industry	336.5	434.6	524.2	532.9	430.6	4.3	4.0	4.2	4.1
185	Computer rental	2559.3	6223.0	10573.9	10540.7	6182.1	14.8	12.9	12.9	14.7

investment figures and the other 1975 numbers, we calculate 1975 output. Then we go back to the investment calculations, revise them in the light of the computed 1975 outputs, and then recompute the 1975 outputs. This process may be repeated if necessary to get agreement between the assumed and the implied growth in output.

We turn now from the making of the forecasts to their applications.

APPLICATIONS

We will illustrate first an application to two questions of public policy—(1) import quotas and (2) the economic effects of reduced military spending—and then discuss an application to a problem of business forecasting, namely forecasting the demand for lathes.

Import Quotas

In our standard forecasts, imports are calculated as a function of domestic demand for the product, and that function is determined from a comparison of the growth in imports and domestic demand over the period from 1958 to 1968. (A simple linear regression of imports on domestic demand was used.) These functions go into the 1975 and 1980 forecasts of industry output that are shown in the second and third columns of Table 12.2. The growth rate between 1969 and each of these two years is shown in the columns labeled "69-75" and "69-80" of that table.

During the last several years, there has been growing pressure in the United States for import quotas in certain industries. There are already quotas on oil, and the steel and shoe industries are ardent suitors for quotas. These quotas are usually set at a certain percentage of domestic production, and the privilege of importing is allocated to domestic producers in proportion to their production. Thus they not only get their market protected, as a tariff would do, but they also pocket the difference between what they pay for imported goods and what they sell them for, the sum that goes to the government under a tariff. Now if "infants" like the oil, steel, and shoe industries get quotas, surely just about any industry that wants one would be entitled to one. What would happen if they all got one?

To pose this question to the model we replaced the estimated import equation by a quota, at the 1968 ratio of imports to domestic production, for all industries in which imports were rising faster than output. By 1980, nonfinancial imports would be $22.5 billion (1967) or 29 percent below their value in the standard forecast.

Our export equations, it will be recalled, relate the exports of each commodity to the total imports of all commodities in the previous year. Consequently, the reduction in the import forecast automatically reduces the export forecast—as it happens by $17.4 billion (1967). Of course it is more efficient to acquire those imported goods by importing them and paying for them with exports than it is to make them here. Consequently, it is not surprising to find that the level of 1980 real personal consumption expenditure with quotas falls $3 billion short of the level without quotas.

These aggregates, of course, are not the starting point but the summing up of the model's calculations. The greatest interest lies in seeing which industries grow faster and which grow slower under a quota system. A comparison of the columns labeled "69-80" and "Quota" in Table 12.2 enables one to see just that. Among the major beneficiaries of quotas (besides steel and shoes) are, such cornerstones of our national security as toys, motorcycles and minibikes, whiskey, pottery, watches and clocks, radios and TV sets, optical goods, textiles, and apparel. Oil does not appear in this list because the present quota strongly influences the standard forecast.

The industries that suffer from quotas are the strong exporters—aircraft, fertilizers, pesticides, electrical measuring instruments, mechnical measuring devices, scientific instruments, X-ray equipment, construction equipment, engines and turbines, and pumps and compressors. What the quotas give to the weak industries, they take away from the industries that have been supporting the balance of payments. (Note that Table 12.1 shows in detail the effects of the quotas on machine tools.)

Reduced Military Spending

What would happen if defense procurement were reduced by 1975 to 20 percent below the planned 1972 levels and taxes were cut enough to keep employment the same as in the standard forecast? Insofar as the answer can be summarized by industry outputs, the columns labeled "1975 Dis" and "Disarm" in Table 12.2 tell the story. The "Disarm" column shows the growth rates between 1969 and 1975 under the above "disarmament" assumption. It is therefore to be compared with the column labeled "69-75," which reflects maintenance of 1972 defense levels to 1975 and 1980 in the standard forecast. A few industries can be seen to be hard hit by disarmament, but the vast majority of them grow a little faster when military spending is reduced.

This analysis, by the way, has entered public discussion in articles in Business Week[3] and Fortune[4] (both in September 1970),

175

and in a published report to the Arms Control and Disarmament Agency.[5]

Lathes

From disarmament to lathes is a complete change of focus, and it is perhaps remarkable that the same "camera" will take both pictures. And indeed a special attachment, a sort of close-up lens, is necessary for looking at lathes, for they are just a part of one of the 185 sectors. But it is worth fitting the model with the close-up lens because the demand for lathes is far removed from consumer demand. Consumers buy clothes, clothes makers buy cloth, cloth makers buy synthetic fibers, synthetic fiber makers buy special industrial machinery, and special industrial machinery makers buy lathes. That is but one of the countless threads tying the demand for lathes to the final demands that determine the direction of the economy. The model has already taken all of these threads into account down to the level of investment spending by the machine tool buyer. Consequently, the place to begin the study of the demand for lathes is with their share of the investment dollar of the lathe-using industries. Those figures are not directly known. What is known is the 1969 stock of 15 different kinds of lathes bought in the previous ten years by each of 35 of the 94 investment industries. (The other industries bought a negligible amount of lathes.) We attached 1967 prices to each of these 15 different kinds of lathes, and added them together to get an estimate of the value, in 1967 prices, of the lathes purchased by each industry over the ten-year period. That sum was divided by the total equipment investment (in constant dollars) by the corresponding industry in those same years. The results approximate the share of lathes in a dollar spent on equipment by each of the 35 industries. To forecast domestic lathe demand we could just multiply that share by the investment forecast for each buyer and sum over buyers. That sum we will call the constant coefficient indicator (CCI). But before we call the CCI a forecast for the future we had better see how it would have worked in the past. It may differ from actual domestic lathe purchases, A, by a proportionality factor, a, a time trend, b, or by a cyclical factor. We therefore estimated the equation

$$\log (A/CCI)_t = a + bt + c \frac{(CCI_t - CCI_{t-1})}{CCI_{t-1}} \qquad \text{(t is the year)}$$

The last term, which is low or negative in recessions, is the cyclical factor. Figure 12.3 shows the historical fit and forecast with this

176

FIGURE 12.3

Lathe Demand

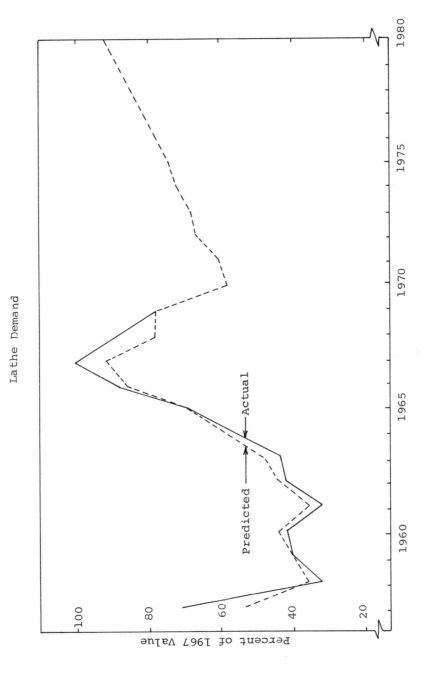

TABLE 12.3

Sales of Lathes (Millions of 1967 Dollars)

BUYER	1958	1960	1962	1964	1966	1967	1968	1969	1970	1971	1972	1973	1974	1975	1980
Ordnance	1.8	2.2	3.2	2.3	4.3	5.0	4.7	3.8	3.8	3.8	3.7	3.3	3.5	3.6	3.8
Household and office furniture	.2	.2	.4	.6	.5	.5	.7	.4	.4	.4	.6	.5	.5	.6	.7
Iron and steel	4.6	7.6	4.9	8.2	11.5	11.8	11.2	8.9	7.6	7.8	8.5	9.0	9.2	9.6	10.0
Nonferrous metals	1.4	1.2	1.1	1.5	3.1	3.5	3.1	2.6	2.5	2.3	2.2	2.6	3.0	3.1	3.8
Metal containers	6.8	12.3	9.8	12.6	16.6	17.1	17.6	14.1	14.3	14.3	14.4	16.2	17.9	18.8	24.1
Hardware, plating, hire plating	2.8	4.0	4.1	5.7	7.7	8.3	7.2	4.9	4.9	5.0	6.3	7.7	8.7	8.5	10.5
Plumbing and heating	1.3	1.4	1.3	1.6	2.1	2.2	2.1	1.8	1.8	1.7	2.1	2.4	2.4	2.7	2.9
Structural metal products	3.6	4.2	3.8	4.4	6.1	7.5	6.9	5.6	5.2	5.2	5.4	5.8	6.2	6.6	7.9
Stampings	13.0	18.2	18.2	30.6	40.6	45.3	36.0	37.1	34.5	36.8	40.9	36.5	38.2	40.9	53.7
Engine and turbines	4.1	2.8	3.4	4.4	7.4	11.2	14.5	11.9	10.1	9.6	10.3	10.9	11.2	11.8	15.8
Farm machinery	1.7	2.4	1.6	2.7	3.4	4.1	3.7	4.1	2.8	2.9	2.9	3.7	3.9	4.2	4.6
Construction, mining, mater, handling	8.2	13.9	9.3	12.4	20.7	26.5	20.4	17.2	16.5	16.5	19.6	22.3	19.9	23.3	27.7
Metalworking machinery and equt.	12.5	15.6	14.5	22.2	42.1	38.6	35.5	34.0	30.1	28.9	32.9	36.5	40.1	41.4	52.3
Special industrial machinery	6.1	9.5	9.6	11.5	19.2	20.7	18.0	17.0	15.7	14.7	15.0	16.9	18.9	18.8	24.4
General industrial machinery	10.9	16.1	13.6	17.8	31.2	33.6	38.9	29.4	29.0	26.2	26.3	27.6	32.1	32.8	41.7
Office and computing machinery	1.1	1.6	2.0	1.9	3.2	3.4	3.2	3.5	3.2	3.3	2.9	3.5	4.0	4.2	4.6
Service industry machinery	1.3	2.1	2.1	2.2	5.2	6.2	5.9	5.0	5.0	4.9	4.9	4.9	5.0	5.6	7.4
Misc. machinery and shops	22.9	19.9	19.2	28.7	34.6	51.2	39.7	35.4	30.7	36.9	39.1	39.2	44.1	48.6	67.0
Electric measuring, transformer	2.3	3.4	3.3	2.8	5.0	7.4	6.1	5.4	4.9	4.5	4.7	4.7	5.0	5.2	7.0
Electric apparatus and motors	4.8	6.8	6.3	7.8	14.0	18.1	15.6	13.9	11.5	11.0	13.2	14.5	15.5	16.0	20.5
Household appliances	.5	.9	.3	1.0	1.5	1.5	1.5	1.2	1.1	1.2	1.5	1.7	1.7	1.8	2.2
Electric lighting and wiring	2.6	3.9	3.8	4.6	7.8	8.2	7.6	5.9	6.0	5.7	6.3	6.9	7.5	8.3	9.8
Radio-, TV-sets, and phonographs	.1	.2	.2	.2	.7	.5	.2	.3	.2	.3	.4	.4	.4	.4	.5
Communication equipment	2.5	4.5	4.2	4.8	7.9	10.5	10.5	7.5	7.3	7.2	8.2	8.1	8.1	8.2	9.8
Electronic components	1.8	4.6	4.2	5.1	11.0	9.9	8.5	7.2	6.2	7.3	9.0	8.9	9.6	9.7	13.0
Batteries, x-rays, and engine equt.	.6	1.0	1.1	1.2	2.0	3.0	2.7	2.0	1.9	1.7	1.7	1.8	1.9	2.1	2.8
Motor Vehicles and parts	7.9	13.5	11.7	22.5	29.6	20.5	17.3	21.2	16.5	17.7	21.1	23.7	25.5	26.9	34.0
Aircraft and parts	11.0	13.3	18.0	19.1	40.9	49.9	37.4	31.5	26.5	26.8	26.6	28.5	29.8	30.5	42.3
Ships and boats	.3	.4	.4	.4	.6	.8	.7	.5	.5	.5	.6	.6	.6	.6	.7
Locomotives, railroads	.3	.4	.4	.6	1.1	1.7	.9	1.3	1.0	.9	1.2	1.3	1.4	1.3	1.7
Engr. and scient. instruments	1.1	2.2	2.0	1.9	1.8	2.9	3.5	3.0	2.0	2.1	2.3	2.5	2.7	2.7	3.3
Mech. measuring devices	2.7	6.0	6.0	5.8	7.3	6.7	6.3	6.0	5.3	5.6	6.4	7.1	7.4	7.9	9.5
Optical and photographic supplies	1.5	2.2	2.2	2.2	4.8	7.6	6.5	5.1	5.3	4.8	5.4	5.7	5.5	6.7	9.1
Surgical and medical instruments	.6	.9	1.1	1.1	1.6	2.0	2.0	1.6	1.5	1.5	1.7	1.8	1.9	2.1	2.5
Misc. manufactured products	3.6	4.3	4.7	4.7	5.9	6.5	6.0	5.4	5.7	5.9	8.6	8.7	6.3	6.9	8.9
Private demand	148.4	203.6	181.2	257.0	402.8	454.6	402.5	355.8	265.9	277.0	303.8	313.0	331.3	344.4	410.4
Government demand	6.2	11.6	15.8	14.7	22.3	27.0	27.6	25.8	25.8	25.8	25.8	25.8	25.8	25.8	25.8
Domestic demand	154.6	215.3	207.0	271.7	425.1	481.6	430.2	381.6	291.7	302.8	329.6	338.8	357.1	370.2	436.2
Exports	17.1	12.0	40.5	41.1	20.6	21.6	18.1	20.7							
Imports	5.1	10.0	9.6	10.0	38.7	47.7	36.7	35.4							
Domestic output	166.6	217.3	237.9	302.9	407.0	455.5	411.6	366.9							
CT output series 567	122.2	159.3	174.5	222.1	298.4	334.0	301.8	269.0							

Note — equt. = equipment
engr. = engineering

178

equation; Table 12.3 gives the full detail of the forecast, showing which industries will be buying the lathes shown in total in Figure 12.3.

Other Applications

Similar close-up lenses have been fitted to the model for nine other types of machine tools, for various types of railroad cars, copper and steel shapes, and work on various types of paper and plastic products is under way.

It is not always necessary to fit so complex a close-up lens to get a detailed product picture. For example, a good idea of the demand for web-fed printing presses versus sheet-fed presses can be had by comparing the investment forecast for newspapers with that for commercial printing. Or the forecast of looms versus knitting machines can be read from the difference between investment by woven fabrics and knit fabrics.

These forecasts do not, by themselves, decide many issues in business planning. But if they are readily available they can add an important element to the process: a forecast that is detailed enough to be relevant yet is a consistent part of a larger picture that covers the entire economy; a forecast that is based upon explicit assumptions that can be changed explicitly, but not implicitly; a forecast that is not colored by the aspirations or anxieties of the user. Such forecasts should, we hope, make possible decisions that are better from the point of view of the firm. And if, through those forecasts, firms can avoid the economic wastes that occur when they are not ready for what happens, the forecasts will have benefited all of us as well.

NOTES

1. Statistical Abstract of the United States, 1970, Table 3 (Washington, 1971).
2. Ibid., Table 317.
3. Business Week, September 5, 1970, pp. 66-68.
4. Fortune, September, 1970, p. 111.
5. "Adjustments of the U.S. Economy to Reductions in Military Spending," Prepared for the U.S. Arms Control and Disarmament Agency, December, 1970, edited by Bernard Udio, University of Colorado.

13

A SYSTEM APPROACH
TO CORPORATE PLANNING
IN LARGE ENTERPRISES
John Grieve Smith

Planning in large public and private industrial enterprises in the Western world has many similarities arising from the fact that both are functioning in a market economy. The publicly owned industries in Great Britain, however, have most in common with those large private enterprises whose major interests are mainly limited to one field (e.g., steel, oil, chemicals). Their problems differ in emphasis, and to some extent in substance, from those of the conglomerate holding companies with a large variety of interests in different industries, which seem to have dominated public discussion of corporate planning in recent years.

This chapter is concerned with the problem of planning, and the economic use of resources, in a large organization in one industry. While the particular approach is specific to the problems of planning in the British nationalized steel industry, the problems tackled have their counterparts in many other large industrial organizations, and have received most public attention in the electricity generating industry.

STEEL AFTER NATIONALIZATION

Following the nationalization of steel in 1967, the British Steel Corporation (BSC) took over the assets of 14 steel companies

The author is indebted to discussions with his colleagues in the Planning Economics and Operational Research departments of the British Steel Corporation for the evolution of the analytical approach in this chapter. The views expressed in it are his own and not necessarily those of the Corporation.

accounting for 90 percent of the industry in terms of crude steel production and two-thirds by value of sales. There had been a period of relatively low investment immediately prior to nationalization, but virtually every works had prepared a plan for the development of its own site designed to ensure its expansion and survival. The immediate planning problem was to decide which works to allow to expand, and in what order of priority. To do this, it was necessary to establish a central planning organization capable of thinking in terms of the needs of the BSC as a whole rather than the individual works or company. With the passage of time, and changes in organization, the emphasis has shifted away from choosing between rival schemes for expansion at different works and toward first analyzing the factors involved and then trying to determine those investment strategies that (from the point of view of the BSC as a whole) are best directed toward improving its profitability.

MARKET FORECASTING

It was possible from the start to take a Corporationwide view of the market position, because demand forecasting for steel had been undertaken on an industrywide basis prior to nationalization. As far as home demand is concerned, forecasting techniques have been elaborated over many years and have benefited from the exceptionally detailed statistics of steel deliveries broken down by product and by industry that are available for Great Britain. Such forecasts are based on projections of the long-term rate of growth of the economy, the pattern of such growth in terms of the main items of national expenditure (e.g., the principal categories of personal consumption, fixed investment, etc.), and in terms of the rate of growth of output in different industries. In addition, estimates have to be made of the trends in the consumption of steel products per unit of output in steel-consuming industries (such as the motor industry or construction), taking into account price movements for steel and competitive materials, changes in design and methods of manufacture, and other factors. It is then possible to forecast the total consumption of each category of steel products. This is usually done year by year for the next ten years.

The resulting estimates show the total U.K. market likely to be open to the BSC, other British steel producers in the private sector, and imports from foreign producers. It is then necessary to assess the share of the market that the BSC is likely to, or should aim to, achieve in view of the strength of competition from other producers and its own pricing policy. For all products the share of the market taken by imports is potentially important; in the case of some products, competition from the private sector within the U.K. is also important, but for other products, e.g., sheet and tinplate, the BSC is virtually the sole U.K. producer.

The assessment of long-term market opportunities abroad is considerably more complex and difficult than assessing the growth of the home market. There is the problem of assessing the growth in steel demand and imports in various countries, the prices that might be obtained, and the strength of competition from other major producers. Long-run forecasting in this field was less highly developed than for the home market before nationalization and a major effort is being devoted to the groundwork needed for the preparation of such estimates on a regular basis.

Once information was assembled on existing and proposed capacity, it became possible to see what combinations of additions to capacity and closures would satisfy any assumed future level of demand for different products and to adopt a "system approach" in physical terms. The task of adding the economic and financial dimension to this physical framework has, however, been a longer and more difficult one.

COST DATA

One essential precondition is to establish the necessary information on costs: estimates of future costs at existing plant, and estimates of the cost of building and operating new plant. The starting point of any such estimate of future conditions must be a reliable picture of current costs at existing works. The fact that such data have not been strictly comparable between works has been a major handicap, which is now being overcome by the introduction of a uniform standard costing system throughout the BSC.

A further difficulty (which to some extent afflicts planners in all such organizations) is that of estimating the probable cost of new plant whose technical characteristics have only been specified in the broadest terms. In many ways the most important point in the decision-making process comes at a relatively early stage when the broad strategy is determined and a particular set of investment proposals is chosen for further examination. Yet often it is only after this crucial point that more detailed engineering work makes it possible to refine the cost estimates. The need to examine alternative development strategies thus has led to more work having to be done by engineers and accountants on schemes while they are still "hypothetical," and on some alternatives that are bound to be discarded.

The remainder of this chapter is devoted to a discussion of some aspects of what may be termed a "system approach" to economic planning for steel. It should be made explicit that the discussion focuses on the problem of determining the course of action that is most profitable for the BSC. The general assumption underlying the establishment of this type of organization (i.e., a commercial but publicly owned enterprise) is that the yardstick of its own economic and financial calculus is also, as a general rule, a guide to the desirable course from the wider point of view of the national economy; and that the effective application of this yardstick is essential if the organization is to make the most efficient use of the community's resources with which it has been entrusted. There are, of course, in some cases, other important factors to be taken into account, either by the BSC in formulating its strategic plans, or by the government in approving them: for example, the relation between the size of the industry and the country's balance of payments; or the effects on regional development and employment of closures or investment at different locations. In such cases, consideration of the effects on the BSC must be supplemented by analysis of the wider impact on the national economy as a whole.

DEFINING THE SYSTEM

By a "system approach," I mean the need to consider the impact of a development scheme on the whole system of which it is a part, rather than (as in much conventional financial and economic analysis) treating the investment project as an independent entity. Such an approach becomes necessary wherever the sales or the capacity and production costs of individual works are interrelated, and hence development at one site is liable to affect the profitability of the BSC's other works.

The system for this purpose can be defined differently according to the ramifications of the project or problem under consideration. If the system is defined as the total activities of the BSC, then one can be sure of evaluating the effect of the project on the profits of the BSC as a whole. But while such a wide definition is necessary for certain major projects, or strategic problems, it may be unnecessarily comprehensive for a good many other purposes. The object should be to define the system in such a way as to encompass the smallest area necessary for the purpose in hand, i.e., including all areas of activity significantly affected, but excluding the remainder. Thus, for example, in the case of strip mill development it is often sufficient to regard the system as synonomous with the various strip mill works and exclude other works. For other purposes the system may be taken as an individual works only.

In many cases the more limited definitions of the system correspond to the layers of organizational devolution within the BSC:

first, the six product divisions (each comprising works producing a limited number of products, e.g., the Strip Mills Division comprising the strip mill works); second, within each product division, the works groups (comprising a major works or group of works); third, the individual works. But while definition of the system may coincide with organizational boundaries it can also be defined in such a way as to cut across them—it may take in particular parts of two or more separate divisions where necessary. (The concept of the system as an analytical tool differs in this respect from that of the profit center for organizational and accounting purposes, since the former is more flexible and its boundaries can be defined most appropriately for the purpose in hand).

THE CHARACTERISTICS OF THE SYSTEM

One field in which economic analysis of the system has been highly developed is the electricity generating system. This is an extreme example of a system with a number of plants producing the same product, with the maximum interconnection between plant, and freedom within certain technical constraints to meet demand from any plant in such a way as to minimize operating costs. The problem of system analysis in steel is, however, more complex for a number of reasons, in particular the variety of products and the evolutionary nature of much of its investment. (Whereas the British steel industry is rarely in a position to build a complete new integrated works, the electricity generating system can absorb more than one new power station a year).

The main characteristics of the BSC's iron and steel activities viewed as a system for economic planning purposes might be summarized as follows:

1. The BSC makes a wide range of steel products.

2. Each product is produced in several works.

3. Each works can produce a number of different products in varying proportions.

4. Sales to different markets realize different ex-works prices for any given product.

5. Subject to certain constraints, the Corporation can decide from which works it will supply a particular market.

6. The production process consists of a series of successive stages, with the early stages at each works providing a common supply of crude steel for one or more rolling mills each producing a particular group of finished products.

7. New units of capacity are large in relation to the annual growth in demand.

BASIC APPROACH

The first thing that a system approach to the BSC's steelmaking activities has to take into account is the fact that a particular product can be produced at a number of works each with different costs, and sold in a number of markets each yielding a different price. The position at any particular point in time can be depicted as in Figure 13.1. The lower stepped line (which I shall call the capacity curve) shows the capacity and costs (or unit of capacity) at each works (W_1, W_2, etc.) arranged in ascending order of costs reading from left to right. The width of the step shows the capacity of the works; its height above the horizontal axis shows its costs per ton. Similarly, the upper stepped line (the market curve) shows sales and prices in each market (M_1, M_2, etc.) in descending order of prices reading from left to right. For the purpose of the immediate discussion the price in each market is taken as given and the problem is to decide what new capacity to build, or existing capacity to close, in order to maximize profits.

Such decisions focus attention on point X where the market and capacity curves cut, and the works and markets around this point can be regarded as marginal. If costs at the marginal plant are above the price obtainable in the corresponding marginal market, then the

FIGURE 13.1

Market Demand and Costs at Different Works

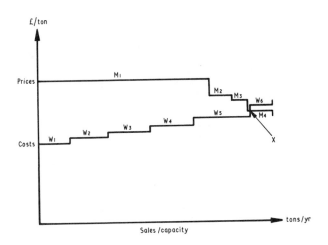

profits of the system would be higher if that capacity were shut down, or not built, and the corresponding marginal market were not satisfied. Conversely, if the costs of marginal works were below the price in the marginal market, the works would be profitable to add to, or keep in, the system. Hence if the objective is to maximize profits, works W_5, in Figure 13.1 should be constructed or kept in operation and works W_6 should not.

DEFINING COSTS

The relevant costs for this purpose are those that can be avoided by not operating an existing works or building a new one. In the case of a plant that is already operating (or where an irrevocable decision to construct it has been taken) the relevant costs are running costs (i.e., all material and operating costs, but excluding all capital charges). Where the question at issue is whether to close W_5 or W_6 the avoidable costs are the running costs of these older, higher-cost works (and expenditure on replacement needed to keep them in operation less any special costs involved in closure, e.g., redundancy pay, etc.).

If, however, the question is whether to install new capacity, then the relevant costs are capital and running costs, both of which are avoidable. Thus, Figure 13.2 shows the total capital and running

FIGURE 13.2

Costs at Existing Works and at a New Works

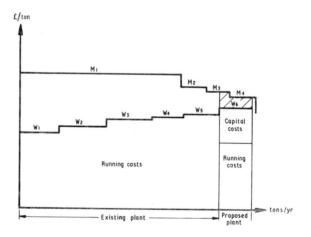

186

costs of the new capacity at issue, W_6. These are lower than the price obtainable in M_4 and the new capacity should be installed because it would increase profits by the amount of the shaded area between the two curves. (It will be seen that the total costs of W_6 are higher than W_5, which is the existing works with the highest running costs. If the total cost of W_6 were lower than the running costs of W_5, the latter should be replaced by new capacity. But, the running costs of W_6 are lower than the running costs of W_1, the most modern plant already in the system.)

ECONOMIES OF SCALE

Where the additional capacity W_6 represents a complete new works, potential economies of scale may affect the picture. In Figure 13.3 the right-hand section of Figure 13.2 is repeated showing both the original W_6 and an alternative larger works W_6' with lower costs per unit of output. In this case profits would be increased if the new works W_6' both replaced the old works W_5 (whose running costs are higher than the total costs of W_6') and also supplied part of the additional market M_5. The increase in profits through installing W_6' (and closing W_5) is shown by the shaded area in Figure 13.3, and would be

FIGURE 13.3

Effect of Economies of Large-Scale Production

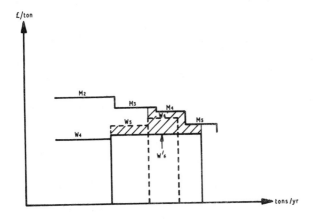

greater than the increase in profits through installing W_6 (the shaded area in Figure 13.2).

THE MARKET CURVE

On the market side, the market curve is not a demand curve in the usual sense of the term. Each step in the curve depicts the tonnage sold in each market at a particular (uniform) ex-works price. But for the home market in particular, the prices charged by the BSC can be varied, with consequent variations in the amounts that can be sold in the face of competition from foreign producers and (for certain products) the private sector. Thus the horizontal lines depicting tonnage sold and prices obtained in any particular market could be lower and wider, or higher and narrower, e.g. M_1' in Figure 13.4. (The curve linking all the alternative price and volume assumptions for a particular market is the conventional demand curve for that market.)

Now assume for the sake of simplicity that the Corporation raises prices (and sells a lower tonnage) in the first market so that M_1 becomes M_1', but that prices and tonnage for other markets are given. (This is an oversimplification, because there is some room to maneuver in pricing exports, but it is a useful approximation of reality.) Then we get two sets of market functions as in Figure 13.4, with the dotted line showing the new market curve with all the subsequent steps, M_2, M_3, etc., shifted horizontally to the left.

In this situation it will pay to penetrate further into marginal markets because there will be more low-cost capacity available for export, e.g., the market and capacity curves will cut at X′ instead of X. The total volume of sales in markets other than M_1' will then be higher; but regarding M′ as the home market and the remainder as export markets, the increase in the volume of exports will not be as great as the loss in home sales so that output as a whole will be lower.

The difference in system profits between the two situations with higher and lower prices in the home market (M_1' and M_1)* will depend on:

_____

*If the BSC were to follow a pricing policy in the home market (and other markets) designed to maximize profits, it would aim to fix home prices at the point where the marginal revenue (taking into account the long-term competitive effects of price changes) was equal to the capital and running costs of the marginal works at X.

FIGURE 13.4

Alternative Market Demand Curves

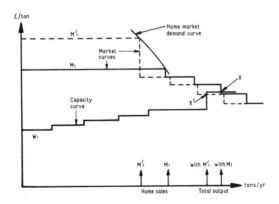

1. the elasticity of demand in the home market; (the greater the reduction in tonnage sold as the prices are raised, the lower will be the increase in profits);

2. how rapidly prices decline as sales are pushed into less profitable export markets M_6, M_7, etc. (the slower the decline, the greater the rise in profits);

3. how rapidly costs rise as more marginal plant (W_6, W_7, etc.) is used (the slower the increase, the greater the rise in profits).

THE PICTURE OVER TIME

The analysis so far relates to a snapshot of the picture at one moment of time—or for practical purposes, one particular year. But decisions on new investment or closures need to take into account the effects over a longer period of time. It is thus necessary to make a series of such snapshots for each of a number of years in order to produce a moving picture of the situation.

The market curve tends to change in two ways over the course of time. First, economic growth in the United Kingdom and elsewhere increases the size of markets. Thus typically a given level of capacity would tend to supply relatively higher-priced markets with the passage of time (i.e., the market curve tends to stretch out to the right while the capacity curve remains fixed). Second, changes in competitive

189

conditions alter the prices obtainable. Prices will be affected by inflation, changes in real costs of labor and materials, technological progress bringing down the cost of production in new plant, the commercial policies followed by major companies, government policies, and the general state of the market.

In the case of the capacity curve, the tonnage obtainable from existing plants will not alter appreciably without further investment, although there will be some scope for stretching capacity by more efficient operation (which will also improve costs); conversely, output and costs may deteriorate at older works as the equipment wears out. Then again costs at successive generations of new plant may improve with technological progress. In addition the cost of production at all works will also alter with changes in the costs of factor inputs.

Thus over the course of time the shape and position of both the market and capacity curves will change. Hence the question whether a closure or an addition to capacity will increase profits has to be evaluated by examining the effects on the system over a number of years and cannot be judged simply by examining the snapshot for one year.

THE WORKS VIEWPOINT

Returning to the basic diagram in Figure 13.1, it is clear that from a system point of view the works to the right of X are uneconomic if the object is to maximize profits. From the point of view of the individual works, however, the position looks different. Each works may be selling in a number of different markets and there is no reason why the highest-cost works should actually be selling its output in the lowest-priced market. Hence examination of profitability works by works on the basis of the actual prices obtained by each works does not provide an accurate guide to profit maximization. In particular, it can make the marginal works look profitable, even when it may be reducing rather than adding to the total profits of the system. In Figure 13.5, the average price obtainable is shown when markets M_1 to M_4 are satisfied by works W_1 to W_7. While costs at each works are below (or in the marginal case equal to) the average price, system profits are less than if the capacity from X to X were not in operation. The maximum profit is the area between the market and capacity curves to the left of X; the area between X and $\overline{X}$ represents a reduction from the maximum profit.

This may seem a simple enough point to the economist used to marginal analysis; but in changing from a situation where a number of works are operating as separate companies to a situation where they constitute a system under one corporation, the magnitude of the

FIGURE 13.5

Maximum Profit Output

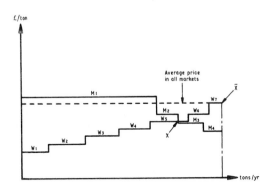

change of approach required from management can hardly be exaggerated.

Indeed a number of large organizations do not, for a variety of reasons, conscious or unconscious, maximize profits in this way. Their objective may be to make a certain specified profit (e.g., a particular return on assets) that may be below the maximum indicated above. They will then put in more capacity W_6, W_7, etc., until the addition of further capacity would reduce profits below the specified level. Their ability to do so, however, depends on the profits obtainable at X being more than sufficient to enable the corporation to survive and expand.

RAW MATERIAL SUPPLIES

One further aspect of these problems, where a system approach may be essential to get a true picture of the situation, is that of the cost of fuel and raw material supplies. The cost of materials may in certain instances be a function of the quantities required and hence of steel output—the recent need to import marginal supplies of scrap at prices well above home market prices is a case in point. In such cases the cost of marginal capacity should reflect the marginal cost of material supplies, which may be appreciably higher than the average cost. This principle applies irrespective of the source of the actual material consumed in that particular works, and again gives rise to a potential difference according to whether the question is looked at from a works or system viewpoint.

ORDER ALLOCATION

The need for a system approach in the way outlined above arises basically from the limited size of markets available and the fact that the BSC has a number of different works producing the same product. It also assumes that at any particular level of sales, the sales opportunities not satisfied are all worse than those satisfied. Hence it assumes enough coordination of the sales of any particular product from different works to ensure that the most profitable markets are satisfied first, but it does not necessarily assume a high level of integration of sales and operations or a system approach to operations. There are, however, potential economies through a system approach to operations and these will in turn affect the approach required for planning purposes. A key factor here is the extent to which the loading of different plants producing the same products is centrally determined (e.g., by the management of a product division).

A basic feature of a multiplant system is the ability to allocate its order load between different works. In the case of the BSC, it charges customers the same delivered price for a specific product irrespective of which works produces it. Hence, subject to customers' preference for a particular source or desire not to be dependent on only one works, the BSC has an incentive to determine the pattern of output between works in such a way as to minimize its costs in the face of a given order load. The problem in principle is to devise a pattern of production that will minimize transport and variable production costs; but in practice there are three essentially different aspects of the problem.

The first is that of minimizing the cost of transport. The pattern of sales inherited from the individual steel companies prior to nationalization involved sales from individual works to markets spread widely over the country. This involved expensive cross-hauling, which is gradually being eliminated. The possibility of reducing transport costs by this form of allocation (i.e., supplying customers from the nearest works) applies even when demand is strong and all works are fully loaded.

The second aspect (which again can produce a potential saving whether or not works are fully loaded) is that of specialization. This is mainly a matter of loading finishing mills rather than iron and steelmaking capacity. Here the object of the exercise is to move away from a situation in which a number of mills are all making a number of different products, and, so far as possible, get longer runs of fewer products on each mill.

The third aspect is that of differential loading of plant when demand is weak and sales are below capacity. This arises partly because steel demand is intensely cyclical: The amplitude of fluctuations in steel demand about trend is several times that of fluctuations in the gross domestic product. It is also a reflection of the fact that additional units of capacity may have to be of such a size that capacity temporarily exceeds demand. Given the inability of the government to regulate demand firmly enough to secure a smooth rate of growth of gross domestic product, quite sharp fluctuations in steel demand are inevitable and must be taken into account in planning. Given the difficulties in forecasting the timing of such fluctuations, and the long lead time between deciding to install new plant and first commissioning it, the industry is bound to go through periods of operating below capacity. Its costs in such a situation will depend partly on the extent to which it can keep its lowest-cost plant operating as fully as possible at the expense of its higher-cost plant.

Taking all these three aspects of allocation together, the problem is to devise a pattern of production that will minimize transport costs and variable production costs. This is a fruitful field for exploration by linear programming techniques. But it remains difficult to represent the problem entirely satisfactorily by such models, partly because cost variations with output are not linear. The customary division of running costs into fixed and variable is an arbitrary one only really applicable to small changes from a specified level of output. In practice, such factors as the size of discrete units of plants, labor agreements, and the technical characteristics of the plants all give rise to discontinuities and nonlinear relationships between costs and output.

From the point of view of planning, the extent to which order allocation is feasible will affect the economic evaluation of development schemes. The profitability of installing new plant will be improved if it can be kept operating at high utilization in periods of recession, and any substantial reduction in activity can be concentrated on the plant with higher running costs. To the extent to which this is possible the introduction of new plant will not only provide additional output, it will also reduce total running costs at times when there is already enough capacity installed to meet the available demand.

Assume the investment in new plant adds C tons a year to system capacity and an average of KC to output: where $K < 1$, reflecting the fact that there is some spare capacity either because the increment in capacity is greater than the growth of demand or because demand is temporarily low. Let the addition to fixed costs (capital and operating) be £F a year. Variable costs are £f per ton at the new plant and average £v per ton for the old capacity C, which has the highest running costs in the system. Now if the new plant is always fully utilized and any underutilization falls on the old plant, the additional cost of producing kC will be:

the total additional costs at the new plant less the saving in running costs at the old plant, i.e.,

$$F + fC - (1 - k) vC$$

which is equal to

$$F + fkC - (v-f) (1-k)C$$

or the cost of producing the additional output at the new works plus the saving in variable cost through using the otherwise spare capacity of the new works to replace the equivalent output at the oldest works.

THE USE OF COMPUTER MODELS

Once the system considered has any degree of complexity, it becomes a fruitful field for the use of computerized models, with the associated advantage of providing a facility for prompt evaluation of alternative strategies and assumptions.

Economic planning models of this kind fall into three main categories. First, there is the continuing model embodying a considerable amount of cost and capacity data, periodically updated and used for a succession of planning problems. The key feature of such a model is the use of the computer to cope with the complexity of the data and evaluate alternatives rapidly. The fact that it continues in use should lead to its acceptance by management as a proven and generally understood tool. In this category a computer model of the BSC's main iron and steelmaking units is now being constructed to evaluate the profitability of different strategies for plant development and closures.

The basic data typically involved in this first category of model are as follows.[1] On the supply side it will embody data on capacity and operating costs (fixed and variable) for each production unit suitably defined, together with the yield loss between successive stages of production. Given a specified demand for each product, in tonnage and price terms, the model must have a set of rules for determining the output of each unit and hence its operating costs. It will then calculate total revenue, operating costs, and operating profits. By adding or subtracting production units, and altering the data for capacity and costs, development strategies involving new investment and closures can be evaluated year by year. A facility can also be built into the model for changing prices of outputs and inputs over time. The results of such models can, if so desired, be presented in the form of financial accounts for product divisions and the corporation as a whole.

The second category of models comprises those that may still be fairly elaborate and require a considerable amount of data, but are specifically designed to evaluate a particular problem. A good example here is the construction of linear programming models for evaluating the effects on transport costs of locating new plant at alternative sites. The essence of this approach is to evaluate the effects of alternative locations on the BSC's total transport bill both for delivering steel products or for assembling fuel and materials (assuming in each instance that sales or materials are distributed between works in such a way as to minimize total transport costs). The regular use of this approach for port and works location studies is making it familiar to a widening circle in management.

The third category of model is the small-scale, ad hoc model constructed to evaluate a particular problem. The use of the computer in this case is mainly to provide a means of evaluating numerous alternatives quickly, not because the inherent scale and complexity of the problem and data makes it essential to do so.

DEVELOPMENT STRATEGIES

One of the advantages of the more general system approach and the associated use of models is that it makes it possible to evaluate development strategies in the sense of a series of related investment projects over the course of time. Revenue, costs, and profits on alternative development strategies (and varying assumptions about the external environment) can be estimated for each of the next 10 to 15 years. The profitability of different strategies can be compared for each year by calculating their net present values and by discounting the different cash flows over time.

The development of this more dynamic analysis helps to overcome the limitations inherent in any attempt to base strategic decisions on estimates of the profitability of individual investment projects considered in isolation. Such estimates start from the definition that the profitability of an individual project is the difference in the profits of the system with and without that project. They run into the difficulty of making assumptions about future development. The traditional way out of the difficulty is to examine the position with and without the new works, on the assumption that there is no subsequent investment in further new plant. This is the implied assumption in most conventional financial assessments, and a useful one in establishing financial discipline because it enables each successive project to be evaluated nominally in its own right. But this process may be misleading, because a key feature of the project may be the impact it has on subsequent development possibilities. For example, if the investment under consideration is the construction of a new works at a virgin site, subsequent investment in new capacity may take place at that site; but if the new works were not constructed, future investment would take place elsewhere and in a different form. Again, a strategy based on construction of a complete new works will involve less subsequent investment in replacement than expansion at an existing works. The concept of evaluating the effect of the strategy as a whole on the profits of the BSC over a period of years, even though at first conjectural and uncertain, may in the event be an essential guide to economic and profitable investment plans.

CONCLUSION

It is natural to emphasize the problem of developing a system approach to economic planning in the nationalized British steel industry at a time when the scale of strategic decision-making has suddenly escalated from a company, and hence in effect very often a plant, basis to an industrywide level. But the problem of the very large enterprise producing the same goods in a number of different plants, exemplified in the publicly owned industries in Western Europe and in a very few major international corporations in such industries as steel and oil, seems to have received less attention in recent years in economic and business school theory (although not perhaps from the operational research world) than their more diversified counterparts. This may be partly a reflection of the fact that the economics of each such industry tends to be a study on its own and something of a closed book to the outside observer. These industries have nevertheless important features in common and provide a rewarding field for joint development by the economist and operational research worker.

NOTE

1. An account of the construction of such a model will be found in R. Holland and S. Hunter, "The Wide Strip Mills Model for the Economic Evaluation of Capacity Developments," paper presented at the June, 1970 Conference of the Operational Research Society in London.

14

LIMITS OF INTERNAL ORGANIZATION, WITH SPECIAL REFERENCE TO THE VERTICAL INTEGRATION OF PRODUCTION

Oliver E. Williamson

That interfirm transactions between technologically separable production stages may be impaired by product market failures and that vertical integration can in these circumstances serve to economize on transaction costs has been investigated elsewhere.[1] But product market failures are only one side of the market versus internal organization issue. A full treatment of this problem requires that the limits of internal organization—organization failures—also be assessed. Although the symmetrical nature of this question was correctly perceived by Ronald Coase in 1937,[2] his treatment—which runs in terms of decreasing returns to the entrepreneurial function and factor price disadvantages in the large firm—can scarcely be regarded as disposing of the organizational failure issue. The matter, nevertheless, has been mainly neglected since.* This chapter attempts a partial remedy of this condition.

The methodological basis for the argument is first developed; certain powers of internal organization are then briefly assessed; and the ways in which progressive expansion of the enterprise leads to size attenuational effects on these powers are examined. The main

Research for this study has been supported by a grant from the Brookings Institution. The chapter is a part of a larger study also supported by the Brookings Institution. The views expressed are those of the author.

*The principal exception has been studies of information flows with cumulative control loss effects in hierarchical organizations. While such a formulation lends itself to formal modeling, it is only a part of the overall problem.

argument, which relies on the transactional limits of internal organization that exist quite apart from size considerations, is developed in the final section.

Although the limits of internal organization in both horizontal and conglomerate structures are similar (and often identical) to the limits developed here, the emphasis on interfirm and interdivisional product transactions gives the chapter a distinctive vertical integration focus. Moreover, horizontal and conglomerate organizations are distinguished by the fact that, in the case of horizontal integration, the additional costs of internalizing the incremental activity may be offset by associated market power effects, while the conglomerate (possessed with the requisite organization form) may permit capital market failures to be internalized to advantage.[3]

The argument also has some relevance for evaluating nonfirm forms of internal organization. For the most part, the indicated limits on firms hold a fortiori for nonfirm forms of organizing economic activity. That firms do not fully displace these other forms of internal organization is because nonfirm alternatives have access to characteristic powers, including a resource base, that firms do not. Developing this set of issues is beyond the scope of this contribution.

METHODOLOGY

The study of the powers and the limits of internal organization is a relatively neglected topic among economists. Many would argue that this is as it should be: with a few exceptions, such as team theory, internal organization is not a subject for which economists, in relation to other social scientists, seem to enjoy a comparative advantage. Unfortunately, however, the study of internal organization in the other social sciences has not produced a strategy for assessing the powers and limits of firms in a way that permits the distribution of economic activities between firms and markets to be treated in a systematic fashion. Among the reasons for this, I submit, is that sociologists, social psychologists, and organization theorists tend not to have a sufficient appreciation of the powers and limits of markets.

The analysis of market (or organizational) failures can be done in a self-contained way by employing an abstract market (or organizational) ideal as the relevant standard. Deviations from this ideal can then be characterized as failures. Frictionlessness standards, however, are rather uninteresting if the problems of firm and market structures are to be examined in an operationally engaging way. The point of view taken here is that the powers and limits of firms and markets are intrinsically joined: one cannot be assessed without consideration for the other. An interdisciplinary, comparative-institutional analysis is required.

A transactional orientation is maintained. Primitive work groups of minimum efficient size, based mainly on technological indivisibility considerations, are assumed to exist. The question is whether transactions between these primitive work groups should be internalized or executed through the market. So as to place the comparison on equivalent terms, a cheek-by-jowl association, if it is desirable, is assumed to be feasible in the market as well as within the firm. (Thus, for example, technological-flow-process economies between otherwise separable stages of production, which require close physical association, are assumed to be available whether the transaction occurs across a market or within a firm.)

Transactional analysis is uninteresting under fully stationary conditions; only when the need to make unprogrammed adaptations is introduced does the market versus internal organization issue become engrossing. It will, accordingly, be assumed that transactions occur under conditions of uncertainty and that the costs of exhaustively stipulating contingent responses to environmental variability are, in a net benefit sense, excessive. It will also be assumed that firms have access to nonnegligible opportunity sets. This is characteristic of virtually all firms in the short run; fixed costs of both organizational and plant and equipment varieties afford the managers of extant firms opportunities for discretion if, as is assumed here, capital markets incur nontrivial management displacement costs. Insularity in the long run relies on monopoly power (at some, not necessarily all, stages) and/or defects in the "natural selection" processes of markets.[5]

The emphasis on "failures" may seem excessively negative; it focuses on the limits and appears to neglect the powers of internal organization. This is partly offset by the treatment in the next section, where the powers of internal organization are briefly assessed. (As will be evident, however, powers of internal organization can be regarded as limits of markets.) But there are also affirmative grounds for studying failures. As Christopher Alexander puts it, "the concept of good fit, though positive in meaning, seems very largely to feed on negative instances."[6] He accordingly proposes that "we should always expect to see the process of achieving good fit between two entities as a negative process of neutralizing the incongruities, or irritants, or forces, which cause misfit." This position is broadly consistent with the spirit of the present analysis.

The argument relies on the proposition that internal organization has both economic and social aspects, and that successive extension of the enterprise alters its social character and/or permits the pursuit of subgoals in ways that impair its economic performance. The usual practice among economists of studying only the economic properties of firms necessarily misses such organizational phenomena, whence the dilemma in attempting to establish the limits of internal organization in anything but a narrow or contrived fashion.

A language for classifying and assessing organizational failures has yet to be devised. That which is advanced here is tentative. It relies extensively on the sociology, social psychology, and organization theory literatures. One suspects that the argument is too much concerned with symptoms rather than causes and that it misses some of the relevant factors altogether. Assuming that the basic approach is sound, however, refinements and extensions to remedy these shortcomings eventually can be made.

INTERNAL ORGANIZATION:
AFFIRMATIVE ASPECTS

Internal versus market exchange is sometimes posed as being a choice between firm and nonfirm. This is not the issue examined here. The choice is between more-or-less integrated firms. Given two related but technologically separable production activities, ought the processes to be integrated or not? This is mainly a transactional issue.

Small Group and Related Effects

Before examining the transactional advantages of internal organization, which is the vertical integration issue, it will be useful to consider first what might be referred to as "small group" advantages of the firm. The argument here relies on the proposition that membership in an organization normally involves more than passive cooperation or acquiescence to authority. Active involvement and concern for the enterprise also result. Partly this is to be explained in quid pro quo terms: the fully engaged employee hopes eventually to receive his just deserts. It is not clear, however, that a detailed effort to "keep books" is warranted on this account. Membership potentially supports an involvement shift from a calculative to a quasi-moral mode (where calculative and moral involvements are used in the sense of Amitai Etzioni).[7] Thus the whole is larger than the sum of the parts, not exclusively because of technological nonseparabilities, but also because internal organization mobilizes energies that, even if they could be monitored costlessly and priced accordingly, could not be exacted in the market by the assured prospect

of pecuniary reward.* The special group compliance pressures that
a membership affiliation affords also warrant mention in this conec-
tion.[9] It should be noted, however, that both of these effects (involvement shift and compliance pressures) are mainly small group consequences and have limited relevance for combining the activities of
what, but for interstage transactional considerations, are otherwise
individually viable economic entities.

Related to but extending beyond these small group effects are
the internal rewards that hierarchical organization distinctively permits. Thus hierarchical structure serves to support an internal value
system and permits status rewards of a sort that cannot be efficaciously
replicated in the market. Consideration for an economy of incentives
favor internal organization in this respect.[10] Also, as Frank Knight
observed, internal organization may facilitate efficient risk bearing
by permitting "the confident and venturesome [to] 'assume the risk'
or 'insure' the doubtful and timid by guaranteeing to the latter a
specified income in return for an assignment of the actual results"[11]
Scarcity of administrative skills might also contribute to vertical integration. As Jacob Marschak notes, there is a lack of homogeneity
among symbol manipulators; there exist "almost unique, irreplaceable
research workers, teachers, administrators; just as there exist unique
choice locations for plants and harbors."[12] Still, it is doubtful that
vertical integration is greatly explained on grounds such as these.

Transactional Aspects

Consider therefore the transactional advantages of firms. The
first thing to note in this connection is that, for the reasons developed
in succeeding sections, internal organization itself incurs very real
costs. But for the existence of market failures, there is no presumption that, once minifirm status has been reached (which permits small-

---

*This does not imply that a reduction in monitoring costs would
necessarily have favorable productivity consequences. It does, however, imply that monitoring has side effects. It is rudimentary that
comprehensive monitoring is humanly oppressive. Chester Barnard
expresses the point in the text in the following way: "It appears
utterly contrary to the nature of men to be sufficiently induced by
material or monetary considerations to contribute enough effort to
a cooperative system to enable it to be productively efficient . . .
over an extended period of time." Whence "efficiency in the offering
of noneconomic inducements" is indicated.[8]

group and related advantages to be realized), any particular transaction should be internalized. Otherwise internalization transforms
what could have been an objective market transaction into an internal
transaction of an inherently small numbers sort—with all of the problems that such internal transactions are subject to (see pp. 213-22).

One of the alleged advantages of internalizing a transaction is
that the adversary interests that characterize exchange between independent parties are harmonized.* What was previously a caveat
emptor relation is transformed into one of joint profit maximization.
Still, the incentives for joint profit maximization operate across markets as well as within firms. Indeed, but for the small-group involvement effects referred to above, firms and markets are virtually in-
distinguishable in this respect under fully stationary conditions.
Greater differences emerge, however, when uncertainty and incomplete information are introduced. Accordingly, such conditions will
be presumed to prevail.**

The properties of the firm that permit internal organization
efficaciously to mitigate market failures would appear to fall into
three categories: incentives, controls, and what may be referred
to broadly as "inherent structural advantages." As will be evident,
these are not independent. It will be useful, nonetheless, to examine
each individually.

The structural advantages of the firm can be illustrated by noting
the important differences between an employment contract and a sales
contract, whether the latter is of a spot purchase or special order

---

*Common ownership by itself, of course, does not guarantee
goal consistency. A holding company form of organization in which
purchaser and supplier are independent divisions, each maximizing
individual profits, is no solution. Moreover, merely to stipulate joint
profit maximization is not by itself apt to be sufficient. The goal
needs to be operationalized, which involves both rulemaking (with
respect, for example, to transfer pricing) and the design of efficacious
internal incentives.

**It would nevertheless be incorrect to suggest that, in the
presence of uncertainty and incomplete information, interfirm exchange is characterized by the absence of cooperation and trust between the parties. (See, in this connection, the interesting discussion
of intercorporate trust relationships by Stewart Macaulay.) It is
sufficient for the argument if the degree of cooperation and trust is
normally lower for external in comparison with internal relations,
which is to say that a qualified caveat emptor conditions still obtains
for market transactions.

variety. This position is to be contrasted with that taken by Armen Alchian and Harold Demsetz, who argue that the firm has "no authority, no disciplinary action any different in the slightest degree from ordinary market contracting between any two people. I can 'punish' you only by withholding future business. This is exactly what any employer can do. He can fire; I can fire my grocer by stopping purchases from him. There is no other difference" (emphasis added).[13] Thus I can "order" my grocer to give me the specified brand carried on his shelf in exchange for the specified price, and his failure to comply with this instruction may lead to my selection of a replacement for him (by taking my trade elsewhere). Similarly, I can "order" a supplier to furnish me with a specified special item under stipulated terms in exchange for a negotiated price.

The apparent similarity between purchase orders and employment relations, however, is incomplete. In the case of the grocer, any procedure for executing the order will do, so long as it is completed in a timely, congenial fashion. Subject to these conditions, his relative efficiency is not a matter on which advice is required. Indeed, any effort on the buyer's part to instruct the grocer on operating matters is presumptuous—clearly outside the scope of the transactional relationship. Although the special order may include some complex delivery terms, the procedure by which the special order is completed is (normally) beyond the purview of the ordering party. An employment contract, by contrast, involves an agreement by the employee to accept, within limits, direction with respect to the time, place, and procedure for executing the task. As James March and Herbert Simon observe, when an employee joins an organization "he accepts an authority relation; i.e., he agrees within some limits (defined both explicitly and implicitly by the terms of the employment contract) he will accept as premises for his behavior orders and instructions supplied to him by the organization." The authority relation is especially important on matters "that are of relatively great interest to the employer, comparatively unimportant to the employee, and about which the employer cannot make accurate predictions much in advance of performance."[14] This contingent instructional relation, which goes both to the timing and procedure by which tasks are to be accomplished, distinguishes the sales from the employment contract. Many would regard this contingency difference as constituting a difference in kind; few would dispute that, at the very least, an important difference of degree exists on this account. In any event, the transactional issue addressed here can be reformulated as follows: should an employment relation be substituted for a sales relation in exchanging products or services between technologically separable production stages?

In addition to this basic contingency difference, employment and sales relations are often further distinguished by human capital effects. Employees acquire firm-specific skills and become familiar with organizational idiosyncracies, the values of which are incompletely transferable. Some are acquired as a result of experience; others are consciously inculcated through training. Although a continuing sales relation may have similar effects, the incentive to invest in transaction-specific infrastructure is less. The differential investment in infrastructure supports a more complex and measured set of disciplinary and grievance procedures than are found in interfirm exchange. An internal control apparatus emerges.*

Constitutional differences between firms and markets reinforce these effects. Thus the firm has the authority to perform internal audits and veracity checks that are unavailable to the buyer.** The resulting low-cost access to the requisite data permit it to perform more precise own-performance evaluations (of both a contemporaneous and ex-post variety) than can a buyer. Ex-post review potentially permits internal organization to distinguish between the effects of random events and of meritorious performance, and in this respect is superior to the market as a mechanism for assigning rewards to deeds. Altogether, internal organization is characterized by a wider variety of sensitive control instruments (including employment, promotion, and internal resource allocation processes) that are available for enforcing interfirm contracts.

The comparative efficiency of the internal, in relation to the external, conflict resolution machinery is of special importance. Thus fiat is frequently a more efficient way to settle minor conflicts (say differences of interpretation) than is haggling or litigation. Frequently such differences are not matters of special importance to employees and, hence, are matters that are subject to an authority relation under the employment contract. To the extent, however, that interfirm profitability effects are implied, similar interorganizational conflict can be settled by fiat only rarely, if at all. What may be a costly arbitration apparatus for settling differences between adversaries, possibly by reference to equity rather than efficiency considerations, must be devised instead.

---

*These emerge even where the employment contract is not with a single employer but is with a common set of employers. The employment, disciplinary, and grievance procedures for longshoremen illustrate the argument.

**Some sales contracts provide for these audits, at least in some degree. Certain military contracts have this property. But the auditing power is limited by the incomplete access of the buyer to the firm's internal reward and penalty apparatus, and by the common interests of the military services with the defense contractors.

Consider in this connection Roland McKean's interpretation of the fiat phenomenon. He asks, "Why is haggling less prevalent (it is by no means absent!) within an integrated firm than between independent components producers and a processor?" The answer that he supplies is that "the manager of an independent firm has a claim on that firm's profits, and lower-level personnel in turn have claims on (i.e., they are rewarded for contributing to) that firm's profits." Employees in the integrated firm find that management fiat is "less costly and/or more rewarding to them than when their rights were linked to the profits of different firms." An implication that he draws from this argument is that where "claims are not linked to increased profits—as in government agencies—it does not follow that integration . . . will markedly reduce transaction costs."[15]

Although this is an attractive argument, it appears to rely on an effort to link profitability with individual employee behavior that is very ambitious and of doubtful feasibility—at least in the policy-relevant large firm to which attention is here addressed. Rather, on the interpretation favored here, employees in the modern corporation accede to the administrative disposition of instrumental issues by fiat not because of detectable profit and corresponding wage effects, but as a condition of employment. By assumption, these are not matters on which employees feel strongly. The efficient disposition of these issues may nevertheless have nontrivial productivity and profit consequences. Such matters are thus properly relegated to the "zone of acceptance" of the employment contract, within which region the employee accepts decisions uncritically, without independent review or resistance. Where frequent adaptations between successive stages of production can be anticipated, an employment relation (hence integration) may accordingly be indicated. Contrary to McKean, the argument applies in public as well as private enterprise, differing only by degree.

Structural differences between firms and markets give rise to information-processing advantages in firms by reason of interest-harmonization and monitoring effects. Risks of contractual incompleteness and strategic misrepresentation are lessened. Investments in organizational infrastructure that facilitate the efficient exchange of information across successive stages of production are encouraged. Economies of information sharing and the convergence of expectations are promoted.

SIZE ATTENUATIONAL EFFECTS

One way of confronting the issue of limits to firm size is to pose the following question: Can a large firm do everything a small firm can do and more? Economists are prone to answer this in an affirmative way. Technological indivisibilities may permit the large firm to realize scale economies that the small enterprise cannot. If, as is assumed here, these are not at issue, the large firm may never-theless enjoy managerial, marketing, financial, or other advantages, and these are not offset by any evident diseconomies. The implica-tions of such a view for the organization of industry are manifestly contradicted by the facts, however. Although something, apparently, is lacking, a different outcome is hard to come by, so long as a strictly instrumental economic orientation is maintained. Recognition that internal organization has social as well as economic aspects and that opportunities for discretion are exercised in ways that favor the individual and group interests of strategically placed members of the organization are, on the argument advanced here, the missing parts. Fundamental internal organization considerations are involved.

Donald Turner and I dealt with one aspect of this problem in our examination of the innovation process. We concluded that inno-vation is not an indecomposable process but instead moves through a series of stages; that large size often is not a precondition for suc-cessful early-stage participation; and that indeed large size, for or-ganizational reasons, can have disadvantageous early-stage conse-quences. Accordingly, we advanced a "systems" view in which dif-ferent firms with different characteristics and capabilities partici-pate at successive stages of the process, with market transactions (possibly mergers) mediating exchanges between stages. In a rough sense, the description appears to accord with observed practice.[16]

The more general problem addressed here is whether succes-sively scaling up the enterprise incurs organizational costs such that, even if technical innovation is absent, a limit to firm size is eventually reached. The size-attenuational effects described are, implicitly, diminishing (including negative) returns limitations on the powers that internal organization enjoys in relation to the market as firm size is progressively extended. Those powers of firms that are not subject to these effects are not considered.

Small Group Effects

The group involvement and compliance effects described above were explicitly delimited by the adjective "small." These effects refer to work groups in which the interaction between the members is extensive and shared interests in large degree can be presumed. Scaling up the enterprise does not intensify these effects, but may weaken or alter them in antiproductive ways.* The quasi-moral involvement of employees may be impaired; aggressive subgoal pursuit may even obtain.

As Robert Dahl and Charles Lindblom observe, large size and hierarchical structure favor impersonality among the parties, which is more characteristic of a calculative orientation.[17] This is attributable partly to the processing of information through an extended hierarchical structural and the corresponding assignment of decision-making to what are perceived by lower-level participants to be remote parts of the enterprise. To the extent that nonknowledgeability impairs moral involvement and larger size results in role incompatibility, which it apparently does,[18] a more calculative orientation is to be expected. The "zone of acceptance" of the employment contract is narrowed, which serves to limit the attractiveness of an employment contract in relation to a sales contract. Put differently, attitudes of voluntary cooperation are supplanted by a quid pro quo orientation. Since, moreover, each individual in the large organization is small in relation to the whole, so that the percentage effects of individual behavior are perceived to be insubstantial, the large organization may be thought to be better able to tolerate deviant or contumacious conduct. Thus both the frequency and tolerance for inharmonious behavior may be expected to increase with firm size.

Similarly, the influence of peer groups on enforcing norms and thereby extending the influence of supervisors is very much a small-group phenomenon. Should alienation from the enterprise develop among members of a group, this power may even be turned against the enterprise in subtle but significant respects. The disaffected group may allocate rewards and sanctions in a perverse fashion. Industrial sabotage is an extreme manifestation of this condition.

Adaptational Limits

The adaptational limits that large organizations experience include a proneness to "overformalization" and a related tendency to "overtraining," both of which have dysfunctional effects. Overformalization is partly a result of the impersonality of the large enterprise,

---

*The argument is related to but is somewhat different from Anthony Downs, who argues that while informal organization contributes to the implementation of the organization's goals, its main effects are dysfunctional. My argument is that the informal organization can have energizing or disabling effects, and that these vary systematically with firm size (organization form held constant).

which gives rise to demands for a more highly elaborated set of rules governing internal due process. This is reinforced by a hierarchical structure, in which felt-needs among managers for defensibility and demands for control and uniformity manifest themselves in extensive rule-making and program specification on functional matters.

Elaborating the internal due-process rules supports equity objectives but tends to limit the flexibility of the employment relation and thus constrains the adaptability of the enterprise. Daniel Katz and Robert Kahn, though they do not make, and perhaps would take exception to, the size distinctions emphasized here, note that the regulatory mechanisms of internal organization "are developed to give some automatic corrections to departures from the norm of organizational functioning. Rules are elaborated and provisions made for their policing. Decisions are made on the basis of precedent."[19] Adversary attitudes between "workers" and "supervisors" easily develop, and antagonistic representations follow. The implicit cooperation on which the small firm can call, and the ad hoc, nonprecedential conflict resolution procedures that it can employ, are both upset.

Program elaboration is a natural result of experience and is a manifestation of organizational learning. The enterprise, when subsequently exposed to a similar stimulus, will have a ready-made response at hand.[20] Performance programs are also important control instruments: "Organizations attempt to control employees by specifying a standard operating procedure and attaching organizational rewards and penalties to it."[21] The amounts and kinds of discretion enjoyed by each participant in an organization are bounded by the programs to which he is subject. Such performance programs are especially important for the control of large organizations; coordinated adaptation between functions and across hierarchical levels in response to changing environmental conditions may otherwise be impossible.

Performance programs are not costless to set up and maintain, however, and such programs may have undesirable operating consequences as well. Even if faultlessly implemented, the expense of introducing and servicing the incremental performance program eventually exceeds the gains. But faultless implementation cannot be presumed.

For one thing, performance programs may be executed in a mechanical, unenthusiastic fashion; they serve as minimum performance standards and insulate the operators from criticism.[22] In addition, programs may have inflexibility effects. Performance programs tend to give formal standing to prevailing practices and relationships and thus acquire symbolic values. The implicit status rankings encourage rigidity. They run the risk of substituting organizational ritualism for instrumental functionalism.[23] Third, even if effects of these two types were missing, highly elaborated

information-processing and decision-making procedures easily lead
to problem recognition failures. Novel developments that require an
unconventional response are misclassified and mishandled because
of their apparent correspondence with existing programs and a common tendency, once programs exist, for perceptions to be biased accordingly. (Although these are partly age rather than size effects,
the increasing reliance on impersonal control techniques that is
characteristic of large size tends to encourage dysfunctional outcomes.)

Internal organization enjoys an advantage in relation to the market in inculcating behavior uniformities. Internal training and social
conditioning, reinforced by the internal compliance machinery, help
to achieve such a result.[24] But social conditioning efforts can likewise be carried to excess. Obedience to authority may become a
hierarchical value in its own right with debilitating judgmental and
performance consequences (see pp. 213-22). To the extent that the
large organization enjoys insularity and is able to cultivate or support
such preferences, overconditioning effects may obtain. In consideration
of the bureaupathological preferences for "complete" control that the
large, hierarchical organization is prone to, this result is commonly
to be expected.

Among the previously indicated advantages of internal organization is that it permits a more highly refined and elaborate status
system than market organization could support. Status awards are
believed to be responsive to deep human needs, permit the economizing of pecuniary incentives, and facilitate communication.[25] Larger
rather than smaller internal structures may accordingly be indicated.
But status systems can also be carried in excess (see pp. 213-22).
What is of interest here is that status systems and hierarchical structure are positively associated and the hierarchical structure of a large
organization is normally more extensive than in small organizations.
Thus the hazards of status systems that are referred to below are
especially serious in the large organization.

As Stewart Macaulay has emphasized and documented, interfirm
contracts (in the American economy or any comparatively high-trust
culture) are neither as complete nor as vigorously enforced as is
commonly supposed.[26] This is supported by the give-and-take attitude of businessmen and by a variety of informal sanctions that are
frequently neglected by legalistic discussions among academic specialists. What is relevant here is that business attitudes toward contracting are not independent of firm size. The large firm may be able, by
reason of greater bargaining strength, to obtain formal contractual
provisions that operate to its advantage in the event of a contract dispute. Also, the management hierarchy in the large firm may require
that its operating parts employ explicit contracting because this has

internal control (accountability) advantages. Such procedures and preferences are not, however, without costs.

For one thing, the costs of negotiating and enforcing comprehensive contracts may themselves be considerable. But there are secondary costs as well. The contract is apt to be interpreted as a minimum performance agreement; what could have been a semicooperative venture is turned instead into an "antagonistic horse trade."

Insistence on contractual completeness and exacting execution thus can run up the cost of doing business beyond what, in a smaller firm, would otherwise be incurred.

Informational Effects

The informational limits of large size are partly attributable to motivational effects, but mainly it is the structural limit of large size in distributing and processing information that is decisive. The more calculative attitude found among employees in the large organization is partly due to the specialization of information gathering and the more limited disclosure of information (on a need-to-know basis) as firm size and hierarchical structure are extended (organization form held constant). Although efficiency purposes are served in this way, there is also a loss of moral involvement. As a result, the nuances of internal communication that come across in a familiar, supportive relationship may be sacrificed. Were this the only informational effect, however, it is doubtful that the large firm could be said to experience a serious limitation in an informational sense.

Surely more important is that the informal organization (which develops within every formal organization)27 experiences very real capacity limits as the enterprise is scaled up, while the demands for informal (nonfunctional or quasi-political) communications are not correspondingly abated. Internal organization is much more prone to politicizing than is market organization. For example (international and love affairs excluded), the concept and language of intrigue apply mainly to intraorganizational conditions. This and other forms of politicizing are more prevalent and complex in internal than in market circumstances. The reason is that the opportunities (and possibly incentives) to allocate rewards on noneconomic criteria are greater internally than in the market. Favors are sought and awarded; animosities, while disguised, are given effect; coalitions are arranged to secure bargaining advantages.28 As a result, the membership of the internal organization is engaged in an internal intelligence, as well as a functional information-gathering, operation.

This is of special interest as a comparative-institutional matter because the informal organization that discharges this intelligence function relatively easily in the small organization is, I conjecture, unable so to perform in the large organization. The demands for intelligence nevertheless continue. As a result, part of the intelligence load is shifted to the formal communication apparatus in the large enterprise. Paperwork proliferates as the practice of resorting to written communications, with multiple copies for distribution to all "interested" parties, is given effect. The ultimate perversion is illustrated by a sign in a railroad office: "Don't say it, write it. You can't file a conversation."[29] Creating a biased record is naturally in the interests of politically vulnerable participants. The expense of bearing this information load operates as a size limit on internal organization (organization form held constant).

Auditing may experience economies of specialization over a considerable range, but it also suffers from what is referred to below as "epsilon connectedness" (See p. 219). Increasing size—organization form and auditing techniques held constant—easily leads to imputation difficulties on account of this connectedness. More generally, imputation difficulties limit the efficacy of internal reward and penalty instruments; free-rider problems multiply and recourse to political (noneconomic) standards increases. Thus although internal organization potentially is able to distinguish between random events and meritorious performance, and in this respect is superior to the market as a mechanism for assigning rewards to deeds, the inference difficulties that it experiences as it grows in size and complexity eventually limit its efficacy.

TRANSACTIONAL LIMITS OF
INTERNAL ORGANIZATION

The above discussion treated the size-attenuational effects that the powers of internal organization are subject to as the firm is successively expanded. But vertical integration also experiences transactional limits that serve to discourage internalization.

It will be convenient in this section to assume that markets "work well" and consider the reasons why internalization in these circumstances is apt to be unattractive. An intermediate market will be said to work well if, both presently and prospectively, prices are nonmonopolistic and reflect an acceptable risk premium, and if market exchange experiences low transaction costs and permits the realization of essential economies. (Actually, if the comparative institutional orientation is to be maintained, what is an "acceptable" premium, a "low" cost, and an "essential" economy must be judged relatively. I assume, however, that rough absolute standards exist that permit a provisional assessment to be reached.)

213

Although large size usually exacerbates the limitational effects discussed in this section, the effects described operate across virtually all firms of any interesting size whatsoever. Certainly all firms of modest size (1,000 employees) or more are subject to them.

As indicated earlier, the internal-versus-market-exchange issue is often posed as a choice between firm and nonfirm whereas the actual choice involves the degree of integration. What economies and diseconomies are experienced by internalizing the incremental transaction with what net effect? Even though it is not really feasible at this time to perform such a netting-out operation, except possibly in very crude terms, an identification of the relevant factors can nevertheless be attempted.

Goal Distortions

Daniel Katz and Robert Kahn distinguish transcendental from pragmatic values and observe that formal organizations have a tendency to overwork values of the first type.[30] This would be of little consequence, perhaps, if the overworking were limited to propaganda statements by the house organ and public pronouncements of the organization's chief officials. Often, however, invoking transcendental values offers the prospect of immediate gains while the eventual goal displacement effects tend not to be fully recognized. Means become an end, ritualism is substituted for functionalism, and severe organizational rigidities appear.[31]

As an example, loyalty may be invoked in support of legitimate goal attainment. Once invoked, however, it may be uncritically extended "to protect the specific means for the attainment of organizational goals so that any criticism of accepted procedures is interpreted as a criticism of the organization itself."[32] Similarly, as David Sills notes, "strong sentiments surrounding obedience to rules are often necessary to protect the organization from the minority of irresponsible members, but these sentiments may cause other members of the organization to concentrate upon the details of behavior involved in abiding by the rules, rather than upon the aims of the organization."[33] Uncritical adherence to the rules easily leads to impairment in the quality of performance, which may result in additional rule specification designed to handle the exceptions. Not only is such an effort itself costly, but it results in organizational rigidities as circumstances change through time. Viability then may be served by widespread rule violation, but this legitimizes attitudes of corruption with disabling effects.[34] It is better that a more "relaxed" attitude toward obedience exists from the outset. Internal organization operates at a disadvantage to the market in that functional attitudes more reliably prevail across markets and thereby serve to discourage the development of ritualistic exchange relations.

Among the more severe goal distortions of internal organization are the biases that it experiences that are favorable to the maintainence or extension of internal operations. Biases of three types should be noted: internal procurement, internal expansion, and program persistence. The internal procurement bias is supported by a number of factors. For one thing, the internal supplier that produces mainly for internal uses may be judged to be at a relative disadvantage in the marketplace. The internal supplier lacks both the large and experienced marketing organization and the established customer connections that nonintegrated external suppliers have access to. In consideration of these conditions, and since fixed costs are sunk, a "preference" for internal procurement might seem appropriate—at least so long as the external price exceeds the variable cost of internal supply.

This may be a specious argument, however, since the fixed costs in question may easily be overstated (there may be a second-hand market for the machinery in question) and individual equipment-renewal decisions ought eventually to be made with reference to the long-run viability of the internal facility. Managers are reluctant, however, to abolish their own jobs. A preference for internal supply may manifest itself by urging that each equipment-replacement decision be made in semiindependent fashion. A fundamentally nonviable internal capability may be uncritically preserved in this way. Internal cross-subsidization may be said to exist.

More generally, the argument is that the existence of an internal source of supply tends to distort procurement decisions. Subgoals of a group or bureaucratic sort are easily given greater weight in relation to objective profitability considerations. This is supported by common membership and the structure of social relations that emerge, including a system of shared beliefs and orientations. A norm of reciprocity easily develops. Equivalence of return between the parties is inessential to this result.[35] The opportunities for reciprocity are more extensive internally (I buy from your division, you support my project proposal or job promotion, etc.) than in the market, where reciprocity is mainly limited to commodity trades that are a matter of record. Distinguishing reciprocal distortion from "constructive cooperation" between internal parties is thus made difficult by the various and subtle forms that internal reciprocity can take. Exceptions from an economic rationality procurement standard are relatively easy both to self-justify and implement in these circumstances.*

---

*The argument is but a particular illustration of the types of politicizing distortions that internal organization is subject to. It is

The expansionary biases of internal organization are partly attributable to its dispute-settling characteristics. Fiat is efficient for reconciling instrumental differences, but it is poorly suited for mediating disputes that have internal power consequences. A common "method of dealing with internal system strain is compromise. The compromise solution tends to make concessions to subsystems rather than requiring them to give up essential functions or resources."[37] This is reinforced by the tendency for both pecuniary and nonpecuniary rewards, at least among the functional parts of the enterprise, to be positively associated with size.[38] An expansionary bias obtains.[39]

Consider now the matter of persistence behavior. Partly this is simply a sunk-cost phenomenon: existing activities embody sunk costs of both organizational and tangible types while new projects require initial investments of both types.[40] The sunk costs in programs and facilities of ongoing projects thus insulate existing projects from displacement by alternatives that, were the current program not already in place, might otherwise be preferred. Moreover, unlike plant and equipment, specialized investments in organizational infrastructure may experience little depreciation. Persistence of a wholly objective variety thus can continue over a long interval.

But persistence is also favored by other factors. "If the . . . administrative system has committed itself in advance to the correctness and efficacy of its reforms, it cannot tolerate learning of failure."[41] March and Simon, in their discussion of innovation, suggest that such commitment is common. They distinguish program elaboration—which corresponds roughly to the program proposal and development stages—from program execution—which involves continuing operations—and note that decisions made at the program-elaboration stage are rarely reexamined at the execution stage.[42]

As a comparative-institutional matter, the question is whether firms and markets can be expected to display differential attitudes toward, or experience differential opportunities for, persistence. Presumably the internal procurement bias referred to above, which

---

to be contrasted with statements such as Coase's that if reciprocity "leads to inefficiency there is no reason why the [firm] should adopt it (since it would reduce its overall profits)."[36] By implication, either the management of the firm is entirely lacking in opportunities for discretion or its interests in single-minded profit maximization can be presumed. Although such assumptions are characteristic of the usual economic treatments of enterprise behavior, severe difficulties are experienced in attempting to address the limits of internal organization issue on these grounds.

is a bureaucratic phenomenon, would support project persistence within firms that is unavailable between firms across markets. Information impactedness may also contribute to this result.[43] Thus it may be impossible, at reasonable cost, to distinguish easily between faulty and meritorious internal performance. Responsible parties who are unable to reveal the objective causes of failure and be absolved of fault are thereby induced to press for program extensions beyond objectively rational cut-off limits in the hope that the environment will change and "save" their reputations.* Sequential decision-making procedures designed to permit project review on the merits, if they exist at all, are apt to be overwhelmed by partisan appeals due to the tie-in of advocacy and administration.[45] Although this tie-in may have the effect of mobilizing energies that would not otherwise be available, the error-admission properties of internal organization would appear to be defective. Fixed costs are not sunk but need to be justified; the decision to proceed is transformed into a commitment to "succeed"—whatever the costs. By contrast, interfirm contracts, which separate advocacy from administration, are apt to provide explicitly for periodic review and have less devastating career implications for their sponsors if "failure" is objectively indicated.

In consideration of these internal reciprocity, expansion, and persistence tendencies, the firm that is considering whether to internalize a transaction or to procure the item in the market needs to consider more than immediate costs. The decision to continue a project, once it is begun, the decision to renew or expand the internal facility, once it is in place, and the decision to procure internally, once that capability exists, may not be decisions for which the ordinary profitability calculus will govern. Proposals to internalize a transaction thus might reasonably be made to "promise" a nontrivial cost advantage. Required rates of return on new programs might be set

---

*Also, "irresponsible" parties may benefit from information impactedness. Thus it may not be possible, at low cost, to demonstrate conclusively to outsiders, who are only remotely familiar with the work, that a task has been discharged badly. Consequently, at high levels at least, "the removal of an official to whom symbolic attributes have become attached, whether for incompetence or for other more reprehensible causes, unless they are very grave and publicly known is felt to be derogatory to the office and to be an injury to the organization both internally and often externally as respects its prestige."[44] To the extent that nonintegration serves better to expose incompetence, which arguably it does, it is less subject to defects of this variety.

at uncommonly high levels to offset these latter-stage distortion tendencies. The widely observed practice of stipulating higher marginal rates of return on new programs than the firm realizes ex post is consistent with the argument.

Chester Barnard notes that status systems have a number of pathological attributes. Some of these involve simple tradeoffs. Thus the importance of status to orderly communication leads to an exaggeration of role to the possible undervaluation of personal abilities.[46] But more complex tradeoffs may also be involved. Even if individuals were ideally merit ranked at any moment in time, conditions and individuals both change. Given the tenacity with which individuals attempt to maintain status,[47] rearranging role assignments and status appropriately through time may not be easy. "Loss of status is more than loss of its emoluments; it is more than the loss of prestige. It is a serious injury to the personality."[48] Since market exchange does not pose these same status problems in adjusting to new circumstances, internal organization may be judged to be less flexible than the market in this respect.

More generally, an employment contract incurs costs that a sales contract avoids (or at least mitigates), since the severance of employment incurs what may be severe psychic costs. Involuntary employment separation may be regarded as a threat to the personal worth of the individual:* "To be a member of a good organization is a personal asset. . . . To be ejected from an organization is a serious, sometimes a catastrophic, injury to the integrity of the person."[49] Discontinuation of sales, by contrast, does not ordinarily carry the same implications. It is a business judgment, warranted by "simple" profit considerations in response to business exigencies.

Status systems may also lead to distortions by insulating incumbents against displacement and permitting them to be rewarded disproportionately.[50] Adaptations to change, for example, are ordinarily the responsibility of those already vested with status; namely, the management. Such adaptations are not performed dispassionately but reflect the interests of individuals initiating the change.[51] Where the adaptation involves adjustments across a market, however, antagonistic interests serve to check the degree of distortion. Status cannot be invoked protectively, while reciprocal favors are less easily arranged.

---

*The personal anguish that an individual experiences is attributable to the web of personal relations that a membership affiliation affords and to his inability to explain easily the discontinuance to others in a way that does not appear to involve excuses and apologetics.

Conflict Resolution and Compliance

Katz and Kahn note that conflict or generalized malfunctioning tends to encourage role proliferation: "The creation of specialized roles is a generalized solution for all organizational problems. . . . It is the modal solution for insuring the role requirements of organization are met; a new role (or many) is added to the organization, the requirements of which are solely to see to it that other role occupants are performing in the required manner, at the approved pace, and in the prescribed relation, one to another."[52] This is not unrelated to the expansionary bias noted above, but here refers explicitly to the extension of the compliance machinery. Policing costs easily become a disproportionate share of the total if these tendencies are not checked. Therefore, where markets may be said to work well, the firm might consciously resist the internalizing of incremental transactions for this reason.

Dahl and Lindblom identify insufficient ruthlessness as a problem to which internal organization is especially subject. Changing an organization imposes status and learning costs on incumbents, who can be expected to resist the change—perhaps vigorously. Hence, "superiors who wish to change an organization must be heavily armed with and ready to use rewards and deprivations against subordinates. Yet superiors frequently . . . identify too much with their subordinates to treat them ruthlessly."[53] The dilemma posed here is akin to that described above concerning calculative and moral involvements. To the extent that ruthlessness in the manipulation of the reward-penalty machinery is relied on, moral involvements are apt to be lessened. Market transactions, by contrast, are calculative in nature. Such relations are inherently impersonal. Since ruthlessness is the norm, vindictive implications or other secondary consequences are mainly avoided. Again, therefore, where markets work well, nonintegration is indicated.

Consider now the compliance limitations to which internal organization is subject by reason of the epsilon connectedness difficulty referred to earlier. One of the distinctive powers that internal organization offers in relation to the market is that it harmonizes interests and permits externalities to be adapted to in a comparatively efficient way. It would be a mistake to assume, however, that inter-firm differences vanish when transactions are internalized. Andrew Whinston notes that free-rider problems often occur when two or more profit centers share a common facility. The frequency and troublesomeness of such issues in the firm that Whinston was studying resulted in a policy of prohibiting asset sharing between divisions.[54] Investments that could be justified only by relying on the joint demands of several divisions thus may be foregone in favor of smaller units that, regarded strictly in technological terms, are less efficient but nevertheless permit exclusive asset dedication.*

The difficulty is that where even small degrees of overlap between otherwise autonomous profit centers exist, imputation problems are vastly greater. Epsilon connectedness prevents imputations from being made with confidence where the size of the epsilon cannot be agreed upon and is costly to establish. Fiat cannot easily be invoked if the distribution of divisional profits is significantly affected. Norms of internal justice, which support quasi-moral involvement, check attempts at vigorously implementing the compliance machinery so long as the "defendant" can establish a reasonable doubt by asserting joint responsibility. The resulting confounding of accountability impairs incentives. Therefore, unless the internalization of externalities is efficacious—in that the affected parts are either efficiently consolidated within a single operating division or internal behavioral rules (including dispute-settling procedures, between semiautonomous parts) provide coordination at low cost—integration, especially in the face of only slight externalities, is not obviously indicated.

Communication Distortion

One of the serious problems to which market exchange is subject is that the information exchanged between the parties in small-numbers bargaining situations may be manipulated for strategic advantage. Internalizing these transactions serves to attenuate these effects. It would be incorrect to conclude, however, that internal communication is not subject to any distortion whatsoever. Thus, although divisional incentives, abstractly regarded, are harmonized by internalization, members of the organization may seek to promote personal goals by diverting the communication system to their own uses.[55] This can take either assertive or defensive forms. Defensively, subordinates may tell their superior what he wants to hear; assertively, they will report those things they want him to know.[56] Recognition of these assertive tendencies is reflected in the common law of testimony in which demonstrated self-interest on the part of a witness can lead to discrediting of testimony.[57] Distortion to please the receiver is especially likely where the recipient has access to extensive rewards and sanctions in his relations with the transmitter, as in up-the-line communication in an administrative hierarchy. The

---

*Alternatively, indivisibilities may give rise to larger, more disparate units than administratively would otherwise be most efficient.

cumulative effects across successive hierarchical levels of these and related adjustments to the data easily result in gross image distortions[58] and contribute to a limitation on firm size.[59]

Related to this matter of communication distortion for assertive personal or group purposes is the possibility that disaffected members of the organization may, rather than quit the organization, choose to subvert it. Members are accorded strategic privileges that are denied to outsiders. Corruption, like intrigue, usually refers to internal affairs. Misinformation may be deliberately planted; sensitive information may be disclosed to outsiders. To the extent that large, complex organizations are more easily subject to such subversion—which presumably they are—smaller, less complex (hence nonintegrated) organizations are preferred.*

Donald Campbell notes that human links in communication systems are prone to a whole series of biases. Some of these biases are little affected whether transactions are organized through the market or internally. There are circumstances, however, where specialized (hence nonintegrated) organizations may have a special advantage.

"Evolutionary considerations lead to the expectation that no constant errors will be found in an environment ecologically typical. . . . Where constant errors have [an ecologically atypical] origin, they will be found to be part and parcel of psychological processes of general adaptive usefulness."[60] To the extent that organizations are required to deal with ecologically atypical conditions, an isolated organization that trains its personnel to be sensitive to the special characteristics of the atypical environment and faithfully to reproduce observations—without introducing adjustments that in general have "adaptive usefulness" but which in the particular case are dysfunctional—is indicated.** Although structural disjunction in the integrated enterprise is possible, integration easily leads to the violation of this isolation condition.

---

*The argument needs to be qualified in that integration may remove a potential entrant (especially where vertical integration is involved) or an actual rival (horizontal integration) and in this respect reduces the risk of disclosure to interested outsiders.

**A similar argument holds where the serial reproduction of transmissions across successive levels—which is usually accompanied by gap filling and other plausibility adjustments—requires that data be retransmitted in original, unadjusted, and perhaps counterintuitive form.

"All members of a person's role set depend upon his performance in some fashion; they are rewarded by it, judged in terms of it, or require it in order perform their own tasks. . . . [Expectations develop which] in the aggregate . . . help to define [a member's] role, the behaviors which are expected of him."[61] The critical structural question for role-design purposes is whether the formal role, in terms of the organizational assignment and objectives and the experienced pressures, in terms of the role expectations that naturally develop to surround the position, are congruent. Structural design error that results in incompatibility between formal and experienced roles produces strain. Formal goals are apt to be sacrificed in the process. Although structural errors can produce such strains in the medium-sized organization, the large, complex enterprise appears to be especially vulnerable.*

A special limitation that integrated forms of organization may experience in relation to nonintegrated is that wage bargains may be insufficiently discriminating in the former—especially in firms that have access to monopoly power. An example is afforded by seat-belt manufacture in the automobile industry. Despite small-numbers supply, with the attendant bargaining problems, as well as indications of supernormal profits among its suppliers, General Motors has not integrated backward into own-supply but rather contracts for these items. A principal reason for this refusal to integrate backward is that General Motors would be required to pay higher labor costs under its labor contract with the United Auto Workers than are its much smaller, independent outside suppliers.[62]

CONCLUDING REMARKS

Both internal organization and market exchange, under conventional assumptions, are anomalies. If the costs of operating competitive markets are zero—which, as Kenneth Arrow notes,[63] is usually assumed in economic analysis—why integrate? But the issue is symmetrical. If the costs of executing transactions within the firm are zero, as is assumed in most theories of the firm, why resort to markets? However useful frictionlessness assumptions are for some purposes, they clearly pose a dilemma in an effort to distribute

---

*The problems that are characteristic of large, functionally organized (unitary form) firms illustrate the argument.

functions rationally between firms and markets. Indivisibilities aside, anything that can be done within the firm can presumably be done as well by successive independent enterprises—since, by assumption, there is no difference in cost. The dilemma is overcome by recognizing that both firms and markets experience frictions, and these must be assessed in deciding whether or not to internalize the incremental transaction (or related set of transactions).

The treatment of organizational failures in this chapter relies on the proposition that <u>internal organization is a syndrome of characteristics</u>: Distinctive strengths and distinctive weaknesses, in a comparative institutional sense, appear nonseparably—albeit in variable proportions—as a package. The principal thrust of the argument is an unsurprising one: Where markets work well, both presently and prospectively, don't integrate. Internal organization, while it possesses distinctive strengths, experiences very real limitations. Thus although the existence of market failure constitutes a presumptive basis for internalizing transactions, only if the "defects" associated with market exchange exceed some nontrivial threshold is internalization apt to be attractive.

The difficult cases, of course, are those where markets experience defects of only modes proportions. An examination of the frictions of both market and organizational types is indicated here, but the current state of the art is hardly able to support a refined net evaluation. Having access to a systematic treatment of the sources of both market and organizational failures, as these bear on vertical integration, should nevertheless serve to distinguish real from bogus issues and thereby facilitate a more accurate assessment. This chapter paired with earlier discussion of market failures,[64] attempts to provide the requisite conceptual apparatus.

It would be useful to develop a rough feel for the relative importance of the various organizational failures discussed. Rather more detailed studies of internal organization than economists have previously undertaken will be required if such an ordering is to be established. Moreover, it will not do simply to replicate the intensive studies of internal organization that sociologists and organization theorists have performed in the past. Typically, these have focused on a particular aspect of behavior and have lacked a comparative-institutional orientation. "Failures" are frequently reported that, in a comparative-institutional sense, are irremediable.

But, for size qualifications, the discussion may appear frequently to suggest that the indicated limits of internal organization apply uniformly to all firms. This would be unfortunate. Recognition of differences in organization form (which includes both the hierarchical structure and internal control apparatus) is also vital to a full assessment of the powers and limits of firms in relation to markets.

Development of this aspect of the argument is beyond the scope of this chapter. It is nevertheless relevant to observe that divisionalization (of an appropriate kind) has attractive properties as a means of restoring incentives and attenuating control-loss experience in the large enterprise although such divisionalization may be more easily accomplished when horizontal or conglomerate rather than vertical integration is involved. Efficacious internal rule-making (on transfer pricing, for example) is of special importance where vertical relationships obtain.

An effort to move the argument to a more elementary level of analysis and develop a more definitive classification of organizational failures would be useful. I am dubious, however, that an attempt to motivate the argument entirely in economic terms would be successful. Some phenomena would be missed altogether, others would be explained imperfectly or with great strain. Rather, comparative-institutional analysis of firm and market structures, inherently it would seem, is an interdisciplinary undertaking. Specialists from the various social sciences may each usefully make their contribution to the organizational failures issue, but eventually I would expect that an interdisciplinary attitude will be required if the parts are to be made to hang together and a "complete" explanation achieved.

NOTES

1. See my treatment of vertical integration in Oliver E. Williamson, "The Vertical Integration of Production Market Failure Considerations," American Economic Review, Vol. 61 (May, 1971), pp. 112-23, for a discussion, including references to the earlier literature.

2. Ronald H. Coase, "The Nature of the Firm," Economica, N.S. Vol. 4. (1937), pp. 386-405, reprinted in George J. Stigler and Kenneth E. Boulding, eds., Reading in Price Theory (Homewood, Ill.: American Economic Association, 1952), pp. 331-51.

3. Peter F. Drucker, "The New Markets and the New Capitalism," The Public Interest, No. 21 (Fall, 1970), pp. 44-49; Oliver E. Williamson, Corporate Control and Business Behavior (Englewood Cliffs, N.J.: Prentice-Hall, 1970).

4. See, for example, Jacob Marschak and Roy Radner, The Economic Theory of Teams (forthcoming).

5. Sidney G. Winter, "Satisficing, Selection, and the Innovating Remnant," Quarterly Journal of Economics, Vol. 85 (May, 1971), pp. 237-61.

6. Christopher Alexander, Notes on the Synthesis of Form (Cambridge, Mass.: Harvard University Press, 1964), p. 22.

7. Amitai Etzioni, A Comparative Analysis of Complex Organizations (New York: Free Press, 1961).

8. Chester I. Barnard, The Functions of the Executive (Cambridge, Mass.: Harvard University Press, 1938), p. 94.

9. For a general discussion, see Barnard op. cit., pp. 170-71; Peter M. Blau, "Exchange Theory," in Oscar Grusky and George A. Miller, eds., The Sociology of Organizations (New York: Free Press, 1970), p. 128; Peter M. Blau and W. Richard Scott, Formal Organizations (San Francisco: Chandler Publishers, 1963), pp. 29, 143-44; George C. Homans, The Human Group (New York: Harcourt, 1950), pp. 294-95; Daniel Katz and Robert L. Kahn, The Social Psychology of Organizations (New York: John Wiley, 1966), pp. 55, 175, 362; J. G. March and H. A. Simon, Organizations (New York: John Wiley, 1958), pp. 59-60.

10. Chester I. Bernard, "Functions and Pathology of Status Systems in Formal Organizations," in W. F. Whyte, ed., Industry and Society New York: McGraw Hill, 1946), p. 68.

11. F. H. Knight, Risk, Uncertainty and Profit (New York: Harper & Row, 1965).

12. Jacob Marschak, "Economics of Inquiring, Communicating, Deciding," American Economic Review, Vol. 58 (May 1968), p. 14.

13. Armen Alchian and Harold Demsetz, "Production, Information Costs, and Economic Organization," Department of Economics, University of California, Los Angeles, Discussion Paper No. 10, May, 1971.

14. March and Simon, op. cit., pp. 90-91.

15. Roland N. McKean, "Responses to Market Imperfection: Discussions," American Economic Review, Vol. 61 (May, 1971), pp. 124-25.

16. Donald F. Turner and Oliver E. Williamson, "Market Structure in Relation to Technical and Organizational Innovation," in J. B. Heath, ed., International Conference on Monopolies, Mergers, and Restrictive Practices (London: HMSO, 1971), pp. 127-44.

17. Robert A. Dahl and Charles E. Lindblom, Politics, Economics and Welfare (New York: Harper, 1963).

18. March and Simon, op. cit., p. 98.

19. Katz and Kahn, op. cit., pp. 87-88.

20. Anthony Downs, Inside Bureaucracy Rand series, (Boston: Little, Brown, 1967), pp. 59-60.

21. March and Simon, op. cit., p. 145.

22. R. M. Cyert and J. G. March, A Behavioral Theory of the Firm (Englewood Cliffs, N. J.: Prentice-Hall, 1963), p. 105.

23. Katz and Kahn, op. cit., p. 88.

24. See the discussion of the command society in Benjamin N. Ward, The Socialist Economy (New York: Random House, 1967).

25. Geoffrey Vickers, "The Demands of a Mixed Economy," Wharton Quarterly, Spring 1971, p. 6; Barnard "Functions and Pathology of Status Systems," op. cit., pp. 68-70, 64-67.

26. Stewart Macauley, "Noncontractual Relations in Business: A Preliminary Study," American Sociological Review, Vol. 28 (February 1963), pp. 55-69.

27. The literature on informal organization is extensive. This aspect of internal organization has been almost entirely neglected by economists. For a discussion of the informal organization and its operations, see Barnard The Functions of the Executive, op. cit., pp. 115-23.

28. For a discussion of politicizing in the context of government bureaucracy, where it is even more prevalent, see Gordon Tullock, The Politics of Bureaucracy (Washington: Public Affairs Press, 1965).

29. Cited in Katz and Kahn, op. cit., p. 88.

30. Katz and Kahn, op. cit., p. 54.

31. Ibid., pp. 54, 88; Robert K. Merton, Social Theory and Social Structure, rev. ed. (New York: Burns & MacEachern, 1957), p. 199; Blau and Scott, op. cit., pp. 228-29.

32. Katz and Kahn, op. cit., p. 55.

33. David L. Sills, "Preserving Organizational Goals," in Oscar Grusky and George A. Miller, eds., The Sociology of Organizations (New York, Free Press 1970), p. 229.

34. Theodore Morgan, "The Theory of Error in Centrally-Directed Economic Systems," Quarterly Journal of Economics, Vol. 78 (August 1964), pp. 414-16.

35. For a general discussion on this and related matters, see A. W. Gouldner, "The Norm of Reciprocity," American Sociological Review, Vol. 25 (1961), pp. 161-79. Gouldner asserts that the norm of reciprocity is as universal and important as the incest taboo.

36. Ronald H. Coase, "Working Paper for the Task Force on Productivity and Competition: The Conglomerate Merger," Commerce Clearing House, Antitrust Trade Regulation Reporter, No. 419 (June 24, 1969), pp. 38-39.

37. Katz and Kahn, op. cit., p. 101.

38. Williamson Corporate Control and Business Behavior, op. cit., pp. 51-52.

39. Alfred Marshall, Industry and Trade (London: Macmillan, 1932), pp. 321-22.

40. March and Simon, op. cit., p. 173; Downs, op. cit., p. 195.

41. Donald T. Campbell, "Reforms as Experiments," American Psychologist, Vol. 24 (April 1964), p. 410.

42. March and Simon, op. cit., p. 187.

43. Barnard, "Functions and Pathology of Status Systems," op. cit., p. 82.

44. Williamson "The Vertical Integration of Production Market Failure Considerations," op. cit., p. 119.

45. Williamson and Turner, op. cit., p. 137; Campbell, op. cit., p. 410.

46. Barnard "Functions and Pathology of Status Systems," op. cit., p. 75.

47. Ibid., p. 78; Sills, op. cit., p. 229.

48. Barnard "Functions and Pathology of Status Systems," op. cit., p. 69.

49. Ibid., pp. 60-61.

50. Ibid., p. 78.

51. March and Simon, op. cit., p. 109.

52. Katz and Kahn, op. cit., p. 203.

53. Dahl and Lindblom, op. cit., pp. 250-51.

54. Andrew Whinston, "Price Guides in Decentralized Organisations," in W. W. Cooper, et al., New Perspectives in Organization Research (New York: John Wiley, 1964), p. 416.

55. H. A. Simon, Administrative Behavior, 2nd ed. (New York: Macmillan, 1957), p. 171.

56. Katz and Kahn, op. cit., p. 246.

57. Donald T. Campbell, "Systematic Error on the Part of Human Links in Communication Systems," Information and Control, Vol. 1 (1958), p. 340.

58. Kenneth E. Boulding, "The Economics of Knowledge and the Knowledge of Economics," American Economic Review, Vol. 56 (May, 1966), p. 8.

59. Williamson Corporate Control and Business Behavior, op. cit.

60. Campbell "Systematic Error . . .," op. cit., p. 340.

61. Katz and Kahn, op. cit., p. 175.

62. U.S. Federal Trade Commission, "Official Transcript of Proceedings in the Matter of Allied Chemical Corporation, et al.," Docket No. 8767, (Washington, 1969).

63. Kenneth J. Arrow, "The Organization of Economic Activity: Issues Pertinent to the Choice of Market versus Nonmarket Allocation," in The Analysis and Evaluation of Public Expenditures: The PPB System, Vol. 1, (Washington: Joint Economic Committee, 1969), p. 48.

64. Williamson "The Vertical Integration of Production Market Failure Considerations," op. cit.

15

RESEARCH ON
SELF-DEVELOPING
FORMS OF ORGANIZATION
Karl-Olof Faxén and Reine Hansson

The research that the URAF, the working group for research of the Swedish Development Council, has set itself starts from greater productivity and greater job satisfaction as the two fundamental objectives that were laid down in the 1966 agreement between the SAF (Employers' Confederation), the LO (Confederation of Trade Unions), and the TCO (Central Organization of Salaried Employees). (All these bodies are described in the Appendix to this chapter—see p. 241). What this means concretely is not easy to express. What can be said, however, is that the URAF could hardly accept a research project with the starting point that the only way of increasing job satisfaction is at the expense of productivity. Correspondingly, the line of reasoning could not be accepted that productivity improvements can be attained only at the expense of reduced job satisfaction.

Another important basis of these experimental activities on new forms of cooperation within enterprises is that the formation of wages in Sweden takes place through collective agreements that are concluded mainly on the national level.* This procedure limits the freedom of movement of the individual enterprises in wage questions.

---

*It should be added that in the manufacturing industry, which works mainly in international competition, the control of wages created through national agreements is such that about half of the annual wage increase—about 4 percent—takes place outside the national agreements, through wage drift. In trade and service industries, where there is no international competition, wage drift is much smaller, and the development of wages is in the main determined by negotiations through national agreements. The development of wages in the industries sheltered from foreign competition is on the whole adapted to

It is true that special collective agreements are often concluded between management and labor in the enterprise, but the scope of these negotiations is restricted by the provisions of the national collective agreements in force.

The same is true not only of wages but also of a number of other questions that are subject to negotiation and collective agreement. Management's contacts with labor organizations on questions for negotiation are normally far more intense than those on questions for joint consultation in works councils.

This means that when decisions about organizational changes are taken in special development groups (containing elected representatives of workers and salaried employees along with management representatives) in those enterprises where experimental activities are carried on, related questions of forms of payment, wage levels, etc., have to be settled through negotiation between the management and local labor organizations.

PRODUCTIVITY AND JOB SATISFACTION AS A STARTING POINT FOR RESEARCH

A considerable part of the work within the URAF has been devoted to a closer analysis of the interpretation of the fundamental concepts of productivity and job satisfaction, as laid down in the 1966 agreement between the SAF, the LO, and the TCO.

The Concept of Productivity

The development of productivity in an enterprise, in an industry, or in the total economy can be divided into three components; labor productivity, capital productivity, and a "residual factor." Labor productivity means the conditions that relate to the individual employee's way of performing his job, such as his utilization of time,

---

wage developments in export industries, through the technique of central agreements and what is called the wage policy based on solidarity. As the growth of productivity in the sheltered industries is lower than in those exposed to international competition, there is a continuous increase in prices, conditioned by costs, in the sheltered industries. This price increase, however, does not exceed what would have been expected on account of wage and productivity development. In this way, the "economywide" bargaining system has contributed to stabilizing general economic development.

the degree of skill with which he does his job, how often he makes mistakes and is forced to repeat certain tasks or perhaps ruins materials.

Capital productivity relates to the qualities of particular capital goods. A new lathe that runs at greater speed is more productive than an older one; a big pulp digester is more productive than a small one since the volume increases by the cube of the size while capital costs increase by the square, etc. The productive capacity of individual capital goods is not proportional to the cost, and this relationship changes in time as a consequence of technological progress.

A certain part of the productivity increase in industry can be referred to these two factors. The educational level of the labor force rises and professional skill grows; capital goods become more efficient through technological progress.

When it comes to measuring the size of the share of the total productivity increases that can be attributed to labor and capital, one must take into account the problem of defining the volume of labor and volume of capital in the course of technological progress. We cannot enter into these well-known and fundamental difficulties here, but we make the assumption that they have been solved in one way or another, e.g., by an index measuring the volume of labor, and by measuring the volume of capital on the basis of historical costs, corrected by a price index.

As to the residual factor—that part of the total productivity development that is of primary interest for URAF's research—the analysis must be more far-reaching. Let us start from the following hypotheses:

1. The so-called residual factor represents an independent cause (or group of causes) of productivity growth. Consequently, it does not rest (except possibly in part) on errors of measurement in the variables (volume of labor and volume of capital), or on interaction effects, that arise when these two variables change. It accounts for a considerable part of the total productivity increase.

2. The residual factor can be attributed to development in a certain system as a whole, not to any particular part of it. By "system" we mean a subdivision of a certain complexity within an enterprise, an enterprise as a whole, an industry, or the total economy.

3. The residual factor is purely dynamic. To study it, a dynamic method is necessary—comparative statics will not capture it. Consequently, the residual factor in the productivity development of an individual enterprise can be attributed to the ability of the enterprise as an organization—independently of which persons form the management—to utilize market changes, changes in production techniques, improved methods of internal organization, etc.

230

It may be a question of how to assimilate a new production technique that is already applied abroad or in other enterprises with similar activities; it may be how to coordinate production and sales internally; it may be how to recruit staff. The aim of research here is to identify the organizational forms or patterns of behavior that characterize a certain enterprise as an organization, regardless of which persons take the various positions in the enterprise or which capital goods the company owns at the moment. Attention is directed at the ability of the firm, seen as an organizational unit, to increase its productivity continuously.

The same dynamic process that characterizes a process of continuous adaptation between the enterprise and the environment is assumed to be important when the internal development of the enterprise is studied. It is assumed that there are internal factors in the organization of the enterprise (some of them will be discussed in more detail under the heading "Job Satisfaction") that, under certain conditions, release productivity growth, which can be ascribed to the residual factor. It is not only a question of interaction between the enterprise and the environment but also of internal interaction.

4. The theory of learning may contribute to the comprehension of the interactive processes sketched above. We refer here to complex learning processes that solve problems. Attention is directed not only toward learning itself but also toward how the organization as a whole increases its ability to learn. The theory of simple learning processes, which can be studied with the help of the theory of conditioned reflexes, does not provide any important contribution in this context.

Of central importance in the URAF research is the role of the joint consultation organization in the total learning process of the enterprise. Up to a certain point, it may be interesting to study how joint decision-making between workers and supervisors in a certain production process leads to increased productivity under stable conditions—for instance, where technology and market demand are concerned. But we know that each production process is exposed sooner or later to important changes in technology, market conditions, or some other similar development. It is far more interesting to look into the conditions under which consultation and joint decision-making can manage great steps in development than to study the decision-making process in the course of continuous development. Is it possible for an organization to "learn how to learn" during a period of stable conditions, in such a way as to improve its ability to solve the problems arising from great changes in, for instance, technology or market conditions?

5. In a variable environment and with the great changes in which we are primarily interested, the criterion of increased

productivity in an enterprise can hardly be expressed by productivity measures based on static theory. The change in the product mix, in the composition of the labor force, etc., becomes so great that index numbers will be inadequate.

Profitability must then replace productivity as an indicator. This is easier to do in enterprises that are divided into divisions or other smaller units for which separate profitability estimates are carried out.

Finally—beyond the profitability criterion—it becomes a question of the ability of the organization to survive in competition with other organizations in the economy. The criterion of an organization's ability to increase its productivity continuously is, consequently, that the organization survive and develop further.

The result of this discussion is that no attempt should be made to measure productivity growth in experimental enterprises or special departments within them by ratios of index numbers for input and output during certain periods, but that profitability should be used as a criterion at an early stage. The accountancy system and internal organization of the enterprise should provide relevant profitability estimates for the decision-making units that have been created during the period of experiment. These profitability estimates should comprise the aggregate effect of all changes that the experimental activities bring about in job organization, in marketing, in the interplay between production and sales, in methods of investment decision, etc. An important part of the effects of an altered organization of work may be a change in sales methods, such as shorter delivery times and better service for customers, which cannot be covered by productivity measures in the form of index numbers, but show up in profitability measures.

However, it is in the end a question of the organization's ability to survive; profitability is not an ultimate aim in itself but only a criterion.

Job Satisfaction

Job satisfaction is an expression of human experiences and emotions, of the relationship between the person who has these experiences and emotions and his work and work environment. Satisfaction or dissatisfaction is something that is felt by the individual employee.

The concept of job satisfaction has developed gradually and has more and more taken on a dynamic meaning. During the 1940s and 1950s, there was a "debate on well-being" that was aimed largely at the physical work environment. Research efforts were directed to physiological and medical factors and questions of industrial safety. Various norms were obtained of what could be characterized as a good or acceptable work environment: Well-being and job satisfaction were defined in terms of physical work environment. (This research has continued and has been intensified in the last few years, for instance in connection with the general debate on the environment.) The general debate on well-being also took the external physical environment as its target and was directed at flowers, color schemes, music-while-you-work, etc. In the 1950s and 1960s, sociological research broadened, the result of this being to supplement the concept of job satisfaction based on physiological and medical factors.

ATTITUDE TO THE ENVIRONMENT

This branch of the sociological research deals with employees' attitudes to various aspects of work and work environment (external physical environment, work tasks, fellow workers, work supervision, time studies, staff policy, wages, etc.). Employees have been asked to say, usually in questionnaires, whether they find conditions of work and work environment satisfactory or unsatisfactory. The answers have been quantified, and then subjected to statistical analysis. Through comparisons between different groups of employees, attempts have been made to express the degree of job satisfaction for whole enterprises or parts of enterprises. The co-variation between the replies to attitude questions and independent judgments of various aspects of work and work environment has also been studied. In this research, the concept of job satisfaction is mainly defined in terms of attitudes.

Job satisfaction is usually measured as the percentage of the group studied that found itself satisfied or dissatisfied with the aspects of work and work environment studied, or as averages (or corresponding measures) on an attitude scale. Surveys of this kind have attempted to classify jobs and work environments as, generally speaking, more or less satisfactory. With a few exceptions, the starting point is work and work environment and it is then assumed that some jobs and environments give rise to satisfaction, and others negative answers to the attitude questions, i.e., to dissatisfaction.

In many of these surveys there is a built-in idea about cause and effect that implies that satisfaction or dissatisfaction is an effect of work and work environment. It is possible to go further along this line and classify jobs and work environments along a general job-satisfaction scale. This point of view agrees with that taken in industrial physiology and medicine that formulates standard values for noise, light, etc., for instance. The concept of job satisfaction is then linked to the "average individual" or a similar standard, and is given the character of a rational empirical concept, primarily based on environmental conditions. A great deal of important information has certainly been obtained about various jobs and work environments, but results have appeared that cannot be explained within the conceptual framework used. There are, for example, jobs and work environments that, seen from the outside, have been judged as decidedly negative, but that have nevertheless yielded positive replies. In many cases, employees in simple, repetitive, strictly governed jobs state that they are on the whole satisfied with their jobs and their work environment. Correspondingly, one work environment has yielded both positive and negative judgments, both satisfaction and dissatisfaction, as defined by the questions.

There are also results that indicate that middle-aged and elderly workers are generally more satisfied than their younger fellow workers with the same kind of work and work environment.

EXPECTATIONS AND EXPERIENCES

These observations have given rise to developments in both theory and method. Psychological and sociopsychological research has led to job satisfaction now being regarded as an expression of a relationship, comprising the individual's needs and personal expectations of his work on the one hand, and his experience of how his work and work environment fulfill these expectations on the other. If expectations are too high or too low in relation to what work and work environment can offer, the result is a feeling of dissatisfaction. If expectations agree reasonably with what work and environment can fulfill, the result is a feeling of satisfaction. Consequently, job satisfaction is an expression of the subjective experience of the individual toward himself and his job situation. These expressions include: (1) the individual's idea about himself, his own value, his ability, his chances of development, his integrity, his identity; (2) how job and work environment correspond to the individual's idea about himself; and (3) the individual's emotional experience of satisfaction or dissatisfaction with himself and his work situation.

The degree of job satisfaction is expressed as the difference between expectations and experience. A comparison of job satisfaction between individuals, or between groups of individuals, can be made through measuring subjective expectations and experiences and estimating the difference between them. Such measures of job satisfaction are clearly more complicated than traditional attitude measurements.

SATISFACTION/DISSATISFACTION:
CAUSE AND EFFECT

The individualized or subjective interpretation of the concept of job satisfaction has also led to a growing interest in how feelings of satisfaction and dissatisfaction change in individuals over time; the dynamic aspects of job satisfaction have attracted greater attention.

In earlier research and discussions, job satisfaction was regarded: (1) in research oriented toward environment, as an effect of job and work environment; (2) in research oriented toward relationships, as an effect of differences in expectations in relation to fulfilled expectations.

At the same time that job satisfaction can be seen as the emotional result of the adaptation process between the individual and his job, feelings of satisfaction or dissatisfaction also become an important part of the actual process, forming a great part of the driving force and motivation.

A lack of agreement between expectations and their fulfillment in work and the work environment leads to dissatisfaction, conflict, and tension, which the individual tries to dissolve. Consciously or unconsciously he tries to get away from this situation. The feeling of dissatisfaction is a driving force toward some kind of activity or action. The effect, dissatisfaction, then becomes the cause of the next phase in an adjustment process between the individual and his work and work environment. This phase in its turn leads to an effect, a feeling of dissatisfaction or satisfaction, which then forms the driving force in the subsequent phase, etc.

In the course of the adaptation process, an individual forms his opinion about himself, his ability, his chances of development, his identity.

The needs and expectations of the individual are adjusted in accordance with, among other things, the demands his work and work environment make. If these demands are too one-sided and simple— if his job is seen as uninteresting and routine—the individual tends to adjust his expectations downward and becomes resigned. If they are more varied and complex—if he finds his job meaningful and interesting—the individual will adjust his expectations upward and becomes active and engaged in order to live up to these expectations.

The feeling of dissatisfaction, the lack of agreement between expectations and fulfillment in work and the work environment, leads to different kinds of activities or actions, depending inter alia on the demands that work and the work environment make. This dynamic element in the adjustment process between the individual and his environment is well-documented empirically. There are a great number of clinical studies among children and adults and also many experiments with so-called levels of aspiration[1] and with expectations and subjective probability.[2] A feeling of dissatisfaction, a lack of agreement between expectations and their fulfillment, is consequently an important driving force in the adjustment process between the individual and his work and work environment. This driving force leads to behavior by the individual that can go roughly in two directions, depending on the demands and opportunities the job and the work environment offer. The individual either becomes passive, and adjusts his expectations and self-esteem downward, or he becomes active, engaged, and develops and adjusts his expectations and self-esteem upward.

It follows that the concept of job satisfaction does not denote a permanent state but forms the emotional driving force in a continuous adaptation process between the individual and his work and work environment. Consequently, job satisfaction becomes not only a goal, a state to be reached, from the individual's point of view, but an instrument, a driving force, that may lead to different courses in the adaptation process.

A SEQUENCE ANALYSIS OF THE INTERPLAY BETWEEN INCREASED PRODUCTIVITY AND INCREASED JOB SATISFACTION

A study based on the comparative statics of an organization in the course of change toward a more democratic decision-making process contains no analysis of why the changes have taken place and of the course of events while they took place. Consequently, it does not supply a basis for a forecast of future development after the experiment has ended. We are not told anything about how the new organization would react if there were a change in market conditions or in production technique. Can the new organization master that task, or will the result be a return to the former state of affairs? How would productivity and job satisfaction appear after such a change, which might be imagined to occur after the specialists have left the enterprise and everything is back to normal?

The main objective of the URAF—to study "self-developing forms of organization"—draws attention to the ability of organizations to adapt themselves, both when there are changes in external conditions and as a result of internal dynamics. The latter is not the least important element. It is all too easy to get stuck at the adaptation to external conditions—the rising educational level of the labor force, increasingly rapid technical development, which shortens the average life of products, increasing difficulty in forecasting the direction of consumers' preference—which all the time get more volatile—and similar factors.

The problem of analyzing self-developing forms of organization and their dynamics is most easily shown if we use a set of concepts that belong to the dynamic theory developed in the economics of the Stockholm School in the 1930s. It rests on a division of time into periods. There is, further, a distinction between discrete changes, which take place at the boundary point between periods, and another type of continuous change, taking place within periods. Among these continuous changes would be found, in this connection for instance, successive learning about a new production organization and gradual shift of the level of ambition, so that the tension between the level of ambition and actual experience of the job situation changes. Discrete changes, at the beginning or end of periods, could be held to correspond in the first place to organizational changes.

Naturally, this is only a pedagogical model that is not intended as a record of what actually happens. But if we systematize the subject matter in this way, we may clarify the concepts. The course of events can be described as certain shifts in a number of continuous variables, which occur gradually during each period, so that certain tensions at the end of the period release an organizational change (a noncontinuous change) at the junction with the following period. When the following period begins with a new organization, a number of new learning and adaptation processes start, which run up to the next period, and so on. In this way, there is an interplay between continuous and noncontinuous changes.

The point of this analysis is that it may enable us to establish a recurring pattern of how changes from one period to the next are connected with changes within the period, and how changes at the previous boundary point influence continuous changes in the following period. If causal relationships of this kind are found, it is possible to discuss various types of cumulative processes and to separate processes that stop after a number of periods and reach an equilibrium from those that continue indefinitely. It is obvious that the latter are the most interesting. The work at URAF rests on the assumption that research workers will be able to determine the character of this process by studying development during a limited number of periods—two or three only. Will it stop, or will there be a continued development toward higher productivity and greater job satisfaction?

Let us take a concrete example. We imagine a change on the shop floor, a change in work organization, such as a new way of arranging for substitutes in case of sickness. Earlier this was a matter for supervisors, but now the working group arranges it among themselves. Is it likely that a change of this character will be the first step in a cumulative process of change, which will later mean other changes, for instance in the functioning of the time-study department? Or is it likely that this change will become permanent but will not release any impulses for continued self-development within the organization?

Let us take another initial change, a change in the first period, for instance a broadened consultation process over questions of scrapping, or in the long-term planning of the enterprise. Is the choice of initial change of decisive importance to the subsequent course of events? And further: What are the similarities and the differences in the processes of learning for different categories within the enterprise, or the shifts in attitudes and levels of ambition, that accompany initial changes of various kinds?

The fundamental hypothesis of this argument is that some types of starting points for self-development lead, reasonably regularly in different kinds of enterprises, to about the same kind of dynamic process, regardless of other conditions. Alternatively, these other conditions may be analyzed and explained, so that actual experience can be systematized in this way.

If we are to hazard a guess, it would be that an initial change in an engineering company that brings about changes only in attitudes and altered levels of ambition among the workers, but has no corresponding effects among salaried employees—who work on time studies, planning, preparation, and similar tasks—will not lead to a cumulative process. It becomes an initial change that will lose its effects relatively rapidly and not lead to continued self-development in the organization. The prerequisite for self-development probably is that impulses pass on in an efficient way to other groups of staff, in this instance to people who are engaged in time studies, planning, and preparation, and that these impulses alter the way of thinking and working among the groups of staff affected. In the following period, this brings a new change in job organization for workers, which in its turn leads to new impulses back to planners, etc.

A cumulative process of this nature probably loses its effect after a number of periods, if it does not reach other parts of the enterprise such as accountancy or sales departments. It runs the risk of being arrested by the accounting system, when the changes brought about during the process are such that the system can no longer adequately measure their profitability effects. Each accounting system is adjusted to a certain work organization. It may answer questions arising from the given organization, and from closely related modifications of it, but after a certain stage in development the system must also be drawn into the process of change. The same is true of, for instance, sales. If a different method of production has evolved, it must influence the method of selling. The enterprise may have learned, for example, to switch between different models within a given interval more quickly and smoothly than before. This production advantage must then be utilized in market competition, so that new varieties can be offered more rapidly than those of competitors. A new, more flexible way of selling in its turn affects the production organization, since sales add greater weight to the new advantages in competition that are already partly developed. In the same way, construction, product development, and other functions of the enterprise may be involved.

The general planning of research must aim at creating opportunities for following a process of change through the various departments of an enterprise. Efforts should be directed at identifying and analyzing the systematic causal relationships through which one function influences another in a cumulative process, so that the organization as a whole develops toward greater productivity and greater opportunities for providing job satisfaction for the individual employee.

The question that the URAF wishes to pose is: Is there a recurring pattern in this process of change, so that certain features are repeated, for instance, in the dispersion from the shop floor to the planning department, in the dispersion back from planning to the shop floor, in the further dispersion to the construction department, in the dispersion back from construction to planning, back to the shop floor, then from there perhaps to sales, etc.?

The specialists engaged in this research cannot stay in an enterprise more than for a few of these phases of dispersion, or periods, using the term borrowed from the sequence analysis of economics. Consequently, no particularly long chain of periods can be observed in any single project. But one might hope to obtain knowledge of what a long chain in an actual process of change can look like by combining systematized information about different components, for instance from a project on the shop floor, a project on supervising, one on time study departments, and so on.

For the purpose of its research, URAF has tackled the problem with the help of a schedule, under which different projects are set in motion from different starting points. The next step is to find out if there are similar courses of events—if any regularly recurring patterns can be discerned in the processes in different departments of the enterprise that we can observe from the different projects.

Consequently, what is interesting and generally valid is not whether a certain step leads to a great or small increase in productivity and job satisfaction, measure in a certain way, but whether this step may be a link in a longer chain of changes of an interesting character. For example: When assembling certain kinds of engines, workers, supervisors, and production technicians carry out an experiment together, which leads to a relatively limited increase in productivity and job satisfaction. This is what happens in the first period.

In the second period, the production technicians go home—they analyze their experiences and draw certain general conclusions. Then the interesting element enters: The production technicians transform these conclusions into a new expansion of production, and they then have an entirely different degree of freedom regarding the old manufacturing process. They can order new machinery and design a new layout on the basis of their fresh ideas.

The third period begins with the new plant being put into operation. There may not be a very great increase in productivity and job satisfaction in the third period, but a new pattern of joint consultation is established, and on a much larger scale. During this period, perhaps several hundred workers are involved, since production is now on a considerable scale.

The pattern of joint consultation leads to a new form of organization, which in the fourth period utilizes the new machinery and the new layout of the factory in a better way than the production technicians had devised for the third period. Only then—in the fourth period—does the truly interesting change take place in productivity and job satisfaction.

At this stage the experiment ends. Are there prospects for further development? There are if the management draws conclusions from what has happened and brings new units into the chain of events, initiates new joint consultation processes, and so on. The condition for this to be meaningful is that the pattern for self-development formed during the first four periods of the process can be transferred to other relationships within the enterprise, for instance between production and sales, bringing positive effects for productivity and job satisfaction.

What we believe to be important in our research is to identify the mutual causal relationships between, on the one hand, the gradual shifts in knowledge, levels of ambition, and whatever variables are used in the periods and, on the other, the changes in organization that take place at the boundary points between periods. In this way, the conditions are created for constant self-development. A basis is also laid for a discussion of the stability of the process.

This line of thinking is important also from another point of view. The form of organization and the fundamental ideas that characterize this area are old and have a long history. They have not developed by chance. They are connected in a fundamental manner with the structure of society as a whole. It is largely the same pattern that recurs, whether it is the way in which the Ministry of Education governs the school system, or the way problems of command in military organizations are solved, or the way business enterprises tackle problems. If we wish to create real democracy at the place of work, there must be far-reaching shifts in attitudes, ambitions, and expectations among employees in different positions. There are no magic tricks that can change these relationships significantly.

The only possibility of obtaining something different from what already exists lies in finding feasible initial changes, relatively marginal changes in previous forms, that can actually be carried out, in agreement with the parties involved, but that are of a nature to give rise to a sequence of events through their own momentum. There may, for instance, be many ways of changing the organization of work, so that it adapts itself better to the higher educational level of the labor force, but that do not have the potential for self-development. That kind of change is not so interesting as those that are largely propelled by their own dynamic force. Only the latter kind of change can start a continuing process of self-development, a stable cumulative process of interaction between increased productivity and greater job satisfaction.

APPENDIX: SWEDISH WORKS COUNCILS—HISTORY AND CONTRACTUAL FRAMEWORK

The first agreement on works councils in Sweden was made in 1946 between the Employers' Confederation (SAF), the Confederation of Trade Unions (LO) and the Central Organization of Salaried Employees (TCO). The basis for workers' participation in management in Sweden was thus established through collective agreements between the central organizations in the labor market and not through legislation. There is no provision in Swedish legislation for the representation of employees on the boards of corporations or other decision-making bodies within the enterprises in which they are employed.

A works council in a Swedish corporation is a medium for information and joint consultation within the firm, between the management and the employees through their trade union organizations. According to the 1946 agreement, a works council could discuss questions concerning techniques, organization, planning, and development of production. The employer was obliged to provide the council with continuous production reports, to explain proposed or implemented alterations or other important changes in production or working conditions in the firm. The employees' representatives were encouraged to submit suggestions to the employer on the same matters.

It should be noted that Swedish works councils were set up as tripartite bodies, with not only manual workers but also salaried employees, including special representatives for supervisors and foremen.

A works council cannot commit its constituent parties by binding agreements in matters of substance. Wage and salary questions, including the application of piece rates, or other "bargaining matters," are handled exclusively through negotiations between employers and trade unions. The task of the works council is to pave the way for practical cooperation in the daily business, by acting as a channel of regular two-way communication between the employer and his workers and salaried employees. This is to be done along three main lines: through regular <u>information</u> on the conditions of production, with past achievements and future changes, to be given by the employer; through <u>consultation</u> about all issues of common interest except personal matters and issues normally dealt with by the negotiating bodies; and finally by arranging for <u>suggestions</u> from all employees to be encouraged, evaluated, and passed on for practical application wherever possible.

In 1966 a new agreement on works councils was concluded between the SAF, the LO, and the TCO. One novel feature was a clause authorizing the employer to delegate to the works council the right to make decisions in certain restricted areas, e.g., welfare questions within the given budget framework and awards for suggestions. Personnel policy, but not individual cases, was now included among the items to be discussed.

Another important change was an obligation on the employer to inform and consult the works council in advance of important decisions by the management or by the board of directors. An exception was made, however, when the disclosure of a certain fact might result in damage to the interests of the firm.

The representatives of the employees have put special emphasis upon this provision in relation to decisions about layoffs, or when it is decided to close down a whole plant. In many corporations, works council meetings regularly precede board meetings by a few days, in order to enable the managing director to consult the works council before decisions are made by the board of directors.

A number of studies have been made both by the Employers' Confederation and by the trade union organizations about the activities of the works councils and their effects. A general conclusion is that they have meant a great deal for spreading understanding of management problems among council members. This is not unimportant, since local trade union leaders are often members of the works council. In this way, the chief bargaining agents within the firm have access to an institutional channel for regular information. There is also an established procedure for giving information about changes in production, employment, etc., in extraordinary situations. On the other hand, the average worker or salaried employee is not affected very much by the exchange of information and improved understanding in the works council. His attitudes to his own problems, relating to his immediate surroundings—the tasks he has to perform, working conditions, safety and health factors at his place of work, his relations with fellow workers and first-line supervisors—are not influenced to any great extent.

Against the background of these experiences, an important feature of the 1966 agreement was the establishment of the Development Council (with five representatives of the SAF, three of the LO, and two of the TCO) with the purpose of promoting new forms of labor-management cooperation that would permit the individual employee's influence on his own working conditions to increase and thus have a real meaning for him. In the 1966 agreement, the SAF, the LO, and the TCO formulated the objectives of future development in the following way: The organizations wish to lay down two fundamental objectives toward which local collaboration should aim—regardless of the forms in which it is carried on. These are greater productivity and greater job satisfaction. It is obvious that these objectives, which are more fully discussed and defined below, are closely connected; at the same time it is clear that each of them is in itself a desirable aim.

Productivity

The chief function of business in society is to bring about profitable production. In order to exist, modern society must have an efficient and well-developed production apparatus in which human and material resources can be coordinated for the best possible production result to be attained, while at the same time due consideration is given to those engaged in the process of production. Efforts to create as efficient a production apparatus as possible are therefore in everybody's interest. Important prerequisites for high productivity on the part of firms in a dynamic society are that everyone is engaged in the structure of the undertaking and prepared, where necessary, to acquire new knowledge and skills, and that in the work of rationalization, due attention is paid to the employees' need for information, consultation, training, and security of employment.

Job Satisfaction

For the employee it is a cardinal necessity to have a job he finds interesting and meaningful. Job satisfaction, the objective of collaboration with which we are concerned here, therefore calls attention to the fact that the place of work must afford a good working environment and to certain other requirements affecting the work itself. The firm must not merely produce goods and services—it must also endeavor to see that this is done under such conditions that the knowledge and abilities of the employees are utilized to the greatest possible extent. In this connection the management must pay particular attention to the framing of the individual employee's duties and to the selection of persons for various jobs. As far as the exigencies of daily work permit, the individual should be given the opportunity to contribute to the formation of his own working environment.

In 1969, the Development Council formed a special working group for research, the URAF (The Development Council for Collaboration in Firms). The URAF issued its first Annual Report in February 1971.

NOTES

1. K. Lewin, Field Theory in Social Science (London: Tavistock Publications, 1952).

2. J. W. Atkinson, ed., Motives in Fantasy, Action and Society (New York: Van Nostrand, 1958).

16

PUBLIC
RESPONSIBILITY IN
THE PRIVATE CORPORATION
Kenneth R. Andrews

For the past 40 years, the enterprise system serving as the engine of the American economy has been increasingly modified by a doctrine of social responsibility. By "social responsibility" we mean voluntary restraint of short-term profit maximization. This restraint, not required by law, is purportedly exercised in the public interest. It reflects a judgment by the managers of a corporation that their powers are ultimately subject to public expectations that extend beyond the stockholders' interest in profit. The emerging doctrine recognizes that the "invisible hand" of competition, postulated in the Wealth of Nations as the ethical balance wheel preventing the self-seeking of men striving against each other from harming the public, does not adequately check the power of great corporations capable of shaping their environments. A central assumption of this adaptation of economic theory is that regulation by government, while to some degree essential under imperfect competition, is not sufficiently knowledgeable, subtle, or effective to reconcile the self-interest of corporate entrepreneurship and the needs of a society being sore-tried as well as served by economic activity.

I should like in this chapter to acknowledge the difficulties of specifying precisely this theory of social responsibility, to assert nonetheless its powerful impact upon management behavior, to defend its validity as a partial substitute for increased regulation of private enterprise by the state, and to indicate how consideration of the public interest is brought into the strategic planning and policy-formulation processes of the professionally managed corporation. The evolution of the American economic system, the security of the franchise granted by the American public to the private firm, the relationship between the individual and the company for which he works, and the very quality of national life will be crucially affected by the extension in practice of the concept of social responsibility. The world importance of this concept becomes apparent as we draw analogies between national and regional economies, and its perplexity is not only a provincial concern, eccentrically American.

Discussion of the ways in which profit maximization is or should be modified by attempting to foresee the impact upon society of economic activity has indeed been confused. Issues have been clouded by imprecision of vocabulary. Practical ethics have not been disciplined by a developed theory. Ideologically inspired emotion, equating (for example) responsibility with state socialism or profit-seeking with piracy, sometimes makes discussion incoherent. Hypocrisy offers noble words to mask business as usual and honest intentions may be doubted by observers or fail in the marketplace. Hopes for the perfectability of managers in some quarters are paralleled by suspicions in others that all businessmen are venal. Men who mean well rationalize costly social investment as, in the long run, economic either because of government regulation fended off or expected discrimination in the marketplace in favor of responsibility. The distinction between a rationalized and a genuine social contribution is as difficult to draw as between short-term and long-term profits. Where opposite tendencies must be reconciled by experience and skill in successive particular situations, as is clearly the case in balancing public and private interests, generalization becomes difficult.

The subject is above all controversial. The American public is generating these days a passionate interest in consumer protection, rescue of the environment from pollution, and social justice. Even shareholder meetings are disturbed by insistence upon corporate involvement in these movements. Although the proponents do not command majorities in the voting of shares, they have alerted institutional holders of corporate securities, who own 40 percent of securities listed on U.S. stock exchanges, to the need to take stands. They have contributed already to new legal standards for corporate activity and have influenced managements, not insensitive to the future significance of today's youth movements, to reexamine settled policies and old industry practices. Under no obligation to produce return on shareholders' investment themselves, these critics expect much greater investment in, for example, pollution control than is compatible with making a large enough return to satisfy shareholders and to sustain the growth of the corporation. They generate resistance from people like the president of General Motors, not because of the direction recommended but the speed expected.

THE CASE FOR ABSTENTION

Led conceptually by Milton Friedman, the opponents of the
burgeoning doctrine of social responsibility fight back. In Capitalism
and Freedom, Friedman argues that the doctrine of social responsibility is a "fundamentally subversive doctrine" in a free society.
In such a society, "there is one and only one social responsibility
of business—to use its resources and engage in activities designed to
increase its profits so long as it stays within the rules of the game,
which is to say, engages in open and free competition without deception
or fraud."[1] The manager is the agent of the corporation's owners;
his primary responsibility is to them. The desires of the stockholders are assumed to be making as much money as possible while
conforming to basic rules. The manager who makes decisions
affecting immediate profit by reducing pollution more than present
law requires, for example, is in effect imposing taxes and acting
without authority as a public employee.

Friedman's argument assumes that the stockholder is "economic
man," interested only in maximum short-run profit with minimum
deference to legal and ethical restraints. U.S. courts, in upholding
against stockholder suits the legality of corporate contribution to
education, have suggested that stockholders themselves have responsibilities as citizens. The legality of corporate contributions to the
public welfare implies that the managers of corporations are entitled
to use their judgment in reconciling immediate return with future
growth, maximum present profit with future return, corporate interests
with the interests of the community. In actual practice, the stockholders of large publicly held corporations do not pick directors,
hire managers, or set the dividend rates. Except in recourse to their
legal powers in case of emergency or rebellion, stockholders and
institutional investors vote shares as management suggests. The
actual power of an individual stockholder to give effect to his preference
for maximum short-run profit is exercised not by changing management policy but by selling his stock.

The notion that the shareholder of a large, publicly held corporation is its owner grows increasingly indefensible. He owns shares,
which represent so small a commitment on his part that he may,
through the mechanisms of the stockmarket, shed it instantly.
Management, to whom has come a virtually permanent delegation of
authority for continuing direction of the publicly held corporation,
is still bound to run the company to serve shareholder interest. But
neither by law nor by custom does it have the simple obligation to
pursue maximum profit. There is no reason in any case to suppose
that over time a socially responsible management will necessarily
make less money, pay fewer dividends, and achieve less appreciation

of share price than the firm run by managers who are only as responsible as the law requires. Since the single-minded profit maximizer is likely to be so shortsighted that he misjudges changing market opportunity and the needs of his own organization, the shareholder, as economic man, needs both clairvoyance and the agility to sell in a hurry.

Beneath the argument that the corporate strategist should confine himself to his economic function is often a bleak view of the typical general manager's personal values and capability. Ranging from scepticism to contempt, this estimate of business leadership is accompanied by the assumption that expertness in the social problems partially caused by industry lies outside industry in the universities or legislatures of the country. Even nearer the root of the argument for isolationism is the undeniable central conflict in responsibility between the need, on the one hand, to make and show continually impressive profits in order to sustain price/earnings ratios and the market values of stockholders' equity, and the costs, on the other hand, of dealing with such by-products of economic activity as water and air pollution. This conflict persists, long after we condemn gross forms of greed and corruption.

Business is most heterogeneous. It has, even more than other areas of human activity, back alleys of self-interest in which the struggle for survival breeds desperation. It has comfortable front offices, as well, in some of which greed fed by success produces various forms of piracy. The rigors of competition, no less harsh for being "imperfect" in the economic sense, develop in the morally weak the temptation to cut corners and to conceal as long as possible the social costs of careless economic activity and other offenses against the public.

But the morality of cutthroat competition or occasional fraud in more elegant surroundings is not really our concern here. For even well-meaning, honest, and educated men the pressure to attain profit targets compels postponement of socially directed projects more often than it prompts unethical acts. The pressures of the present at the expense of the future, the motives of the profit-centered manager to win the approval of his superiors by meeting his profit commitments, the system of control of decentralized operations, and the need to satisfy quantitative measures of performance divert effort away from social problems that otherwise might be susceptible to effective but expensive attention.

The central conflict between self-interest and social concern cannot be explained away. So long as it exists, it can be used with a dash of cynicism to note that it is not easy to reconcile them nor likely that business leaders should even wish to. If we add to the difficulty of striking a balance between divergent interests the problem of establishing standards for ethical behavior in complex situations, we may conclude that those who wish to argue against corporate involvement in noneconomic activities will always have something to say. Piracy, hypocrisy, and naiveté can always be alleged or detected in business activity.

THE CASE FOR INVOLVEMENT

The arguments for the active participation of corporations in public affairs and for the assumption of responsibility for the impact of economic activity upon society are nonetheless gaining ground. It appears to be propelled by four fundamental ideas. The first is that government regulation, certainly essential for the provision of ground rules for competition and the prohibition of grossly improper and dishonest behavior, is neither a subtle instrument for reconciling private and public interests nor an effective substitute for knowledgeable self-restraint. The second proposition is that in an industrial society, corporate power, vast in potential strength, must be brought to bear on certain social problems if they are to be solved at all. The third proposition is that corporate executives of the integrity, intelligence, and humanity required to run substantial companies cannot be expected to confine themselves to narrow economic activity and ignore its social consequences. Finally, the dangers and problems of corporate participation in public affairs can be dealt with through research, education, government control, and self-regulation. To each of these propositions we must give some attention.

The idea that businessmen should be free of the need for self-restraint rests on the assumption that government regulation can be sufficiently specific, knowledgeable, and timely to check or forestall abuse without being damaging to initiative. We have had much experience in the United States with regulation. Besides surveillance of business activities by the courts and numerous administrative agencies, we have the influential hearings into industrial activity by the Congress.

Our national experience with government regulation should tell us that, necessary as is regulation, it cannot possibly design the ideal relationship between the corporation and society. the leaders of virtually every industry, as a matter of ideology and desire to exploit unchecked newly discovered opportunity, once fought all regulation as evil and whatever practical made captive in one way or another the agency assigned to regulate them. With a decline in the hostility between business and government developed during the recent history of the relationship between the Defense Department, the Space Administration, and the Atomic Energy Commission with large-scale business, and with greater understanding in government of the problems of doing business, the present disposition of business leaders is to recognize the need for standards in such matters as drug quality, tire and automobile safety, advertising claims, and other matters in which bad practice by one firm makes good practice economically impossible for all. Even acquiescence to a simple rule-setting role for regulation has been hard to achieve, but no responsible voice commanding a following now argues that government regulation can be dispensed with. The realization that it should be designed in negotiation between lawmakers and affected industries to make it fair and effective is a recent consequence of a redirection of business interests away from evading all regulation toward seeking rules that would make ethical competition feasible.

At the same time, it is clear that new forms of regulation come late to the problem, as in the case of water and air pollution. When the problems are far advanced, it is hard to design incentives and restraints equitably. They become expensive and cumbersome to administer over the protests of competitors not acceding to the justice of the regulation. The incentives and rewards for members of regulatory agencies do not attract talent equal to their problems. Our economic system is based on the fertility of entreprenuerial initiative; we seek, therefore, to leave as much room for initiative as possible. Freedom is predicated more on responsibility than police power. If corporate power is to be regulated more by public law than by private conscience, a large part of our national energy will have to be spent keeping watch over corporate behavior, ferreting out problems, designing and revising detailed laws to deal with them, and enforcing those laws even as they become obsolete.

The alternative to much greater but still inadequate intervention by the state in economic affairs is for businessmen to assume responsibility early as a matter of conscience rather than accept it late as a matter of law. The principal justification for leaving corporate power relatively unchecked is the emergence of the doctrine of social responsibility. This doctrine is the only alternative we have to an unworkable extension of the role of government in our economic system. It will, of course, never be prudent to rely only on the conscience of individuals, to relinquish the role of fair and sensible laws, or to suspend public criticism of business practice. We cannot dispense, as Friedman would like us to, with every form of regulation. But to argue that a businessman should knowingly ignore the consequences of his company's impact upon its physical and social environment until new laws are passed is, in this day, wantonly irresponsible in itself.

The public expectation that business will behave not only legally but with visible regard for the rights of competitors, customers, and the general public grows rapidly more determined. The critics of business, once content to condemn corporate behavior in clinical ignorance on the basis of ideological assumptions alone are now testing the advertised nutritional value of foodstuffs, checking into the quality of automobile service, measuring the effectiveness of emission control devices, comparing the prices of branded and generic drugs, just as our students are criticizing the relevance of their college educations and the slow pace with which the nation approaches its social problems. The only practical response to this movement is acknowledgment of its power and authority. Because the executive of today is ordinarily as sensitive as other citizens to the upgrading of our goals as a society, he cannot for long be told that concern for the problems of society, especially those that his company wittingly or unintentionally worsens, are none of his business.

We turn now to the second proposition underlying the present redefinition of corporate responsibility. It has become commonplace to assert that in a corporate society corporate power is necessary to solve problems beyond the reach of local and national government, of nonprofit organizations, and of individuals. In the Johnson and Nixon administrations, the invitation to businessmen and corporations to move into the public arena has become more fervent. Corporate involvement in public issues is increasing on two fronts—educational activity as a contribution to community development and entrepreneurial ventures in needed services expected to produce some profit for the service rendered. Business has expanded its search for opportunity to devise reclamation procedures for exhaust gases, and for effluent and solid waste, entering into occasional joint research contracts, as in one instance to find a practical way for utilities to recapture sulfur from the burning of fuel oil. Here, of course, the economic compulsion is to make the process feasible—i.e., at least profitable enough to justify investment in research and equipment. But the principal motive clearly is to make economical the reduction of pollution, rather than to seek profit as such. The supply of free sulfur is indeed abundant.

The entry of a number of firms like General Electric, Litton Industries, Westinghouse, and Xerox into education, and the efforts of Lockheed, Ford, and of many other companies to rehabilitate housing, establish factories and training facilities in ghettos similarly reflect a recognition of obligation even more than a search for market opportunity. The quest to make these ventures profitable is to make them effective and expansible, not to make money out of the misfortunes of the poor.

The suspicion that once would have attended corporate attention to public problems is less virulent today. The arguments that a company should pursue only those growth opportunities that produce the greatest profit possibility are losing force. For even the most successful company there is not much money to be made in the ghetto; the hiring of persons from disadvantaged minority groups does not increase productivity. The need to extend the benefits of a technological-industrial system to these areas are seen as important enough to justify corporate entry. Many social problems are left unattended by medicine, the law, the church, and the schools, and are beyond the reach of legislators. They are complex enough to be worthy of the highest technical, professional, and organizational skills that business executives can muster.

The safeguarding of the public from exploitation at corporate hands has as yet been less of a problem than, for example, corruption in the disbursement of public funds by local public agencies. The visibility of corporate behavior in the community, the quality of corporate concern and its origins in conscience, and the necessity for various constituencies to be satisfied have been automatic assurance of the integrity of most corporate efforts in public problem areas. That great public danger follows corporate involvement has so far not been demonstrated, for the motives of those who have led the way are not suspect. That corporations have not taken advantage of the opportunities for graft and corruption in government-supported projects is in itself a reflection of both rising standards of individual integrity and effective control.

Students of the corporation have noted with interest the transformation of this institution. Under the steady improvement in the ethical level of business practice, sociologists have noted the appearance within corporations of a system of private government that regularizes and makes fair the impact upon individuals of managerial power. Sociologist Philip Selznick, for example, finds that "due process," which in civil life goes far beyond codified law to regulate social behavior, is operative within corporations.[2] A. A. Berle described this development as "constitutionalization."[3] Its impact is to establish norms of what may or may not be done, to restrain actions that curtail the rights of others, and to extend to all employees, for example, the rights won by some in legitimate negotiations between management and organized labor. In corporations of some size, complexity, and visibility to the public, the need for its actions to appear fair to its members and, in fact, to all its constituencies is a powerful check on the irresponsible use of private power. The reality of the corporate conscience, like that of the individual conscience, is essential to an open society valuing responsible freedom.

The third proposition, in effect that present-day corporate executives are increasingly the kind of people who cannot be expected to confine themselves to pursue economic activity while ignoring its social consequences, means merely that managers will concern themselves and their companies with social problems because they find it stimulating to do so. It would be untactful for us to attempt to document the progress asserted in this statement through the appointments now being made to corporate high office in our leading companies. But it could be done. Such men are more and more attracted by the opportunity to apply corporate power to socially desirable ends; they are aware that social, political, and economic affairs are increasingly interrelated; they realize that a large "private" corporation is a public institution and that its management is conducted under the guidance of implicit moral values constituting a corporate conscience.

The concern for the health of the society in which business operates leads these days to managers speaking in support of action not in the immediate interest of their companies. To be sure, minor concessions to the public interest by men like Henry Ford are small recompense for the inaction over many decades of the automobile and petroleum industries in dealing with pollution by the internal combustion engine, estimated in 1970 to be the largest single cause of our own air quality problem. Of small importance in themselves, they may well authorize speaking out on the part of many men in management who would like to do so but until now have not dared.

The fear of controversy diminishes slightly, as experience shows its consequences to be less lethal than feared. Thus, since 1967 the organization called Business Executives Move for Peace in Vietnam has enlisted executives willing to challenge national policy and to subject themselves and their organizations to public displeasure. The members are not acting as private individuals, for their corporate affiliation is always stated forthrightly to document their qualifications as businessmen and to call attention to the importance of their opinions. Speaking out on the war culminated, in a sense, with the testimony before the Senate Foreign Relations Committee in 1970 by Louis B. Lundborg, chairman of the Bank of America. Lundborg said he considered our involvement in Vietnam a tragic national mistake of colossal proportions, morally indefensible and practically unsustainable. He said that people like he were to blame for our continued engagement in an unwise war for not speaking up and speaking out sooner.

John T. Connor, chairman of Allied Chemical Corporation, Thomas J. Watson, Jr., chairman of IBM, and Charles B. McCoy, president of DuPont, have all spoken out against the war with a boldness not usual until recently.

Some executives feel that the corportaion itself should be committed to stands on certain public issues. Thus, Joseph Wilson,

then chief executive officer of the Xerox Corporation, said in 1964: "The Corporation cannot refuse to take a stand on public issues of major concern; failure to act is to throw its weight on the side of the status quo, and the public interprets it that way."[4]
Peter McColough, his successor as president and chief officer of the company, has argued at annual meetings of shareholders, in support of the same view, that individuals in the company must not be prevented from expressing dissenting views so that the corporation does not override their liberty. Similarly, he believes that if all corporations were to take forthright stands on public issues, the variety of opinions would be as great as among individuals, and the public would be protected from excessive influence on public opinion by a few powerful firms. If he were to be deprived of the privilege of stating publicly his views on controversial questions or to contribute to an official corporation position on the same issues, he would lose interest in continuing to be an executive. Both Wilson and McColough have told their stockholders, in effect, that if they do not approve they should either dismiss their management or sell their stock.

Whatever the problems of official corporate positions on controversial issues not directly related to the corporation's own interests may be, the improvement in the lawful, ethical, and humane quality of corporate practice during the last 70 years is in any case quite unmistakable. From close at hand the rate of progress, subject in definition to contentious subjectivity, is harder to realize. Improvement can be directly traced to the aspirations of men moving into top management positions and their sensitivity to public opinion.

Companies choose for positions of top leadership the best men they have the wit to recognize. For years such men were the typical product of the technology upon which their businesses were based. They had learned the hard way how to make technical progress profitable. "This technological world," writes Philip Sporn, himself an engineer and the retired head of American Electric Power Company and the Ohio Valley Electric Corporation, "is, in its final evaluation, a world created by the engineers. Its successes, but also its failures, all are the product of the engineers. Thus in the important sense the pollution problems we are suffering from today represent a failure of engineers and a bankruptcy of engineering." The realization grows that we need top managers with the ability to transcend what has been called the "human limits of technology—the problems of persuasion and decision, limited not by science and mathematics and engineering but limited by our ability to understand the problems of our society and to assemble the necessary public support behind the solutions."[5] But the need for breadth of imagination in recognizing opportunity, for the capacity to change objectives and policy in the face of changing opportunity, for the self-knowledge required to gauge corporate resources and the market opportunities to which they might be applied, and for the sensitivity to win organization support in the company human and political system is beginning to produce the kind of leader whose motivations are not those of the economic isolationist, pursuing his own gain with a steely eyed disregard for the future of his company or of society.

As the levels of formal education and professionalization rise, executives will turn to social problems as concerned individuals simply because they want to. In recognition of their motives and capability, their participation generally will be welcomed. A concerned individual who is president of a substantial corporation cannot act apart from it even if he would; he must bring at least the prestige of his firm with him. To enlist its power by designing its strategy to encompass a chosen set of social conditions is only a second small step. The problem of bringing together personal and corporate aspirations for a better world are attractive because to men who are intelligent as well as concerned they are intellectually satisfying. To populate an organization with younger people who are also intelligent and concerned becomes easier and henceforth will probably be possible only if the stated objectives and observable behavior of the organization include more than self-preservation and meeting the economic needs of its customers and employees.

The prohibition against such interests and activities left over from the laissez-faire doctrine of Adam Smith and fostered still by the suspicious theorists who postulate, in effect, venality and self-aggrandizement as the primary motive for economic activity becomes less compelling. The person humane and experienced enough to be a general manager at a high level in a complex company will join the interventionists' ranks because it is the natural and obvious thing to do. Only two conditions make it necessary to defend his presence: an obsolete set of arguments based on a hostile definition of the role of business in society and the continuing presence in high office of narrowly educated men making intuitive strategic decisions— decisions based on technical tradition, jungle instincts of conduct, skill in emergency improvisation, and a vague loyalty to a self-vindicating economic rationale. A new kind of manager has been emerging from the process of education and natural selection.

The fourth proposition supporting the participation of companies in social problems is mostly an assurance that such activity, conducted by the kind of generalists we are making way for, is neither impractical nor dangerous. The competence to deal with the social consequences of strategic decision can be nurtured through education, experience, and proper selection; it is part of the unitary capacity for strategic planning. The other professions, including law and medicine, distinguished by individual achievement and fully authorized to deal in social problems, are not so far ahead that they are out of sight.

Every profession, to be sure, is subject to capture by complacency with its own achievements or conventions about what is
practical or possible. In recent years, each one has been shaken by
its younger members to reconsider its premises. The corporate
conscience, the inexorable clarification of due process supporting
social justice within the corporation as well as in society at large,
the new muscularity of government regulation, signs of industry self-
regulation, the revitalization of boards of directors, and the availability of criticism from a pluralism of standards and prejudices in
an open society are all available to contain corporate power wrongly
directed. The quality of leadership available to the citizenry in other
walks of life does not suggest that the average will be lowered by
corporate executives. Up to this point, in fact, American society has
been needlessly deprived of the participation of some of its best-
qualified members.

THE CATEGORIES OF CONCERN

That the case for corporate involvement in social problems is
steadily winning converts among managers of private enterprises
cannot be disputed. You may attribute this development to recurrent
melioristic optimism, to defensive ingenuity on behalf of capitalism,
among other possibilities, or to the professionalization of management practice. Whatever its origins, we should in any case proceed
to examine the range of involvement available to a firm and the
considerations that guide its choice of opportunity. The admission
of opportunity to make these social contributions extends the range
of strategic alternatives confronted by the general manager. As we
will see, this complication makes necessary a theory of strategic
decision that includes, but is not confined to, the optimum combination
of market opportunity and corporate resources that constitutes a
firm's economic strategy.

The problems affecting the quality of life in the society to which
the company belongs may be thought of as extending through a set of
spheres from the firm itself to the world community. For multinational firms the primary economic opportunity to contribute to
industrialization of underdeveloped nations replaces irresponsible
exploitation. The potential for peace as well as economic development
makes East-West trade under some conditions as much an issue of
responsibility as of economic return. The maturing of world corporations into fully contributing institutions is assisted of course by
the realization that host countries will ultimately have it no other
way. We have already said that responsibility entails doing early as
a matter of conscience what later may well be required by law.

Voluntary responsibility has, however, large dividends in public acceptance, customer goodwill, and latitude preserved.

At the national or common-market level, the choice of problems susceptible to constructive attention from business firms is bewilderingly large. National firms tend to begin with the environmental consequences of their manufacturing processes or the impact of their products upon the public. Thus, Standard Oil Company of New Jersey or General Motors have no doubt about what to work on—the question is how much and how fast. After such a company has put its house in order or has begun a long program to make it so, it may then take interest in other public problems, either within the context of philanthropic contribution or through business operations that in essence seek out economic opportunity in social need. Once corporate concern for national problems like equal opportunity, race relations, education, and poverty is recognized as legitimate, the question becomes: How does a company decide which ones it should work on?

Besides world and national problems, a third category of concern appropriate for all kinds of firms are the problems of the local communities in which the company operates. In the United States the city has become the special focus of our national interest. Urban problems like housing, unemployment in the poverty culture, substandard medical care, ineffective education, rampant ugliness, and defective transportation appeal to companies as the proper arena for economic and social action because of their nearness and compactness. Because business cannot remain healthy in a sick community, the problems of the city, despite their complexity, will continue to dominate the social action of corporations. Increasing sophistication will make this more effective than it has been so far.

As if world, national, and local social responsibility were not already more than enough, two other less obvious avenues of action must be considered: the industry or industries in which the company operates and the quality of life within the company itself. Every industry has problems that arise from a legacy of indifference, from the stresses of competition, from violation or fear of antitrust laws, or from cartelization, legal or otherwise. Industry self-regulation, designed to pick up where government regulation leaves off, has not been markedly successful in the cigarette, broadcasting, and motion-picture-producing industries in the United States. But it becomes clearer that the strategy of any firm in a roughly competitive industry must include a determination of how the industry's organization can be used or altered to raise the level of responsibility of most of its members.

Finally, within the firm itself, a company has attractive opportunity for satisfying its management's interest in social responsibility. The quality of any company's present strategy is always subject to improvement as new technology and higher aspirations work together. Here as in every other category of social issues, decision is difficult. The kind of detached self-criticism essential to the perpetuation of responsible freedom is especially rare within a business. The proper role of the board of directors in supervising this function, long since lost sight of, needs revitalization.

The actual quality of life in a business organization turns most crucially on how much freedom is accorded to the individual. Certainly most firms consider responsibility to their members a category of concern as important as that to external constituencies. It is as much a matter of enlightened self-interest as of responsibility to provide conditions encouraging the convergence of the individual's aspirations with those of the corporation, to provide conditions for effective productivity, and to reward employees for extraordinary performance. The degree to which an organization is efficient, productive, creative, and capable of development is dependent in large part on the mainte- nance of a climate in which the individual does not feel suppressed, and in which a kind of freedom (analogous to that which the corpo- ration enjoys in a free enterprise society) is permitted as a matter of course. Overregulation of the individual by corporate policy is no more appropriate internally than overregulation of the corporation by government. On the other hand, personal responsibility is as appropriate to individual liberty as corporate responsibility is to corporate freedom.

THE PROBLEM OF CHOICE

What the corporate strategist has to be concerned with, then, ranges from the most global of the problems of world society to the uses of freedom by a single person in his firm. The problems of his country, community, and industry lying between these extremes make opportunity for social contribution exactly coextensive with the range of economic opportunity before him. The problem of choice may be met in the area of responsibility in much the same way as in product-market combinations and in developing a program for growth and diversification.

To guide the policy-maker in private business, a simple prac- titioner's theory of general management has been developed. It postulates that every firm, if it is not to be a chip adrift in economic currents over which it has no control, must develop a corporate strategy, oriented to the future, flexible enough to permit adaptation but firm enough to establish a unique character for the firm and a durable definition of its business. This strategy is developed by matching corporate resources and distinctive competences to imaginatively perceived opportunity in the company's market environment. This combination, a perception of how best a company's present and potential resources and capability can be applied to changing opportunity, is bound to be affected by the personal values and aspirations of the managers making the decision. What a company might do in terms of available opportunity is matched with what it can do in terms of resources; this choice is further narrowed by what the managers of a firm want to do. This preference is modified not only by responsibility—in the case of a publicly owned firm—to the shareholders, but by a consideration of what the company ought to do in the face of the ethical and moral concern previously described in this chapter.[6] Since the identification of economic opportunity, the determination of corporate capability, the personal values of the senior management group, and their aspirations to social responsibility might lead in four different directions, reconciling the outcomes in such a way as to leave the firm economically viable and its leaders unfrustrated constitutes the art of strategic decision.

Even from this spare reference to strategy formulation it is clear that the choice of avenues in which to participate in public affairs will be influenced by the personal values of the managers making the decision. To be strategic rather than improvisatory, participation must take place within a set of social and economic objectives that reflect the company's definition of itself not only as an economic entity but as a responsible institution in society. Its social action would include issues most closely related to the economic strategy of the company, to the expansion of its markets, to the health of its immediate environment, and to its industry and internal problems. The extent of involvement relates importantly to the resources available. A company struggling to avoid bankruptcy will omit contributions to good causes. A company easily able to meet its dividend and growth-in-earnings targets can be more generous not only in its support of education and other acceptable causes but to national and world issues not directly related to its economic function. What its competence in such areas might be is open to question. The question is so serious as to suggest a principle that a company should not venture into good works that are not strategically related to its present and prospective economic functions.

We lack space here to elaborate the doctrine that makes strategic the concern for social responsibility, which (as we saw earlier) is radically redefining the corporate manager's view of his function in circumstances where freedom of choice is open to him. We see that he needs to relate his firm's aspirations to social responsibility to a predetermined strategy as explicit in its social as in its economic terms and one presenting a clear view of the kind of organization it intends to be and the kind of people it will enroll in its membership. From this point of view, "social responsibility" becomes strategic corporate response to the needs of society.

For the leader of a private corporation, a strategy including economically feasible and socially desirable objectives serves many purposes. It makes clear the quality of his claim to remain free— within the limits of economic and social responsibility and the essential but flexible specifications of the law—to set his own course, chart his own future growth, decide on and develop his own product line. It enables him also to secure the commitment to corporate purposes of the members of his own organization, whose motivation to contribute to competitively effective performance does not arise only from their economic needs. The professional general manager, in an environment where some measure of freedom of choice is available, has as his most important function the continuous examination of alternative objectives and the determination of purpose. In these days, his decision is not only the result of economic analysis but an act of intellect, will, desire, and character. Since freedom without responsibility is intolerable, and entrepreneurship must ultimately be disciplined, issues of public responsibility will always attend strategic decision in private corporations.

NOTES

1. Milton Friedman, Capitalism and Freedom (Chicago: University of Chicago Press, 1962).

2. Philip Selznick, Law, Society and Industrial Injustice (New York: Russell Sage Foundation, 1969).

3. A. A. Berle, Jr., The 20th Century Capitalist Revolution (New York: Harcourt, Brace and Company, 1954).

4. Joseph C. Wilson, Unpublished speech, 1964.

5. Philip Sporn, Technology, Engineering and Economics (Cambridge, Mass.: M.I.T. Press, 1969).

6. A fuller treatment of this idea may be found in the author's The Concept of Corporate Strategy (Homewood, Ill.: Dow Jones-Irwin, 1971).

AUBREY SILBERSTON is an Official Fellow in Economics at Nuffield College, Oxford. He was until recently a Fellow of St. John's College, Cambridge. He has published a number of books and articles in the field of industrial economics and the theory of the firm. He has sat on a number of government committees including committees on the automobile industry and the patent system. He has been a Member of the Monopolies Commission and is currently a Non-executive Board Member of the British Steel Corporation (the nationalised steel industry in Britain) and an economic adviser to the Confederation of British Industry. Mr. Silberston holds an M.A. from the University of Cambridge and an M.A. from the University of Oxford.

FRANCIS SETON is an Official Fellow in Economics of Nuffield College, Oxford. He has specialised in the economics of Socialist countries and, more recently, in the economics of developing countries. He has written a number of articles on the Soviet Union and on Socialist problems and has recently published a book on 'Shadow Wages in the Chilean Economy'. He has been Visiting Professor at the Universities of Osaka, Columbia, Pennsylvania and others, and a consultant to the United Nations and to the Governments of the U.K., Iran, Chile and Indonesia. Francis Seton is an M.A., D.Phil., of Oxford University.